KIRSCH'S HANDBOOK OF PUBLISHING LAW

Kirsch's
Handbook *of* Publishing Law.

for **Authors, Publishers, Editors and Agents**

by **Jonathan Kirsch**

ACROBAT BOOKS
Los Angeles

To Ann, Adam, and Jennifer

"God's novel has suspense."
Isaac Bashevis Singer

Acknowledgments

The idea for the book you are now reading was first suggested by Ann Benjamin Kirsch on a drive through the Florida Keys on the first day of hurricane season in 1993. We had spent a few days at the Miami convention of the American Booksellers Association, where I customarily give a couple of talks on recent developments in publishing law, and it was Ann's good idea to do *something* in the way of publishing the notes that I gather every year as ABA approaches. I am not surprised that Ann came up with the idea: all good things in my life start with her.

Then, a few weeks later, I had the good fortune to meet Tony Cohan for lunch at Cafe Montana in Santa Monica. Tony, the publisher of Acrobat Books, suggested a way to turn raw notes into a book. Over the next year or so, I learned that Tony is an author, editor and publisher whose vision, intelligence, good taste and professionalism make him the archetype of what a book publisher ought to be.

I am not surprised that a man like Tony thought to bring a number of his gifted colleagues to work on the project, including Clive Piercy, who designed the book and the cover; Victoria Gold, who copy-edited the manuscript; and Winnie Li, who designed and executed the typography.

I owe a special debt of gratitude to my law partner, Dennis Mitchell, whose encouragement, good counsel and friendship have always been indispensable to my work; Jan Nathan, Executive Director of Publishers Marketing Association, a dear friend, an incomparable professional and one of the real treasures of the publishing industry; Larry Zerner, a valued colleague at Kirsch & Mitchell, who patiently read every page of the manuscript and offered much good advice; Judy Woo and Angie Yoon, whose charm, grace, and patience make it a pleasure to come to the office every day; and Raye Birk, Candace Barrett Birk, and Harvey Mindess, each of whom supported and encouraged my efforts in important ways at various crucial moments.

Several of my colleagues in law and publishing were kind enough to read various chapters of the book. Lon Sobel, Mike Hamilburg, Ted Gerdes, Andrea Jane Grefe and Lou Petrich were especially generous in accepting thick manila envelopes full of manuscript pages for comment and correction—and always with good cheer and abundant *menschkeit*.

I am especially grateful, too, to Ed Komen, Stanley Fleishman, David Nimmer, Lyle Stuart, Carolyn See (O Radiant One!), Doug Dutton, Lisa See, George A. Crawford, Lyle Stuart, Gwen Davis, Susan Fassberg, David Gerber, Jessica Algazi, and Karen Vogel for their willingness to share their expertise and experience.

During my research, I also called on the kind assistance of numerous friendly folk in various aspects of publishing, including Suzanne Bedell, Jo Bradley, Carolyn Glaisek, Gordon Grayson, Deborah Kirschman, and Ann McCarthy.

To my father, Robert Reuven Kirsch, of blessed memory, who taught, nurtured and inspired so many writers and readers, I owe a passion for hot type, a reverence for words on printed page, and a generous splash of the printer's ink that seems to run through the veins of *all* of his progeny.

Finally, to my children, Adam and Jennifer, I hasten to declare not only my love but also my special thanks for their willingness to let me on the home computer once in awhile. In a house where *everyone* is a writer, what greater gift could they bestow?

Contents

Introduction

Kirsch's Handbook of Publishing Law is a survey and discussion of the law that applies to the publishing industry in general and the work of authors, editors, agents and publishers in particular.

The main text is presented in eight chapters that follow the trajectory of a typical book project and explain how basic principles of publishing law are actually applied in the real world of book publishing.

▷ Chapter 1: **Idea Protection**. The rights of an author in her ideas and how to protect them when submitting a proposal for a book project.

▷ Chapter 2: **Co-Authorship and Copyright**. The dealings among co-authors and collaborators, and the mechanisms for acquiring rights in the copyrighted work of another writer, artist or publisher.

▷ Chapter 3: **Agents and Packagers**. The relationship between an author and the agent or book packager who represents or acquires the author's work.

▷ Chapter 4: **The Book Publishing Contract**. A clause-by-clause analysis of a typical book publishing contract, including a discussion of the "deal points" that an author and publisher must consider and resolve in negotiating a book deal.

▷ Chapter 5: **Preparing the Manuscript:** A summary of the perils that an author or publisher may face, including copyright and trademark infringement, defamation and invasion of privacy, and so on, and how to spot and avoid such claims during the research, writing and review of the manuscript.

▷ Chapter 6: **Copyright Formalities.** A survey of the legal mechanisms for protecting the copyright in a book project, including copyright notice, registration of copyright in the Copyright Office, recordation of copyright documents and other "formalities."

▷ Chapter 7: **Electronic and Other Subsidiary Rights.** A comprehensive analysis of the ownership and exploitation of subsidiary rights in a typical book project, including electronic or "multimedia" rights, audio rights, motion picture and television rights, merchandising rights, and "future technology" rights.

▷ Chapter 8: **Remaindering, Reversion and Copyright Termination.** The practical and legal mechanisms by which a book, a publishing agreement and copyright itself come to an end, including returns and remaindering of books, reversion of rights in a book, and the right of an author to terminate a transfer of copyright to a publisher.

▷ **Briefs.** Short summaries of the law of trademark and unfair competition, the "moral rights" of authors, insurance for "media risks," international copyright, a list of publishing law reference works, and other sources of information and services.

▷ **Forms Library:** A collection of legal forms for various publishing transactions, including Collaboration Agreement, Agency Agreement, Work-for-Hire Agreement, Interview Release, Permissions Agreement, and so on.

▷ **War Stories.** Some of the more colorful lore of publishing law— case histories, court opinions, war stories and horror stories that illustrate the practical application of legal principles—are presented in sidebars in each chapter. By setting off the anecdotes, you will be able to concentrate on the "nuts and bolts" of the text—but you may find some inspiration and some entertainment in sidebars that show how the law plays out in real life.

▷ **Tips and Techniques.** The main text also includes sidebars that offer tips and techniques for applying the abstract principles of law in specific settings and situations. Because the tips are drawn from real-life problem-solving in the publishing industry, they tend to reflect the cutting edge of the law.

▷ **A Note on Gender.** The hypothetical author to whom I refer from time to time is imagined to be a woman in some chapters, a man in others.

A Special Caution to Readers!

Kirsch's Handbook is intended to be as free of dreary legalisms and lawyerly circumlocutions as possible—but I must call your attention to some important cautions.

Kirsch's Handbook is *not* a "do-it-yourself" book and does *not* take the place of expert advice and assistance from a lawyer with experience in publishing law. Although *Kirsch's Handbook* may help you determine *when* you need to see an attorney—and help you make better use of an attorney's services if you consult one—the fact remains that *no* book on the law can replace a consultation with an attorney.

Bear in mind the following limitations that apply to *any* book about the law for lay readers:

▷ The law changes constantly as new cases are decided, new laws and regulations are enacted, and new products and technologies enter the marketplace. *Kirsch's Handbook* reflects the law that was in effect on the date of publication, but the reader ought to make sure that he or she is relying on the most current state of the law.

▷ Various legal forms are provided in the Forms Library of *Kirsch's Handbook* as examples of typical agreements and other legal documents now in use in the publishing industry. However, no single form can serve all readers as an all-purpose, off-the-rack legal document. Before using any "standard" form, including the ones in the Forms Library, be sure that it adequately covers the particular goals and concerns of *your* project.

▷ The explanation of legal principles in *Kirsch's Handbook* has been greatly simplified and summarized, both to make the material accessible to non-lawyers and to prevent the book from swelling up into several volumes. That's why you will often encounter certain cautionary words and phrases: "For example," "as a general proposition," "typically," and the like. These phrases are intended to remind you that the subject under discussion is much more complex than it may seem. For that reason, please remember that there may be various exceptions to each rule of law. Make sure that the general principle of law actually applies to *your* legal problem!

▷   As you will see in the pages that follow, publishing law is a complex and highly sophisticated body of law. A general survey of the law cannot anticipate and answer every problem that an author, editor, publisher or agent is likely to encounter in real life—and, more often than not, the solution to any such problem will be determined by the specific circumstances of *your* project and the specific laws of *your* state. Only an attorney who is familiar with your problem can render effective advice on how to solve it.

So be cautious in making use of *Kirsch's Handbook*, and when in doubt see a lawyer!

CHAPTER ONE

Idea Protection

Nowadays, the book proposal or "pitch letter" has taken on a grand role in the marketplace. An unusual premise, a little-known fact, a unique plot twist, or a catchy title may command a sizable advance on the strength of an idea alone. Even a pitch letter to a magazine editor may represent the opportunity to pick up a writing assignment worth several thousand dollars to a freelance writer. And, now and then, an author can win the lottery with a "mere" idea—John Grisham, it is reported, picked up a $1.5 million advance on the strength of a one-page outline of his next book!

So the fact is that ideas *are* a commodity in the media industry. But, as we shall see, the law continues to afford only scant protection for the idea itself.

The Idea That Belongs to No One

An idea, according to the old common law, belonged to no one. And, for that reason, the law simply did not recognize any right of ownership in mere ideas, no matter how clever or original or marketable the ideas might turn out to be. One author was perfectly free to copy the ideas and information in another author's work as long as the words and phrases were original.

"The noblest of human productions—knowledge, truths ascertained, conceptions, and ideas—become, after voluntary communication to others," intoned the venerable jurist Louis Brandeis, "as free as the air to common use."

The law of copyright, which protects the ownership of "works of authorship," provides little or no protection for ideas or information. Rather, copyright protects only the particular *expression* of ideas and information. For that reason, the particular words or images by which ideas or information are expressed—in the form of an article, a book, a photograph, a sculpture, or other "works of authorship"—may not be copied without the risk of copyright infringement. Under certain very limited circumstances, even the particular selection and arrangement of ideas or information may be entitled to copyright protection. But, as a general matter, copyright will not protect the story ideas or the information in a work of authorship.

Thus, even if *Moby Dick* were still protected under copyright, you would be perfectly free to write a novel about an obsessive sea captain who sails in pursuit of a rogue whale, but it would probably be a good idea not to start the book with the line: "Call me Ishmael."

Even the law of trademark, which recognizes the ownership of property rights in something so ephemeral as a squiggle, a sequence of musical tones or even a scent, does not prevent the expropriation of a "mere" idea, no matter how valuable that idea might be. ➤ *Chapter 9: Briefs (Trademark and Unfair Competition)*

Still, there's something deep in the heart and soul of an author that prompts her to regard her ideas as something rare and precious. Every author is haunted by the same terrible fear: *If I propose an idea for a book to a*

WHO OWNS THE RIOTOUS KNIGHT? Exactly when do "mere" ideas and information, which are not protected under copyright law, turn into "expression," which is protected? We cannot draw a bright line between ideas and expression; like so much else in the law, the line is where a judge or jury draws it in a particular lawsuit. But we know that at some sublime moment in the creative process, an idea is sufficiently clothed in the trappings of plot, dialogue, characterization, setting and circumstances to turn into "expression." Here's how the venerable Judge Learned Hand put it in Nichols v. Universal Pictures Corp.:

"If Twelfth Night were copyrighted, it is quite possible that a second comer might so closely imitate Sir Toby Belch or Malvolio as to infringe, but it would not be enough that for one of his characters he cast a riotous knight who kept wassail to the discomfort of the household, or a vain and foppish steward who became amorous of his mistress. These would be no more than Shakespeare's 'ideas' in the play, as little capable of monopoly as Einstein's Doctrine of Relativity or Darwin's Origin of the Species. It follows that the less developed the characters, the less they can be copyrighted; that is the penalty an author must bear for marking them too indistinctly."

publisher, the author frets to herself, *if I pitch a story idea to a magazine editor, what prevents a rapacious editor from simply ripping off the idea and assigning it to someone else?* Unhappily, the answer is: Not much. The legal protection of ideas is difficult to obtain, narrow in scope, and hard to enforce. But some scant legal protection is available.

The Law of Idea Protection

Essentially, idea protection begins (and, in most cases, ends) with a contract in one form or another. Sometimes the contract is in writing; sometimes it is merely "implied" by the nature of the dealings between author and agent, editor or publisher. But the essential point of agreement is that one party, whether straightforwardly or tacitly, promises not to use or disclose the ideas or information of the other party without getting (and paying for) the permission of the other party.

But be forewarned: The most effective form of idea protection—a straightforward written agreement between author and agent, editor or publisher regarding idea protection—is so alien to the way business is actually done in the publishing industry that such contracts are rarely, if ever, actually used in ordinary publishing deals. But an anxious writer seeking to protect a story idea or book proposal can use some of the legal tools described here.

Non-Disclosure and Non-Competition Agreements

A formal contract that obliges the parties to keep a secret is known as a "non-disclosure agreement," and such agreements are commonplace in business and certain aspects of the media. A clause or provision regarding non-disclosure might also appear in a collaboration agreement, an agency agreement, a publishing contract, or some other form of contract.

Essentially, a non-disclosure agreement obliges the parties to keep each other's secrets—that is, not to disclose any of the information that one party shares with the other party—except under specified circumstances.

Frequently, a non-disclosure agreement is used in conjunction with a non-competition agreement, especially when one party is disclosing his "trade secrets" such as customer lists or manufacturing processes. A non-competition agreement is a promise by one party to refrain from going into business in competition with the other party. When combined with a non-disclosure agreement, a non-competition agreement prevents one party from disclosing *or* using the information that the other party has shared.

When it comes to idea protection, a non-disclosure and non-competition agreement is probably the single best way to protect the ownership of ideas and information that are not subject to the laws of copyright or trademark. Unfortunately for the anxious author, however, the fact is that such agreements are rarely used in conventional dealings between an author and a publisher.

The Unopened Envelope. Authors who make unsolicited "over-the-transom" submissions to studios, networks, and producers are likely to be asked to sign a submission agreement that simply and flatly rules out any right to sue if the story ideas are used without the author's permission. As a rule, unless an agent or attorney makes the submission, all unsolicited scripts and treatments are returned, unopened, along with a release which asks the author to waive any right to sue if the story materials are used without the author's permission. And if the author doesn't sign, the story materials are not read at all. Happily for authors, the practice is not found in the publishing industry—or, at least, not yet.

As a practical matter, non-disclosure and non-competition agreements in the publishing industry are appropriate only in very limited circumstances. Any author who actually *asks* an editor or a publisher to sign a non-disclosure agreement before pitching a book idea is at risk of being regarded as something of a crank—and, even if the author's mental health is not openly called into question, it's unlikely that the editor or publisher would agree to sign one.

Nor are non-disclosure and non-competition clauses found in agency agreements. In theory, at least, the author might want to extract a written promise from the agent that he will not use another writer to develop a project based on the same idea that the author pitched. But such clauses are virtually never seen in agency agreements; in fact, most agency agreements include a clause that specifically permits the agent to represent other authors and other books, even if these projects directly compete with the author's work! ➤ *Chapter 3: Agents and Packagers*

A more appropriate setting for a non-disclosure and non-competition agreement is the collaboration between two authors, or a collaboration between an author and a ghostwriter, especially if the ghost is being "auditioned" for the writing assignment. ➤ *Chapter 2: Co-Authorship and Copyright; Form 1: Collaboration Agreement*

The collaboration agreement might well include a clause that prevents the ghostwriter from disclosing or using the contents of the book project except with the permission of the author, especially if the ghost is not actually hired to complete the project. (Sometimes, of course, even the fact that a book is ghostwritten must be kept a secret!) And we might imagine a project in which the publisher or the packager approaches a prospective author or ghostwriter with a story idea—and asks for a promise not to disclose the project in the form of a non-disclosure agreement.

A Model Non-Disclosure and Non-Competition Clause

The crucial language of a confidentiality and non-disclosure agreement is fairly concise and straightforward. Here is an example of the non-disclosure and non-competition clauses that I used in a contract for an author who was engaging the services of a ghostwriter to develop a book proposal based on the author's life experiences.

> Reservation of Rights in Story Materials. In consideration of the mutual promises set forth herein, AUTHOR agrees to disclose to COLLABORATOR various details of his life experiences, and other ideas, information, and story materials based in whole or part on his life and professional experiences. All of the foregoing is collectively referred to as "the Story Materials." All right, title and interest in and to the Story Materials are hereby reserved wholly and in perpetuity to AUTHOR alone.

> Non-Disclosure of Story Materials. COLLABORATOR acknowledges and agrees that the Story Materials are disclosed by AUTHOR to COLLABORATOR in strict and complete trust and confidence, and shall be held in trust and confidence by COLLABORATOR and shall not be disclosed to third persons except pursuant to the provisions of this Agreement. COLLABORATOR acknowledges and agrees that AUTHOR has relied on this promise of confidentiality as a material inducement for this Agreement and for disclosing the Story Materials to COLLABORATOR.

> Non-Competition. COLLABORATOR shall not prepare or publish, or participate in the preparation or publication, of any work embodying the Story Materials, or any work that may tend to compete with or otherwise injure the exploitation of any work of AUTHOR based on the Story Materials.

While a co-author or collaborator may be willing to sign such an agreement, an editor or agent is unlikely to do so. So what can an author do to protect a story idea, a plot line, a set of characters, or perhaps just information that might be turned into a book or an article? Only one other legal mechanism is available for protection of "mere" ideas, a legal concept known as "idea misappropriation" that may allow the aggrieved author to file a lawsuit even if no contract has ever been signed.

The Legal Remedy for Idea Misappropriation

What happens if the author's worst nightmare comes true: she pitches a story idea to an agent, editor or publisher who says "No"—and then the same idea shows up in the next issue of the magazine or in a book on the shelf of the local bookstore with someone else's byline on it?

Under the so-called law of "idea misappropriation," as the legal claim is known, the courts have fashioned a remedy for the person who pitches an idea with the notion of selling it to a publisher, packager, producer, or some other buyer and user of ideas—and then finds that the idea has been used without permission or compensation.

Essentially, idea misappropriation is based on a contract, although the contract is rarely put in writing and signed. Rather, the contract in an idea misappropriation case is usually "implied" in the dealings between the parties. If an author pitches a book idea to an editor at a publishing house—and the author can prove that both author and the editor understood that the author's idea, if used, would be paid for—the law will presume that author and editor have entered into an enforceable contract.

A LITERARY FISH STORY. John Ed Bradley, writing in _Esquire_, recalls an episode of apparent "idea misappropriation" involving the late poet and short story writer Raymond Carver. One of Carver's friends told him a story about an incident that had taken place when the friend was taking a walk: A salmon fell out of the sky and landed on the hood of a nearby Jeep. A pelican passing overhead had probably dropped the fish, but the experience appeared almost magical. When the story appeared in one of Carver's poems, the friend accused Ray of stealing it. "I guess I must have," Carver said after a moment of reflection, "since I don't take walks."

If the agent, editor or publisher later decides to make use of the story idea without assigning the project to the author—or at least getting the author's permission—the law gives the author the right to sue for idea misappropriation. Generally, the author will have to prove certain basic elements in order to prevail in an idea misappropriation case, and all of these elements are designed to prove the existence of an "implied" contract to pay for the idea that was pitched by the author.

The Elements of an Idea Misappropriation Case

The basic elements of an idea misappropriation case may vary from state to state. But the following elements are likely to arise in most idea misappropriation cases:

▷ **Did the author submit the story idea?** The first step in an idea misappropriation case is proving that the author submitted the story idea to an editor, a publisher or someone else who actually used it. A copy of a submission letter from the author, or her agent or attorney, is usually enough to prove the point that a submission was made.

A carbon copy of a letter is less effective than, for example, a signed receipt for a Federal Express or a Certified Mail delivery. Of course, the author may be reluctant to make such a big point of securing proof of delivery—it may be seen by the publisher as amateurish or even as slightly paranoid. Nowadays, however, Federal Express and other forms of traceable mail are so commonly used that it may no longer arouse the curiosity of the recipient. Then, too, the use of a "fax" followed up with a "hard copy" in the mail also allows the sender to keep a written record of transmission.

Some idea misappropriation cases turn on the question of whether a submission was made directly to the person who actually used the story materials. A submission to an editor's secretary may be enough to prove that the materials were seen and used by the editor herself—but the author who hands her manuscript to a guy whose cousin is

THE MAN IN THE HOLE. The law of idea protection starts with Desny v. Wilder, a 1956 case arising from the Billy Wilder movie, Ace in the Hole. A fellow named Victor Desny telephoned Wilder's office on the Paramount lot and pitched his secretary on the idea of a movie based on the real-life story of Floyd Collins, a man who was trapped in a cave in the 1920s. Wilder later made a movie on the same theme, and Desny was able to convince the Supreme Court of California that he was entitled to be compensated for his idea. The court carved out an exception to the rule against idea protection in order to compensate the "idea man" who provides only a story idea and nothing more.

"Generally speaking, ideas are as free as the air," the court ruled. "But there can be circumstances when neither air nor ideas may be acquired without cost. The diver who goes deep in the sea...knows full well that for life itself, he, or someone on his behalf, must arrange for air...to be specifically provided at the time and place of need. The theatrical producer likewise may be dependent for his business life on the procurement of ideas from other persons...; he may not find his own sufficient for survival."

dating the secretary is probably not enough to show that the materials were submitted at all!

▷ **Was the submission made with the understanding that the idea was offered for sale?** Again, the author must be able to prove that she submitted a story idea to an agent, an editor, a publisher, a packager, a producer, or some other buyer and user of story ideas with the understanding that the material, if used, would be paid for. Sometimes the circumstances of the pitch will be enough to suggest such an understanding; an editor ought to know that a pitch letter or a book proposal is an offer to make a deal. But the author must be able to show that the recipient of the proposal understood that the idea is not being offered freely and for the taking.

The Fine Art of the Pitch Letter. If a dispute over idea misappropriation comes down to a lawsuit, the very purpose of the submission may become a point of contention. Sometimes the fact that a story submission has been made through an agent or an attorney—as opposed to an unsolicited or "over-the-transom" pitch—is enough to prove that the submission itself was a commercial proposition: The agent submitted his client's story materials for sale, and the author expected to be paid.

However, the cautious agent or attorney—and, above all, the author who pitches a book proposal <u>without</u> the assistance of an agent or an attorney—will make it entirely clear that a book proposal or manuscript is being pitched for the purpose of a sale. I usually recommend to my clients that they use something along the following lines:

<u>I am pleased to submit the enclosed book proposal for your consideration. Please note that all rights in the enclosed materials are fully reserved, and I ask that you treat these materials in confidence. If you wish to acquire rights in the proposal or the ideas embodied in the proposal, please let me know.</u>

▷ **Was the author's idea actually used?** The crux of an idea misappropriation case, of course, is that the author's story idea was actually *used* by the person to whom it was submitted but without the author's permission. In many cases of alleged idea misappropriation, the big fight is whether or not the offending book or movie is actually based upon the idea that was submitted by the author in the first place.

The proof of misappropriation often consists of tit-for-tat testimony by gun-for-hire expert witnesses. The witness for the author will come up with a list of similarities between the story submission and the offending book or movie, and the witness for the publisher or the producer will come up with a list of dissimilarities. Sometimes, after all the expert witnesses have been handsomely paid and given their day in court, a judge (or jury) will simply ignore all of the expert testimony and decide for himself if one project is based upon the other. And, in virtually every case, the similarities are mostly in the eye of the beholder, and the judge or jury is the only beholder who counts.

▷ Was the author's idea new, original, and concrete? Some (but not all) courts in various states across the country have added a new and additional element to the author's burden of proof in an idea misappropriation case. Under some circumstances, and in some jurisdictions, the idea that was submitted by the author to the publisher or producer must be "novel" or "original" or "concrete." But the definition of novelty or originality in the case law is hazy if not unintelligible, and the requirement has been applied with very mixed results. Again, these qualities are mostly in the eye of the beholder.

▷ What are the author's damages? Bear in mind that an idea misappropriation case generally focuses on the wrongful taking of an idea alone, and not the particular words and phrases that the author used in expressing the idea. In such cases, an idea misappropriation is *not* the same as a copyright infringement case, where the author claims that someone has copied her copyrighted work without her permission, and the substantial damages that are sometimes available in copyright cases simply do not apply.

Essentially, the measure of damages in an idea misappropriation case is the "fair market value" of what was actually taken and used—that is, the idea itself, and *not* the magazine article or book manuscript or screenplay in which the ideas were embodied. And, after all, what is the value of the idea alone? Most publishers and producers will argue that they are not in the business of buying story ideas apart from books or screenplays, and thus the idea alone does not have a market value. And, even if an idea can be appraised at a certain dollar value, the price tag will be low indeed.

The fact that story ideas are hard to value at all works a real hardship on authors who believe that their ideas have been misappropriated and want to sue for idea misappropriation. The fact is that most authors simply cannot afford to hire and pay a lawyer by the hour to prosecute a lawsuit against a publisher under any circumstances. A claim of copyright infringement holds out the possibility that the author may be able to force the infringer to pay her attorney's fees—but no such remedy is available in idea misappropriation cases. So the author is usually reduced to the dispiriting task of finding a lawyer who will take an idea misappropriation case on a contingency fee basis—and, because such cases are hard to win and, even if won, don't bring in much money—it's damned hard to find a lawyer who will take one on contingency. ➤ *Chapter 6: Copyright Formalities*

Options and Development Deals in Idea Misappropriation Cases

If the author is fortunate enough to sell a project to a publisher, packager, or producer in the form of a publishing agreement or an option agreement, or some other form of development deal—and then the author finds that her ideas (but not the actual words in her manuscript, screenplay, or treatment) have been ripped off—an idea misappropriation case may be a considerably more attractive prospect.

Under these circumstances, the author may not be forced to rely on an "implied" contract. Rather, the publishing agreement, option, or the development deal itself may amount to a written contract that can be used to prevent the misappropriation of the ideas embodied in a project that has been optioned or put into development.

An option agreement or other development deal is most helpful in an idea misappropriation case if the agreement itself includes language that extends specific legal protection to the *ideas* contained in the project. Otherwise, the author may still have to prove that the agreement covered the ideas that appear in the manuscript or treatment, and not merely the words and phrases of the manuscript, screenplay or treatment in which the ideas are expressed.

Idea Protection Between Authors and Agents

The special relationship between an author and an agent may give rise to a certain degree of idea protection even if the agency agreement itself is silent on the subject. Anyone who enters into a "confidential" relationship with another person—and an agent is one example of a confidential relationship—is entitled to rely on that person to keep one's secrets and to avoid injury to one's interests. ➤ *Chapter 3: Agents and Packagers*

The classic examples of a confidential relationship are attorneys and their clients, for instance, or physicians or psychiatrists and their patients. The basic test is whether one person has reposed his trust and confidence in the other person, and relies on the other person's good faith in carrying out a task. A literary agent, who is entrusted with the right to collect and hold the author's money, stands in a confidential relationship with the author.

For that reason, any agent who takes a story idea from one client— and then tries to sell a book project using the same idea for another client—has breached the trust of the first client and may be facing a claim for idea misappropriation. And the same theory of legal protection may be extended to protect an idea that one author has disclosed in confidence to a collaborator or a co-author.

How to Prove Ownership of an Idea

Authors tend to invest a good deal of psychic energy in worrying about the theft of their ideas, and a curious kind of folk wisdom is passed down from one generation of ink-stained wretches to the next. But, as we shall see, the folkways of proving ownership of ideas are mostly wrong.

One of the most cherished nuggets of folk wisdom among writers (and, by the way, rock musicians) is the so-called "Poor Man's Copyright"—that is, the ritual of sealing a manuscript in an envelope, mailing it to oneself, and then keeping the sealed and postmarked envelope in a safe place against the day when someone challenges the author's rights in the manuscript. Someday, the writer believes, he can prove ownership of the manuscript by pointing to the sealed envelope and the postmark.

But the "Poor Man's Copyright" is mostly (if not entirely) a myth. First of all, the ritual of mailing a manuscript to oneself in a sealed envelope is not equivalent to registration of copyright in the United States Copyright Office. In fact, it has nothing whatsoever to do with the author's ownership of copyright in a manuscript. Under most circumstances, if the author created the manuscript, she owns the copyright from the moment of creation, and then no registration of copyright is necessary to acquire ownership of copyright.

However, registration of copyright is an important and sometimes essential step in protecting against copyright infringement! Since the Poor Man's Copyright is not a substitute for formal copyright registration, the author should be careful to properly register the copyright in her work according to the procedures of the United States Copyright Office.

► *Chapter 6: Copyright Formalities*

At best, the sealed-and-post-marked envelope is *evidence* that, on the day of the postmark, the author was in possession of a copy of the manuscript. But possession of a manuscript is *not* equivalent to ownership of copyright in the manuscript. So the postmarked-and-sealed envelope only establishes the date on which the author possessed the envelope. At least in theory, what is found inside the envelope might very well belong to someone else.

> **WHEN THE POOR MAN'S COPYRIGHT REALLY COUNTS.** I once represented an author who hired a ghostwriter to edit and polish the first draft of his manuscript. Early on, the author fired the ghostwriter, but the "ghost" later claimed to be a joint author of the author's book because of her contribution to the manuscript during her brief period of employment!
>
> Here was one instance where the Poor Man's Copyright might have really made a difference. If the author had been able to produce a sealed envelope containing the original manuscript with a postmark that predated the hiring of the ghostwriter—and the original manuscript itself showed that the ghostwriter contributed little or nothing to the project—then the ghostwriter's claim would have been squarely repudiated.
>
> As it turned out, the author found it necessary to pay a royalty to the ghostwriter in order to "clear" the rights to his own book!

Still, the Poor Man's Copyright is not an entirely useless gesture. The simple fact that the author possessed a certain manuscript on a certain date may suggest that the author is, in fact, the owner of copyright—or, crucially, the ideas that are contained in the manuscript.

Another way to prove possession of a manuscript on a certain date is to register the manuscript with the Writers Guild of America (WGA), which maintains script registries in both New York City and Los Angeles. Guild registration, like the Poor Man's Copyright, has nothing to do with ownership of copyright, but a registration is good evidence that the author was in possession of written materials on a specified date. ➤ Chapter 9: Briefs (Trademark and Unfair Competition)

The WGA charges a modest fee to place a sealed envelope containing story materials treatment in storage in a secure facility. A receipt showing the date of deposit is issued, a WGA serial number is assigned, the envelope is maintained on file for a period of five years, and the envelope can be retrieved and opened under court supervision if necessary. One does not have to be a Guild member to use the service, although the fee is currently $20 per deposit for non-members and only $10 for members.

THE BUCHWALD SAGA. The most celebrated case of idea misappropriation in recent years was the lawsuit that author and columnist Art Buchwald brought against Paramount Pictures for allegedly stealing the idea for Coming to America. Buchwald enjoyed the advantage of a written agreement with Paramount—actually, an option on a story treatment—and he was able to convince a judge that the Eddie Murphy movie was "based on" his treatment. (He also had the advantage of a gifted lawyer and a mammoth law firm, all working for him on a contingency fee basis!) Eventually, Buchwald was awarded $295,000 in damages—a fraction of what his lawyer spent in litigating the case. But, even after Buchwald won his case, a half-dozen other self-styled authors pressed their own claims of idea misappropriation against Paramount and Eddie Murphy, each one claiming that he or she—and not Buchwald—was the creator of the story idea. One of the relentless plaintiffs claimed to be a flesh-and-blood African prince who told his life story to Eddie Murphy in a bar!

Essentially, WGA registration is the functional equivalent of the Poor Man's Copyright, but it offers the advantage of a third-party stakeholder and some formal procedures that enhance the credibility of the evidence itself. Bear in mind, however, that the Guild destroys registered materials after five years!

The Pyrrhic Victory in Idea Misappropriation Cases

Like so many other legalisms and lawyerly advice, all of the theories for the protection of ideas require a lawsuit in order to enforce one's claim of ownership against the literary scavenger who has misappropriated a story idea. And the costs, risks and burdens of litigation are so great that few authors have the heart or the bucks to pursue a lawsuit for idea misappropriation. Even a victory may turn out to be strictly a Pyrrhic one if the costs of litigation are greater than the judgment!

Then, too, the publishing industry—and the entertainment industry generally—tend to regard an idea misappropriation claim as a nuisance suit or, worse, a shakedown. Such lawsuits tend to be vigorously defended out of a fervent belief that a quick settlement will only encourage more lawsuits from frustrated would-be authors who see their own cherished ideas in the success of another author. Idea misappropriation cases, so to speak, get no respect at all.

By contrast, a claim for copyright infringement is much more likely to be taken seriously, and the Copyright Act bestows upon the wronged author a much greater arsenal of legal weaponry. Perhaps the most important differences between a lawsuit based on copyright infringement and one based on idea misappropriation relate to remedies. A plaintiff in a copyright case does not have to prove the reasonable market value of her work in order to win a substantial damage award—she may be entitled to damages that range up to $100,000 per act of infringement even without proof of actual damages. And, crucially, the successful plaintiff may be entitled to recover her legal fees and costs in addition to statutory damages.

➤ *Chapter 6: Copyright Formalities*

But even if an author is not entitled to sue for copyright infringement because only ideas and not copyrighted words and phrases have been ripped off, some small measure of comfort is still available in the form of a lawsuit for idea misappropriation, no matter how cold it may seem to the author who will not or cannot pay a lawyer to pursue the remedy.

Co-Authorship and Copyright

2.

An author, according to the law of copyright, is one who creates *any* work of authorship—a novel, an essay, a poem, a song, a sculpture, a software program, and so on. But when more than one person has taken part in the creation of the work, the rights and duties—and sometimes even the identity—of co-authors and collaborators are not so obvious.

Of course, the author who sits down at the keyboard by himself and simply writes the manuscript will be the sole author of his work, and the sole owner of copyright in the work, at least until he signs a publishing agreement or otherwise sells the rights to his work.

Nowadays, however, co-authorship and collaboration are commonplace in the publishing industry. Sometimes it's a matter of two or three writers—or a writer and an artist—who decide to create a book together. Sometimes it's a celebrity whose autobiography is written by a ghostwriter, or an expert in some technical field whose book is co-written by a professional writer.

Even if a book is authored by a single person, the author may choose to hire an editor to polish a manuscript before it is submitted to an agent or a publisher. And the book as actually published is likely to include copyrighted work owned by a third party—a song lyric or a passage from another book quoted in the text, a photograph or an illustration, a map, a chart, an index.

If the author works with a collaborator of any kind—a co-writer, a ghostwriter, an editor, an illustrator, an indexer—or if the author's work incorporates copyrighted material that is owned by someone else, then a series of crucial questions will arise: Who is really the author of the work in its final form? Who owns the copyright in the work? Who is entitled to authorship credit? Who is authorized to decide how and when the work is published? Who is entitled to cash the royalty checks? And whose permission must be sought before the work can be published?

The questions ought to be answered *before* the project goes very far, and they ought to be answered in one or more written agreements. By the time the work is done and a publishing contract is signed, it will be much more difficult to sort out the rights and duties of the collaborators; indeed, the author may find that he has acquired a co-author without ever intending to do so! And, if the book includes copyrighted material owned by third parties, permission in writing should be obtained to use such material.

Joint Authorship

The simplest and most straightforward form of collaboration consists of two or more individuals who agree to write a book together as co-authors. As a basic proposition, authors who share the work of writing a book—planning, research, writing, revising, and so on— also share ownership of copyright, authorship credit, royalties, and the right to sell the work. They are "joint authors," as the law of copyright puts it, and their work is a "joint work." For most purposes under copyright law, "co-author" and "joint author" are equivalent, and the terms will be used interchangeably here.

The essential test of joint authorship is set forth in the definition of a "joint work" as it appears in the Copyright Act, the federal statute that embodies the law of copyright in the United States:

> "A work prepared by two or more authors with the intention that their contributions be merged into inseparable or interdependent parts of a unitary whole."

"Inseparability" and "Interdependence". Sometimes the collaborators will work together in a manner that makes it literally impossible to say who came up with what, and that's what the law means by "inseparable" contributions. If the co-authors "brainstorm" during the writing process, each one suggesting bits and pieces of the final manuscript, each one revising and polishing the words and phrases suggested by the other, then it will be difficult to untangle the specific contributions of one author or the other—and the resulting work is a classic example of a "pure" work of joint authorship.

Or, if the authors agree on the basic outline of the book, but each author creates a separate element—one author comes up with the text of a children's book, for example, and the other creates the illustrations—then the contributions of the writer and the illustrator are "interdependent," and the resulting work is another classic example of joint authorship.

Each Author Must Make More Than a "De Minimis" Contribution to the Joint Work. Authors of a joint work need not contribute equally to the final work product, but each author is required to make something more than a "de minimis" contribution to the authorship of the project in order to claim rights in a joint work. Exactly what "de minimis" means is, like so much else in the law, mostly in the eye of the beholder, but the law offers us some guidelines.

It's also true that one who contributes *only* ideas or information to a writing project—but does none of the writing—is probably *not* a joint author in the strictest sense. The same is true of one who only conducts research for a book or article, or "packages" a project, or finances a book project, or acts as an agent. That's because one must contribute copyrightable matter in order to be a joint author—and the law of copyright generally does *not* protect ideas and information.

In each of these cases, the person who actually writes the book may agree to give the researcher, packager, publisher, financier or agent a share of the ownership of the project (or, more likely, a share of the revenues), but an agent or publisher, for example, is generally not entitled to the rights of a co-author.

No Contract Is Required to Create Joint Authorship. No formalities are required to create the relationship of joint authorship among the collaborators on a writing project. The co-authors may work in different places and at different times. One author may do most of the work. And the co-authors may work on a project without signing any form of collaboration or co-authorship agreement. Nonetheless, if it was the *intention* of the co-authors *at or prior to the act of creation of the work* that their work be merged into a *unitary whole* according to a *"preconcerted common design"*, then the resulting work is a joint work and the authors are joint authors.

What this means, of course, is that collaborators on a writing project may end up in the legal relationship of joint authorship without ever talking or even thinking about it. And even if two writers fully intend to write a book together as joint authors, they may not pay much attention to how they will handle the details of joint authorship: advances, royalties, authorship credit, and so on.

The Rights and Duties of Joint Authors

Joint authors can allocate the rights and duties of the writing project among themselves. For example, the task of writing of specific chapters may be divided up among the joint authors. A greater share of the advance may be given to the co-author who is expected to carry the greater burden of work. Or the co-authors may agree that one of them will be designated as the "principal" author and will be named first (or named alone) in the byline.

If no agreement is made, however, the law will presume that each of the co-authors owns an equal share of the copyright, each co-author is entitled to equal authorship credit, and each co-author is entitled to an equal share of the advance and the royalties.

For that reason, the best approach is to discuss and decide in advance how the rights and duties of the collaboration will be allocated among the joint authors—and then to write down and sign the agreement. If no agreement has been made to the contrary, however, then these principles will apply to the co-authors and their joint work.

➤ *Form 1: Collaboration Agreement*

▷ Each author is presumptively entitled to an equal share in the ownership of the joint work. Thus, for example, two co-authors will own fifty percent shares of the joint work, three co-authors will own one-third shares, and so on. The equal division of ownership is presumed by the law even if one author clearly contributed a greater quantum of work than his co-authors.

▷ Each author owns an "undivided" interest in the work as a whole. Thus, for example, if a book consisting of art and text is intended by the authors to be a "unitary whole," then the artist and the writer each own one-half of the entire work, including the art *and* the text.

▷ Each of the co-authors may grant rights in the work to third parties on a *nonexclusive* basis without the consent of the other co-authors. (A nonexclusive grant of rights entitles a third party to make use of the work, but the authors are free to grant rights to other users, too.) Thus, for example, a single co-author can authorize the nonexclusive publication of an excerpt from a book in a magazine without the permission—or even the knowledge—of his co-authors, but the co-authors can do the same!

However, a single co-author may not make any use of the joint work that causes the "destruction" of the work—that is, the destruction of its market value. For example, if one co-author grants "nonexclusive" rights in the joint work to a book publisher, it is likely that, as a practical matter, no other book publisher will wish to publish the book. But the fact that other rights in the work are still available for sale—foreign rights, for example, or motion picture and television rights—may mean that the work has not been "destroyed."

Nowadays, of course, the point is probably moot since few, if any, book publishers or movie producers will acquire rights in a book project on a nonexclusive basis. And, once the purchaser of rights knows that a project is co-owned, the purchaser will doubtlessly require the signatures of *all* co-authors and co-owners on a publishing contract or an option for motion picture rights.

▷ Each co-author is under a duty to account to the other co-authors for any profits he may obtain by exploiting the joint work. For example, if a co-author sells nonexclusive magazine excerpt rights to joint work, then the co-author must inform the other co-authors of the sale and pay each co-author his or her share of the fee.

▷ All of the co-authors must consent in writing to any grant of *exclusive* rights in the joint work. For example, if one co-author wishes to sell the joint work to a specific book publisher on an exclusive basis, then *all* of the co-authors must agree to the deal and sign the contract. Otherwise, the publisher will acquire only nonexclusive rights in the work. As noted above, of course, it is unlikely that *any* purchaser of rights will be content with a contract signed by less than all of the co-authors.

▷ Each of the co-authors is entitled to assign his share of the copyright in a joint work to a third party, and to bequeath his share of copyright to his heirs. If a co-author dies without a will, then his share of the copyright will pass automatically to his heirs, and *they* will step into the shoes of the deceased co-author. ➤ *Chapter 8: Remaindering, Reversion and Copyright Termination*

Authorship Credit. The law of copyright does not specifically address the issue of authorship credit and bylines, although authorship may be protected by contract or under the law of unfair competition. Of course, the co-authors are perfectly free to work out an agreement regarding authorship credit and bylines, but unless they do, the best reading of the law is that all co-authors will be entitled to equal authorship credit. Thus, for example, if one author is the "principal" author and expects to be named first in the byline, then an agreement to that effect ought to be written down and signed. ➤ *Chapter 4: The Book Publishing Contract & Chapter 9: Trademark and Unfair Competition*

Compensation of Co-Authors and Collaborators

Co-authors and collaborators are free to share the revenues from a joint work in any manner they choose, or—for that matter—to assign all of the revenues to a single person. Thus, the allocation of *rights* in a joint work need not determine how the *revenues* are shared among co-authors or collaborators. Rather, the compensation of collaborators and co-authors is a "deal point" that can be worked to reflect the deal that the co-authors or collaborators have struck among themselves. Still, compensation of co-authors and collaborators usually falls into one of the following categories.

Flat fee. Many collaborators—and especially ghostwriters, artists and illustrators, and indexers—work on a fee-for-service basis. The collaborator is paid an agreed-upon fee in exchange for the outright acquisition of rights in his work, and no further payments need be made. Of course, the fee may be paid in installments as the work is completed, but the collaborator enjoys no right to participate in the advance, the royalties, or the revenues from exploitation of subsidiary rights.

Advance Against Royalties. The typical publishing contract will include the payment of an advance by the publisher to the author. Co-authors who own equal shares of a joint work will probably expect to receive equal shares of the advance. However, co-authors may agree to allocate a greater percentage of the advance to the co-author who is expected to bear the greatest burden of expense or labor at the outset of the project. The same may be true of a deal between a principal author and a ghostwriter, especially if the principal author is an expert in some field other than writing and publishing.

If one co-author or collaborator receives a greater share of the advance, then it may be decided to allow the other collaborators to recoup their share of the advance out of royalties. For example, if one co-author takes 75 percent of the advance, then the other co-author may take 75 percent of the royalties until each of them has received an equal amount of money.

Royalties. Most book publishing contracts are based on the payment of royalties by the publisher to the author. A co-author is likely to expect an equal division of royalties, but the parties can work out any arrangement that they find mutually acceptable in sharing the royalties. For example, if one author has taken a greater share of the advance, the other author may be allocated a greater share of royalties.

A ghostwriter, even one who is working for a flat fee, may be given a small percentage of the author's royalties as an incentive or a bonus if the book is especially successful.

Other Revenue. A writing project may generate a great deal of revenue from sources other than advances and royalties. For example, if the motion picture rights in a book are optioned or sold, the option payment or purchase price may be substantially greater than the royalties on book sales. Again, the assumption is that co-authors share equally in revenues from the exploitation of subsidiary rights, and so any other split of revenues must be put in writing and signed by all of the co-authors. Even if a ghostwriter, an illustrator, or other collaborator has agreed to work on a fee-for-service basis, some percentage of the revenues from subsidiary rights may be allocated to the collaborator as a kind of performance incentive or bonus for an especially successful project.

➤ *Chapter 7: Electronic and Other Subsidiary Rights*

Time and Manner of Payment. The time and manner in which compensation will be paid needs to be discussed and resolved. As a basic proposition, co-authors will share in revenues generated by the writing project "as and when" received. But a ghostwriter or other collaborator may demand a guaranteed fee paid in installments—and, for

Conditional Royalty. Here is a sample clause that reflects a "conditional royalty" that was granted by an author and his publisher to a freelance editor as an incentive bonus: "CONDITIONAL ROYALTY TO EDITOR. If Editor completes the preparation of the manuscript of the Work to the joint satisfaction of Publisher and Author, then Editor shall receive a royalty of 2% of the suggested retail price for all copies sold less returns of the softcover edition of the Work as published by Publisher in excess of 20,000 copies. If Editor does not complete the preparation of the manuscript of the Work to the mutual satisfaction of Publisher and Author, then the royalty described here shall fully revert and be paid to Author instead of the Editor."

that matter, the principal author may wish to schedule the payments in installments to make sure that the work is performed in a timely manner and in a form that is satisfactory to the author.

Checklist of "Deal Points" in Collaboration and Co-Authorship Agreements

The legal, financial and creative relationship among collaborators involves much more than the ownership of rights in the finished work. The collaborators must answer some very basic questions: How will the actual work of writing the project be divided up? Who will receive authorship credit? How will advances, royalties and other revenues be shared? Who has the right to make decisions about publication of the work? And what happens if the collaboration comes to an end, whether because of the death or disability of a collaborator or simply because the collaborators cannot get along with each other?

Here is a checklist of topics that ought to be considered, discussed and resolved by collaborators. Ideally, the conversation will take place—and the decisions will be made—*before* the work is undertaken. And, ideally, the points of agreement will be written down and signed by all of the collaborators.

Each of these "deal points" is drawn from the model Collaboration in the Forms Library. ➤ *Form 1*

▷ **Allocation of responsibility for work to be performed by the collaborators:** A collaboration agreement ought to be quite specific about the specific tasks that each co-author or collaborator will undertake.

▷ **Deadlines and availability:** Although contracts often express deadlines in soft language—an author will deliver a manuscript "on or about" a particular date, or use "reasonable best efforts" to deliver on a date certain—the agreement can and should be used as a scheduling tool to set goals and keep the project on track. Since money is, after all, an ideal motivator, compensation is often keyed to delivery dates. The agreement should also specify when and where the co-authors and collaborators will make themselves available for the work.

▷ **Ownership of Copyright:** As discussed above, the collaboration agreement ought to specify who owns what rights in the project, and in what percentages. If one party to the agreement is intended to acquire rights from the other parties, then an appropriate grant of

Co-Authorship and Copyright

AND WHO GETS THE ESPRESSO MAKER?
If a writing collaboration resembles a marriage, as many co-authors say, then a collaboration agreement is the functional equivalent of a prenuptial agreement—it's most useful when the agreement anticipates what might go wrong and offers some approaches to solving problems. One pair of co-authors worked out an elaborate arrangement for the byline of their book—one author's name would always come first, and the other author's name would be on the second line in type no greater than one-half the size of the first author's byline. Just to make sure there were no misunderstandings, they went to the trouble of setting a specimen of the byline in type and attaching it as an exhibit to their collaboration agreement!

Another pair of co-authors, at my invitation, made notes on the "deal points" that they wanted to see in the collaboration agreement that they asked me to draft. The notes turned out to be a meticulous and almost encyclopedic list of do's and don'ts—one author, for example, insisted that her co-author should not call her on the telephone before 10:00 a.m. or after 8:00 p.m. Eventually, we simply attached their letters to the collaboration agreement, labeled them "Exhibit A," and wrote the following clause into the agreement:

We agree to cooperate with each other as joint authors of the Work, and to share equally in all tasks and responsibilities as may be necessary to complete the Work and secure its publication and other exploitation, including research, writing, and editing of the Work. However, in order to clarify our respective responsibilities, and to the greatest extent possible, we agree to follow the procedures described in Exhibit "A".

rights or work-for-hire clause ought to be included. ➤ *Work-for-Hire & The Perils of Employment–Below*

▷ **Compensation:** As discussed above, the collaboration agreement ought to address how each co-author or collaborator will be compensated, whether by payment of a flat fee, a share of advances and royalties, or some other method, and the time and manner of payment should also be specified.

▷ **Authorship Credit:** The agreement ought to specify the manner in which each contributor will be credited, especially if the author credits are to be anything but strictly equal. Even then, the order of names in a joint byline ought to specified to avoid hurt feelings—or worse. A sample byline can be attached to the agreement as an exhibit.

▷ **Right to Control:** *Someone* will need to make decisions on the creative, business, legal and other considerations that arise in a writing project. The co-authors or collaborators may agree to share the decision-making authority, but there is always the risk of a deadlock if everyone's consent is required—and some mechanism for breaking a deadlock ought to be included in the deal.

29

▷ **Sequels and Revisions:** A successful book is likely to result in revised editions, a sequel, or other spin-off projects. Unless otherwise specified, the ownership and control of such projects probably belong to the co-authors or collaborations on the same terms that apply to the original project. But if the author, for instance, wishes to reserve the right to exclude a ghostwriter from participation in future projects, the agreement should say so. And a well-drafted co-authorship agreement may include a mechanism for determining whether or how to compensate the co-author who declines to work on a sequel.

▷ **Death or Disability:** Life is short, as the poet says, but art is long. And once a writing project is finished, the rights of the co-authors upon death are governed in most respects by copyright law, but what happens if a co-author dies or is disabled before the project is completed?
➤ *Chapter 8: Remaindering, Reversion and Copyright Termination*

▷ **Termination:** The sad fact is that some writing collaborations crash and burn. A useful way for co-authors or collaborators to extract themselves from a project and divide up what's left is to invoke an arbitration or mediation clause—which may also be useful in resolving other, less dramatic problems that may arise during the collaboration.

▷ **Non-Disclosure and Non-Competition:** Since each collaborator is confiding in the other—and does not want to see his best ideas show up in somebody else's work—most collaborators will want a non-disclosure and non-competition clause that restricts the collaborators from making use of materials outside the collaboration itself. This is especially important, of course, where the principal author is confiding information to a professional writer.

▷ **Expenses:** As a general matter, income and expenses are usually allocated in the same percentages; if the co-authors share equally in advances and royalties, then they will probably agree to share equally in expenses. However, it is useful to include a clause that obliges each collaborator to obtain the other collaborator's written permission *before* incurring a major expense. Bear in mind, too, that a co-author or collaborator may be liable for the debts of the other party if, in fact, the collaborators are held to be partners or "joint venturers"!

▷ **Mediation and Arbitration:** If the parties to an agreement find themselves in dispute, they may choose to forego the right to bring a lawsuit in court and instead submit their disputes to what attorneys like to call "alternative dispute resolution"—that is, mediation or arbitration. *Mediation* is the submission of a dispute to an individual or group of individuals who try to work out a mutually agreeable solution to a dispute. It's non-binding and non-coercive—if the mediator cannot bring the parties to a settlement, then neither party can be forced to accept. *Arbitration* is the submission of a dispute to one or more individuals who consider the arguments and evidence of all parties to a dispute—and then decide one way or another. An arbitration is generally less formal than a lawsuit in open court, and they are almost always faster, cheaper, and more private.

Other Forms of Collaboration

Some forms of collaboration may be undertaken without the intent of creating a work of joint authorship. An author who hires an editor to polish his manuscript, for example, certainly does not intend to put the editor's name on his book as a co-author and share the royalty checks. But, as discussed above, there is a distinct risk that a collaborator may end up as a co-author if the collaborator contributes "independently copyrightable" elements to a "unitary work."

For that reason, the terms of any collaboration ought to be carefully thought out in advance of undertaking the work—and if the roles of the collaborators change along the way, the subject should be revisited. Above all, the relationship among collaborators should be defined in a written agreement. ➤ *Form 1: Collaboration Agreement*

If a single person intends to acquire ownership and control of all rights in a project, then one or more agreements *must* be written down and signed by *all* of the participants in the project. ➤ *Acquiring Rights in Copyrighted Work–Below*

Here are several common varieties of collaboration, and some of the problems that may arise in each one.

Ghostwriters. If an author hires a ghostwriter to assist him in writing a book—and the final version of the book includes copyrightable material provided by the ghostwriter—then the book is probably a work of joint authorship owned by both the author *and* the ghostwriter, even if the ghostwriter is *not* credited as a co-author. And, under the principles of joint authorship discussed above, the author and the ghostwriter will be presumed to own equal shares in the finished work, even if one or the other wrote most of the work.

Of course, the expectation of an author and a ghostwriter, almost by definition, is that the ghostwriter will *not* be credited as a co-author—or, in many cases, not credited at all. And the ghostwriter may agree to accept much less than fifty percent of the advance and royalties in payment for his work. That's why it is essential for an author and a ghostwriter to work out the details of their relationship in advance, write them down in a formal agreement, and then sign it.

Editors. As a general proposition, an editor is *not* a co-author, especially if the editor confines his work to the traditional editorial functions: correcting grammar and spelling, rearranging words, phrases and paragraphs, and polishing the author's prose.

There is little risk that the issue of co-authorship will arise in the dealings between an author and his editor when the editor is employed by the publishing house. But an editor who is privately hired by the author to work on a manuscript may be asked to play a very intimate and extensive role in shaping the project and the written material itself, and—in fact—a private editor may turn out to be a kind of ghostwriter.

The best way to avoid any

THE ACCIDENTAL CO-AUTHOR. Can an author acquire a co-author by accident? Since intent is one important element of joint authorship, the law says no—but sometimes it takes a lawsuit to make the point. In Childress v. Taylor, the court ruled that actress Clarice Taylor was not the co-author of a play by Alice Childress about the life of "Moms" Mabley even though the actress commissioned the play and contributed research material, jokes, scenes and characters to the finished work.

By way of example, the court considered the relationship between an author and an editor or researcher in emphasizing that both collaborators must intend to enter into the relationship of joint authorship.

"For example, a writer frequently works with an editor who makes numerous useful revisions to the first draft, some of which will consist of additions of copyrightable expression. Both intend their contributions to be merged into inseparable parts of a unitary whole, yet very few editors and even fewer writers would expect the editor to be accorded the status of joint author, enjoying an undivided half interest in the copyright in the published work. Similarly, research assistants may on occasion contribute to an author some protectible expression or merely a sufficiently original selection of factual material as would be entitled to a copyright, yet not be entitled to be regarded as a joint author of the work in which the contributed material appears. What distinguishes the writer-editor relationship and the writer-researcher relationship from the true joint author relationship is the lack of intent of both participants in the venture to regard themselves as joint authors."

misunderstanding on the subject is to carefully define the relationship between author and editor in a written agreement for editorial services. The agreement should specifically define the services to be rendered by the editor, and a disclaimer should be included:

> **EDITOR is engaged to provide editorial services only, and no relationship of joint authorship is created by this Agreement.**

Still, it's not enough to include such a self-serving clause if the editor goes beyond "blue-penciling" the manuscript and, in fact, creates and contributes independently copyrightable material to the project. A better (and more cautious) approach is to include a "safety net" clause that transfers to the author all rights in any material that the editor may create. ➤ *Form 2: Work-For-Hire Agreement & The Perils of Employment– Below*

Researchers. Since raw data is not subject to copyright protection except under exceptional circumstances, a researcher—like an editor—does not ordinarily acquire authorship rights in the material that he gathers and contributes to a book.

However, it is possible to claim ownership of copyright in the particular *selection* and *organization* of facts. What's more, if a researcher summarizes and refines his research in a written form—or if the researcher creates maps, charts and graphs, or other forms of graphic or verbal expression—then the researcher's work product is probably copyrightable in itself.

Thus, as a matter of caution, it makes good sense to ask the researcher to sign a simple agreement that confirms that the author owns copyright in the researcher's work product. ➤ *Form 2: Work-For-Hire Agreement*

Artists and Illustrators. Artists, photographers and illustrators who create incidental artwork for a book project *are* the "authors" of their work under the law of copyright, and they start out with complete ownership of rights in what they create. What's more, freelance artists often sell their work without formal agreements regarding acquisition of rights. Often, a simple invoice is the only document that passes between an artist and the author or publisher who acquires artwork. A better approach for both artist and publisher is to set down in writing exactly what rights are being granted and what rights are being reserved.

Under the law of copyright, one cannot acquire *exclusive* rights in the copyrighted work of another person except in a written agreement signed by the person who is granting rights. Unless the freelance artist's invoice includes specific language regarding the grant of rights, it will probably convey only a *nonexclusive* right to the author or publisher. Thus, for example, an illustrator who sells a cover illustration—or a photographer who sells a photograph—on a nonexclusive basis to one publisher is perfectly free to sell the same illustration to someone else!

➤ *Acquiring Rights in Coperighted Work–Below*

Bear in mind, however, that a different situation arises when the artist is collaborating with a writer on a work in which art and text are combined into a "unitary whole." In that case, artist and writer are joint authors for purpose of copyright law, and each one acquires an undivided one-half interest in the work as a whole unless they agree otherwise in writing.

Indexers, Graphic Artists, and Other Contributors. A book or an issue of a magazine may include a number of copyrighted elements that are actually created by someone other than the author or the publisher. A preface or introduction may be contributed by a separate author. An indexer or indexing service may be hired to prepare an index. A graphic artist may be engaged to create the typography, page design, and incidental illustrations. Each of these contributors may have claims to copyright in their work. The legal relationship between the publisher and these contributors ought to be written down and signed.

Agents and Packagers. The legal relationship among authors and publishers, on one hand, and agents and "packagers," on the other hand, is a complex one that is discussed at greater length elsewhere. But agents and packagers, who gather the various elements of a book project and then sell the rights to a publisher, may claim rights of ownership or even authorship. A clear understand-

THE RIGHT STUFF. Care should be taken in drafting the various agreements by which rights are acquired from illustrators, indexers, and other copyright owners whose permission is needed to publish the final version of the work. Among the questions that must be answered is: <u>To whom are the rights granted, the author or the publisher?</u> For example, one author who assembled an anthology of readings for college students used a standard permission form that granted to the <u>publisher</u>—and <u>not</u> the author—the right to use the readings on a non-assignable basis. Later, when rights to the anthology reverted from the publisher to the author, he discovered that the permissions were still controlled by the publisher. As a result, he had to approach each and every copyright owner and ask for permission all over again in order to publish a new edition with another publisher.

ing of the agent's or packager's rights in the project—and a clear agreement signed by author and agent, or author, publisher and packager—are the best way to avoid disputes later on. ➤ *Chapter 3: Agents and Packagers & Form 3: Agency Agreement*

Acquiring Rights in Copyrighted Work

As a general rule, the author or publisher who seeks to make use of someone else's copyrighted material must first acquire the right to do so. Four basic legal mechanisms for the acquisition of rights in copyrighted work are described below, and these approaches may be used when, for example, one author acquires rights from a co-author or collaborator, or when a publisher acquires rights from an author, or when an author *or* publisher acquires rights from an artist, illustrator, indexer, or some other owner of copyrighted work.

Bear in mind that one or more of the following approaches may be used by *any* person who is acquiring rights in copyrighted material from another person who created or owns the copyrighted material. For the sake of discussion, however, we generally will refer to the person *acquiring* rights as "the publisher," and the person *conveying* rights as "the copyright owner."

▷ A **grant of rights** by the copyright owner to the publisher, which actually conveys ownership of some or all rights in the copyrighted material from the copyright owner to the publisher for use in the author's work as published.

> **Fair Use.** No permission from the copyright owner is required to make use of portions of a copyrighted work under the doctrine of "fair use," which generally applies to limited use of a small portion of a copyrighted work for approved purposes such as commentary, criticism or scholarship. The factors that determine whether any particular use of copyrighted work is fair use are discussed in detail elsewhere. But fair use is a narrow and highly technical doctrine, and one only knows with certainty whether the doctrine applies after a lawsuit for copyright infringement has been filed and the court decides the question! So the cautious author or publisher will almost always secure written permission from a copyright owner before making use of copyrighted material in a published work. ➤ *Chapter 5: Preparing the Manuscript*

▷ A **license**, which conveys permission to use (but *not* ownership of) the copyrighted material from the copyright owner to the publisher for certain specific uses.

▷ A **work-for-hire agreement** between the publisher and the independent contractor who provides certain specific categories of copyrighted material for use in the author's work as published, which vests ownership of *all* rights in the publisher. ➤ *The Perils of Employment–Below*

▷ An **employer-employee relationship** between the publisher and the person who is employed by the publisher to create the copyrighted material, which vests ownership of *all* rights in the publisher.

Distinctions Between "Work-for-Hire" and Other Forms of Copyright Ownership

As a general proposition, copyright in a work of authorship automatically belongs to the person—or persons—who created the work in the first place. The creator of the work is known as the "author" under copyright law, and it is the author alone who owns and controls the copyright in the work. The author can convey some or all rights in his work to another person by granting or licensing the rights—but the copyright law allows the author to terminate the transfer and reclaim his rights under certain specific circumstances. ➤ *Chapter 8: Remaindering, Reversion and Copyright Termination*

The author of a "work-for-hire," by contrast, is *not* the person who actually creates the work. Rather, it is the person who *hired* the creator of the work, or who "specially *ordered* or *commissioned*" the work from the creator of the work. For all intents and purposes under the copyright law, however, the commissioning or hiring party *is* the author.

> **FASTER THAN A SPEEDING LAWSUIT.** Back in 1933, when Jerome Siegel and Joseph Shuster first came up with a comic strip featuring a character called Superman, they were freelance artists who sold comic strips to various magazines. Four years later, they went to work for a comic book publisher who signed them to an employment contract that included a work-for-hire clause, and they sold the rights to Superman to their employer "to have and hold forever." The rest, of course, is pop-culture history.
>
> In the mid-70s, Shuster and Siegel sought to win back the rights to their fabulously successful comic book character, and their publisher argued, among other things, that Superman fell under the work-for-hire agreement that the two artists had signed back in 1938. But the court disagreed—Superman was <u>not</u> a work-for-hire because the character had been created long before the two artists went to work for the publisher. In other words, a work-for-hire agreement cannot be retroactive and applies only to work undertaken after the artists actually went on the payroll of the publisher.

A work-for-hire differs from a conventional copyrighted work in the following ways:

▷ The employer or commissioning party, and *not* the actual creator of the work, is the designated author of a work-for-hire in the records of the Copyright Office, and for all purposes under the law of copyright.

▷ The actual creator of the work may *not* exercise the right to terminate transfers.

▷ Works for hire are *not* eligible for protection under the doctrine of "artist's rights" under the Visual Artists Rights Act, and are probably outside the bounds of the doctrine of "moral rights."

➤ *Chapter 9: Briefs (Moral Rights*

> "[Work-for-hire] is applicable only when the employee's work is produced at the instance and expense of the employer," the court ruled in <u>Siegel v. National Periodical Pub., Inc.</u> "Superman had been spawned by the plaintiffs four years before the relationship between his authors and the defendants existed."
>
> But the publisher prevailed on other grounds—an earlier lawsuit in 1948 had resulted in a consent decree that "settled for once and for all that the [publisher] had all right and title to Superman for all time." So it was the publisher of Superman—and not his creators—who turned out to be invulnerable.

▷ The duration of copyright protection for a work-for-hire under current law is 75 years from the year of first publication, or 100 years from the year of creation, whichever expires first, rather than the life of the author plus fifty years. ➤ *Chapter 8: Remaindering, Reversion and Copyright Termination*

From the point of view of the party who is *acquiring* rights, therefore, it is almost always preferable to acquire the work of a ghostwriter or other collaborator on a work-for-hire basis since the rights in the collaborator's work will be fully owned and controlled by the acquiring party.

On the other hand, from the point of view of the party who is *conveying* rights, a grant of rights or a license is preferable since it allows the actual creator of the work to enjoy the benefits of authorship and to maintain a degree of control over the rights even after they are transferred to another person—including, under specific circumstances, the right to terminate the transfer of rights.

Grant of Rights

A basic approach to acquiring rights in a copyrighted work is a grant of rights, that is, an agreement by which the creator of the work conveys the ownership of some or all of the rights in the work to another person. The typical book contract is essentially a grant of rights, and so are many contracts for electronic, audio, motion picture and other subsidiary rights in a book.

A grant of rights *must* be embodied in a signed writing if the acquiring party wishes to obtain *exclusive* rights in the copyrighted work. An oral grant of rights will convey rights on a nonexclusive basis only. If, for example, an author seeks to acquire *exclusive* rights in the work of a ghostwriter or a co-author—or if the publisher wishes to acquire exclusive rights in the author's work—the person conveying the rights *must* sign a written grant of rights. Once signed, the rights belong to the person who acquired the rights, and the acquiring party is now entitled to exploit the rights that he has acquired.

However, the person who grants some or all rights in his work remains an author of the work in the technical and legal sense. This means, among other things, that his name will appear in the records of the Copyright Office, and he will enjoy the right to terminate the grant of rights at a later date and reclaim his ownership of copyright in the work! ➤ *Chapter 6: Copyright Formalities & Chapter 8: Remaindering, Reversion and Copyright Termination*

When rights in a copyrighted work are acquired by a grant of rights, special care must be taken to define the nature and scope of rights that are being conveyed. Copyright in a work of authorship may be subdivided in an almost infinite number of subsidiary rights—book rights, movie rights, foreign rights, electronic rights, and so on—and each right may be conveyed separately. Of course, the acquiring party is only entitled to exploit the rights that have actually been granted to him by the author. Thus, the grant of rights ought to be clear and explicit on the question of what rights are being granted and what rights, if any, are being reserved. ➤ *Chapter 4: The Book Publishing Contract & Chapter 7: Electronic and Other Subsidiary Rights.*

Copyright Licenses

A license, by contrast, conveys the right to *use* some portion of the copyrighted work without conveying *ownership* of any rights in the work. Typically, a license is limited in scope, duration, territory and other particulars. For instance, the right to publish a foreign-language edition of a book in a particular country is often licensed to a foreign publisher for a specified number of years, and the rights expire at the end of the term.

Licenses are also commonly used when an author or publisher seeks permission to quote a passage or copy an illustration from another copyrighted work. Such licenses are almost always nonexclusive—that is, the copyright owner gives the publisher permission to make use of material from the copyrighted work, but the owner is perfectly free to give permission to others, too.

A license must be embodied in a signed written agreement in order to convey exclusive and irrevocable rights. An oral license conveys only nonexclusive rights—and, more crucially, an oral license is generally revocable by the owner of copyright. So the author or publisher who secures permission to quote a copyrighted work—but does not bother to confirm the permission in a written agreement—may find that the permission has been revoked and the material may no longer be used.

➤ *Form 4: Permissions Agreement*

KILLING HER SOFTLY WITH YOUR SONG. Publishers and other copyright owners routinely entertain and grant requests for permission to quote or copy their published works in a process generally known as "Rights and Permissions." But permissions must be carefully negotiated and drafted in order to make sure that the permission covers the intended use of the quoted material. One mystery writer who wanted to use the lyrics of a famous song in a crucial scene in her novel took care to seek permission from the music publisher—and she paid $500 for the right to do so. But, as she later discovered, the permission only extended to <u>print</u> editions of her novel. When the author was asked to license an <u>audio</u> version of the book, she discovered that she needed to go back to the music publisher and start all over again!

Work-for-Hire

Another approach to acquiring rights in the work of a collaborator is work-for-hire (or "work made for hire," as the doctrine is also known). The work-for-hire doctrine is a form of copyright ownership in which the acquiring party is treated as the author of a work that was actually created by someone else. Ownership, control, registration, and all other incidents of copyright proprietorship belong solely to the acquiring party.

In order to qualify as a work-for-hire, a work of authorship must fall into one of two very different legal categories. One category applies to works that are created by an independent contractor, and the other category applies to work created by an employee within the "course and scope" of employment.

Works for Hire by Independent Contractors. A work created by an independent contract—a freelance writer, artist or editor, for example—may be characterized as a work-for-hire under certain limited circumstances.

▷ The work must fall into one of nine specific categories set forth in the Copyright Act: A contribution to a collective work; a part of a motion picture or other audiovisual work; a translation; a supplementary work (i.e., forewords, afterwords, illustrations, maps, charts, tables, bibliographies, appendices and indexes); a compilation; an instructional text; a test; answer material for a test; or an atlas.

▷ The work must be "specially ordered or commissioned," that is, a work-for-hire cannot be an existing work that is transferred from one party to another after its creation. Rather, a work-for-hire must be created at the special request of the acquiring party.

▷ Both the creator of the work and the person who acquires the work must sign a written agreement that characterizes the work as work-for-hire—and, at least under the strict technical requirements of the copyright law, they must do so *before* the work is actually created!

> **The Perils of Employment.** The work of both employees and independent contractors can be acquired as work-for-hire for copyright purposes under proper circumstances. But special care must be taken when characterizing someone as an employee. Under federal law, as well as the laws of most states, an employee is generally entitled to certain benefits, including workers compensation and unemployment insurance, and an employer is under certain obligations, including the withholding of taxes from wages and salaries. So the employment status of <u>anyone</u> contributing work-for-hire must be carefully evaluated according to applicable laws.

Since ghostwriters, illustrators, photographers, and similar contributors are usually independent contractors, and *not* employees, most work-for-hire will be acquired under the rules and procedures described here. A sample work-for-hire agreement may be found in the Forms Library. ➤ *Form 2: Work-for-Hire Agreement*

Work-for-Hire by Employees. The second category of work-for-hire applies to works of authorship created by an employee within the "course and scope" of employment. A work-for-hire by an employee is *not* confined to the statutory categories described above—*any* work by an *employee* within the *course and scope of employment* can be a work-for-hire—and *no* written agreement is required.

However, the hiring party must be able to show that the employee was a bona fide employee, that is, the relationship of employer-employee existed between them at the time the work was created. No single test of employee status is controlling, but the courts will look at various factors to determine if the employer enjoyed the "right to control the manner and means" by which the work is carried out.

Even if an employee-employer relationship exists, the work must have been created within the "course and scope" of employment. The stories filed by a staff reporter on the police beat are work-for-hire and belong to the publisher of the newspaper, for example, but the Great American Novel that he is writing on weekends at home is not.

No written agreement is necessary to create a work-for-hire relationship between an employer and an employee. However, a cautious employer may wish to ask the employee to sign an agreement that confirms the work-for-hire status of the employee's work product—and, for that matter, a cautious employee may wish to ask the employer to sign an agreement that carefully defines the "course and scope" of employment and clarifies what specific categories of work are excluded from work-for-hire status.

3.

Agents and Packagers

The days are long gone—if it were ever truly so!—when the first person an unlucky author called from jail on a Saturday night was his agent. Authors may still cherish secret fantasies of the agent as confidante, mentor, and benefactor, but the reality is that an agent is, above all, a *salesperson* whose job is to sell the author's work to a publisher, collect the advances and royalties on the author's behalf, and then—after deducting the near-universal fifteen percent commission—pay what's left to the author.

Of course, some authors are fortunate enough to find an agent who is able to play a more expansive role than deal-maker. An agent may suggest a project to an author, assist the author in finding a collaborator, alert the author to a publisher in search of a writer for a particular project. Often an agent will shape and sharpen the book proposal to make it more marketable, and the rare agent may be able to guide the author through a rewrite or a polish of a manuscript.

But the highest calling of the literary agent is the ability to generate a market for the author's work and to find a buyer who will pay the highest price. The fondest dream of every author, of course, is an agent who manages to work up so much heat around an author's project that the publishers line up to bid at an "auction" for the right to publish the work. But the agent who manages to place a book with a publisher at a decent advance and royalty rate merits the author's gratitude *and* the fifteen percent commission, even if the agent isn't quite a surrogate parent.

Still, the fact is that the relationship between author and agent can be a troubled one. The friction usually begins when the author begins to worry about how hard the agent is working and how much attention he is paying to the author's book. Indeed, the two most common complaints that I hear about agents is that they are not aggressive enough and that they do not return telephone calls. (The same complaint, by the way, is often heard about lawyers!) And, ironically, the agent with the longest client list and the most impressive record of big advances is precisely the one who may not have enough time to call back every anxious author who wants to know what is going on with *her* book. But at least one agent of my acquaintance insists that the opposite is true:

"A busy agent," he says, "is a *good* agent."

The Role of the Agent

The key to solving the potential friction between author, on the one hand, and agent, on the other hand, is to talk out what the agent will and will not do, to measure each other's style and temperament, to ask some hard questions about the availability of the agent's time and attention, and—as in virtually all business dealings—to write down the deal in a way that both parties can understand and live with. *All of the "deal points" set forth below ought to be discussed and resolved before the agent and author strike a deal with each other.*

As every author knows, it is often as hard to find an agent as it is to find a publisher. But an effective agent plays a crucial and sometimes indispensable role in placing a book project, and he

---

WHEN THE CLIFF NOTES AREN'T AVAILABLE. When I was spending my afternoons working on my first novel and my evenings studying for the bar exam, I was fortunate enough to find an agent who agreed to (and, in fact, did) sell my book. And my agent quickly enlightened me to one of the hard truths of the book business.

"Send me five complete copies of the manuscript," he growled over the phone from his Broadway office in New York City, "and a summary. One page, tops. One paragraph is better."

The fact that he wanted multiple copies of the manuscript was one small revelation about the role of the agent in the publishing business—the agent did not want to shell out for photocopying. But I was curious about the one-paragraph summary, especially since the manuscript of my novel was complete and he could read it for himself.

"Oh, I don't read the stuff," he explained. "I just sell it."

Nearly 20 years later, both agents and editors are demanding outlines and synopses since the first cut among submissions is often made without reading the manuscript at all!

---

brings real value to the work of the author by searching out a market for what would otherwise remain an unpublished manuscript tucked away in a bottom desk drawer—or, nowadays, stored somewhere in the limbo of a hard drive.

What Am I Bid? A curious feature of the book publishing industry is the book auction—a round of competitive bidding among several publishers who are interested in the same book project. Often (but not always), the agent starts out by soliciting a firm offer from one publisher who sets the "floor." (Usually, the bidding focuses on the cash advance to be paid by the publisher to the author, but other deal points may also be specified.) Then the agent solicits bids from as many other publishers as she can, and the highest bidder takes the book. But the "floor" bidder is usually granted "topping privileges"—that is, the "floor" bidder has the right to "top" the highest bidder by adding a specified percentage to the high bid. Bidding may be conducted over a few hours or a few days, and it usually consists of a series of frantic telephone calls by the agent-cum-auctioneer to the various acquiring editors who have expressed interest in the project. Although there may be a confirming letter or two, most book auctions are conducted with little or no paperwork at all.

The Agent as a Fiduciary

The law defines an agent as one who represents another person, known as the principal, in dealings with third parties. As we've seen, a literary agent is, first and above all, a salesperson. But the law regards the relationship between an agent and his client as something loftier. "Agent" is a "term of art" in the law, a word that implies a weighty and solemn relationship between two people—the agent is one who is entrusted with the money, property, or business dealings of another person, and the agent is held to the highest standards of honesty and good faith.

The key concept in the agent-principal relationship is *trust*. An agent is a "fiduciary," a word that derives from the Latin word for "faith" and implies that the agent must act in a way that earns (and deserves) the confidence of the principal. According to the law of agency, the agent is required not only to use "reasonable care, diligence and skill" in the performance of his work, but to go much further: the agent must render complete and accurate accountings of the money he receives on behalf of the author; he must make full disclosure of any facts that might affect the interests of the author; and he must scrupulously avoid any conflicts of interest.

Technically, an agent must refrain from competing with his client or representing someone who is in competition with her. But, as a practical matter, a literary agent will represent many authors who may be in competition with each other for book projects and pub-lishing deals. What's more, the literary agent is more likely to conceive of the relationship with his clients as an arm's length business transaction rather than the intimate relationship that "fiduciary" implies.

Some agents will go to the trouble of including language in their agency agreements by which the author is asked to acknowledge that the agent is free to represent other clients and other projects that may well be in competition with the author and her book project. But the verbiage in an agency agreement does not change the exalted nature of the relationship between author and agent. An agency *is* something more than an ordinary business relation-ship, and the author is entitled to expect a degree of candor and commitment that might not arise in ordinary business dealings.

➤ *Form 3: Agency Agreement*

> **WINNING THROUGH INTIMIDATION.** One agent with a reputation for driving hard bargains—and making big deals—turned over a manuscript to a "reader," who is often an aspiring agent whose hazing consists of answering the phones, answering the mail, and reading the unsolicited (or "over-the-transom") man-uscripts. The reader gave the manuscript a thumbs-down, and—on the strength of the reader's report—so did the agent.
>
> The author, angry and undaunted, shot off a letter that cast some rather dark aspersions on the reader's intelligence, literacy, and acuity—so sharp, in fact, that the reader was literally reduced to tears.
>
> "You made my reader cry," the agent told the author.
>
> "So what?" the author replied.
>
> The agent, recognizing toughness and tenacity when she saw it, promptly signed the author—and sold the project for a six-figure advance.
>
> We do not know what became of the reader.

The Elements of an Agency Agreement

No Contract Is Necessary! No formal contract is necessary to create an agency relationship. Indeed, an agency may be based on an entirely oral agreement—or it may even be *implied* by the circumstances of the dealings between an agent and principal, as when an author submits a manuscript to an agent with a cover letter that says, in essence, "Will you please represent my book project?" And the fact is that many authors and agents deal exclusively by telephone without ever signing a contract or even meeting one another face to face. However, a written contract is *required* for certain kinds of agents, and a written contract is always *preferable* because it's the best way to avoid misunderstandings between author and agent.

A written agency agreement is required by law when the author is empowering the agent to enter into agreements that require a signed contract. For example, some agents may actually seek the authority to sign publishing agreements on behalf of the author—and a publishing agreement must be in writing in order to convey exclusive rights under copyright. So the agent's authority to sign on behalf of the author must be in writing, too.

Even when the law does not require an agency agreement to be in writing, however, some form of written agreement signed by both author and agent is always preferable. As discussed below, there are so many ambiguities and vagaries surrounding the role of an agent that a written agreement will almost always serve the best interests of *both* author and agent. And the written agreement should address each of the following basic "deal points." ➤ *Form 3: Agency Agreement*

▷ **Exclusivity.** Theoretically, an author might engage several agents to represent her work on a nonexclusive basis, and then choose the deal that she likes best. As a practical matter, however, few (if any) agents will accept an author on a nonexclusive basis. Although the agent's right to represent the author's work may be limited in duration or scope, as discussed below, the agent will expect to be given some degree of exclusivity.

However, an agent need not be the exclusive representative of the author for all projects, or even all aspects of a single project. As discussed below, it's not unusual for the author and her literary agent to agree that the agent will be responsible for selling domestic book rights only, and another agent will be responsible for selling movie rights or foreign rights.

The issue of exclusivity is one that ought to be addressed and resolved in a signed contract. A vague understanding of the scope of the agency relationship—or even a specific oral agreement—will be hard to prove one way or the other if author and agent disagree over the commission on a particular deal.

▷ **What Rights Does the Agent Represent?** The key question in any agency agreement between author and agent is the *scope* of the agency. Even if the agent is entitled to represent the author's work on an exclusive basis, the question remains: What rights is the agent authorized to sell?

Any work of authorship embodies a "bundle" of rights. By definition, the right to publish the author's manuscript as a book is usually the most important right in a book project, but—as authors and publishers know so well—a publishing contract may lead to the sale of various "subsidiary" rights: the right to make a movie or a television program based on the book, the right to produce an audiocassette version of the book, the right to use the book in CD-ROM or other electronic media, and so on. ➤ *Chapter 7: Electronic and Other Subsidiary Rights*

As a general proposition, the agent will want to represent as many rights as possible for the simple reason that he will expect to be commissioned on as many deals as possible. The agent argues that it is only fair for him to participate in, for example, a movie deal if the producers were attracted to the project because he sold the book to a publisher. If the agent "creates value" in a project by persuading a publisher to publish the author's work, the agent's argument goes, the agent is entitled to participate in the enhanced value of the project.

Some agency agreements go beyond "all rights" in a single work and claim for the agent the exclusive right to represent *all* of the author's work. Here's a clause from a commonly used agency agreement that bestows upon the agent an exclusive right to represent virtually everything the author may create during the term of the agency:

> Author irrevocably appoints Agent as Author's sole and exclusive agent throughout the world to represent Author in any and all matters relating to the Author's Work, including but not limited to the negotiation of Contract(s) for the disposition of Author's Work.
>
> "Author's Work," as the phrase is used in this Agreement, includes but is not limited to all ideas, story materials, characters, situations, formats, and works of authorship which Author has created or creates during the term of this Agreement, or in which Author has any title or interest, including but not limited to books, articles, playscripts, screenplays, teleplays, treatments and outlines, and any and all rights in and to such work.

The author, on the other hand, may be justifiably concerned about an all-inclusive agency. Indeed, the author may not even want to consign all of the rights in a single book to a single agent, especially if the agent is primarily a literary agent. A New York literary agent who is best positioned to sell book rights may not be the most effective agent to sell movie rights, for instance, or foreign rights. Here's a clause, for example, that carefully restricts the scope of the agency to

English language "print publication rights" in a single work in the English speaking markets only:

> Author irrevocably appoints Agent as Author's sole and exclusive agent
> to represent Author in the U.S. and Canada in any and all matters
> relating to the print publication rights in the English language in Author's
> work titled YOUR FINGERTIPS TOUCHING MY FACE: An Iconography of
> the Music of Van Morrison ("the Work"), including but not limited to the
> negotiation of Contract(s) for the disposition of the Work. All rights not
> expressly described above are reserved to the Author.

Between these two points—an agency for all rights in everything, and an agency for English language print rights in a single market—is plenty of room for a good deal of heated debate between author and agent. Indeed, the question of what rights the agent will be authorized to sell is often a hot point of negotiation at the very outset of the agency relationship.

> Who's Hot, Who's Not. Authors are always attracted to the agent whom they perceive to be the "hottest." Usually, that means the agent whose last deal had the most zeros in the advance. Among the best places to find out who's making the hot deals is Publishers Weekly, the all-important "trade" publication of the book publishing industry—it's virtually the stock market page of the agency business.

Some agency agreements address the issue by authorizing the literary agent to engage co-agents or sub-agents who will handle specialized rights or particular markets. It's commonplace, for example, to provide for the literary agent to work with a foreign rights agent—and, nowadays, it makes sense for the literary agent to work with a "dramatic" agent, that is, an agent who specializes in selling motion picture, television and other dramatic rights. In such instances, however, the author will often be asked to pay a higher commission in order to compensate the two agents.

Here's a typical clause on co-agenting:

> Author acknowledges and agrees that Agent may appoint sub-agents or others
> to assist her at her own expense. However, if Agent engages a co-agent
> for the disposition of any particular rights in Author's Work, then a total
> commission of Twenty Percent (20%) shall be payable on any and all
> Contract(s) on which Agent and the co-agent have jointly represented Author.
> Such commissions shall be shared between Agent and the co-agent according
> to their mutual agreement.

As set forth below—and as the co-agenting clause suggests—the principal agent may demand that the author pay an enhanced commission when more than one agent is working on the project. But the author may prefer to simply enter into two different agency agreements, one for print rights and another one for motion picture and television rights.

▷ **Term.** How long will the agent enjoy the exclusive right to represent an author and her work? The agreement between author and agent may be entirely open-ended, or it may specify a number of months or years.

An agent will expect a fair chance to sell the book project before the agency is terminated—six months or a year, perhaps longer. An author, on the other hand, may be concerned that an agent who has not made a sale within the first six months or so is not likely to work very hard as the months and years go by; a project can appear shopworn if an agent has been flogging it to editors for too long. And a project that has already been "shopped around" will not attract the attention of a new agent.

Generally, an agency agreement that is strictly oral—or a written agency agreement that does not specify a term—may be terminated at will by either party. Thus, if either the author or the agent wants to bind the other party to the agency for a specific term of months or years, the agency agreement must be written down and signed by both parties.

> **What a Difference a Day Makes!** "Rollover" clauses in agency contracts often require that notice of termination be given within a certain number of days or months prior to the expiration of the contract. If the deadline is missed, then the contract automatically rolls over for another full term. Thus, for example, if an author misses the deadline for giving notice of termination on a two-year agency agreement, she may find herself signed up for another two years!

▷ **Commissions.** Although there may be a traditionalist or two among book agents who still charge only a ten percent commission, most independent agents in the publishing industry nowadays are asking for a commission of fifteen percent. And, unless otherwise agreed, the commission applies to *gross* revenues from any deal that the agent has made on behalf of the author. In other words, the agent takes his percentage "off the top."

As discussed above, it's not unusual for a book agent to demand an even higher commission—20 or 25 percent—on the sales of foreign rights, or on sales where the primary agent works with a sub-agent or a co-agent (sometimes called a "cooperating" agent) for the sale of subsidiary rights such as motion picture and television rights. The higher commission is based on the fact that the primary agent will have to split his commission with the sub-agent or co-agent.

Ideally, the author will pay one commission to the literary agent who sells the book rights, and a separate commission to the dramatic agent who sells movie rights. (Generally, agents who sell motion picture rights still charge a ten percent commission.) If the agent insists on representing *all* rights—or if the author judges it to be in her best interest to deal with a single primary agent who directs the work of sub-agents and co-agents—then an enhanced commission rate is common.

Almost invariably, the literary agent will expect to be entitled to collect advances and royalties directly from the publisher (or any other party that acquires rights from the author), deduct his commission (and, if the contract so provides, his expenses), and then pass along what's left to the author. But the money that an agent collects is held in trust for the benefit of the author—it is the author's money, not the agent's, and the agent is entitled to deduct only what the author has agreed to pay him as a commission or an expense reimbursement.

The "A" List. Most agents expect to be commissioned on sales to publishers to whom they first submitted a book project, even if the deal isn't actually closed until after the agency agreement has expired. So, when an agency relationship comes to an end, it makes good sense for the agent to give the author a list of editors and publishers to whom the project was submitted, and the dates of each submission. This protects both author and agent—and provides a benchmark for determining whether a deal with a particular publisher entitles the agent to a commission. And if the agent doesn't offer a list of submissions, the author should ask for one. Ideally, the point should be covered in the agency agreement itself.

Once an agent has closed a deal for a publishing contract or the sale of other rights in a book, the right to receive commissions is "vested" in the agent. That is, the agent continues to receive royalties for the life of the contract, even if the agent no longer represents the author for any other work. Thus, the agency relationship—or, at least, the right to receive commissions for a particular project—will last as long as the publishing agreement or, in some circumstances, as long as the copyright in the work itself.

▷ **Expenses.** Agents generally expect the author to reimburse them for expenses; as a rule, they expect to be authorized to deduct their expenses from the author's advances and royalties. But the mechanism for expense reimbursement may vary significantly from one agent to another.

Some agents impose a yearly charge on *every* client—$100 or $200—in order to spread the burden among their entire clientele. This means, of course, that the author whose royalties are nonexistent is paying the same as the author whose royalties are princely. Other agents agree to pay their own "ordinary and customary" expenses, but ask the author to bear the costs of photocopying, messengering, fax, long distance telephone, and overnight mail services for the author's project. Still others agree to obtain the author's approval before incurring reimbursable expenses, especially if the expenses are unusual or exceed a certain agreed-upon dollar amount.

Unlike the payment of commissions, there is no "custom and practice" in the publishing industry that generally defines when and how an agent is reimbursed for expenses. That's why expense reimbursement ought to be discussed, resolved, and—ideally—written down in an agreement.

▷ **Royalty statements and other communications.** If a publishing contract contains an agency clause, then it's the agent—and *not* the author herself—who will receive royalty statements and other formal communications from the publisher.

➤ *Agency Clause–Below*

One of the implied duties of an agent, of course, is to keep the author informed of communications from the publisher. However, it may be worthwhile to define exactly what the author expects the agent to do in forwarding statements, notices and other communications.

> Agent or Attorney? Sometimes an author may be tempted to negotiate a book deal through an attorney, who charges an hourly fee, rather than an agent, who takes a 15 percent stake in the book project. Generally, I tell my clients that an attorney is more cost-effective than an agent when one or more publishers have already expressed an interest in the project, and it's simply a matter of making the best possible deal with one of them. But an agent is better positioned than an attorney to "shop" a project to as many publishers as possible—and it's always tantalizing to an author to wonder if there's something better out there. Still, an agent must find a publisher who's willing to pay at least fifteen percent more than the best pending offer in order to earn his commission!

The author may ask the agent to promise to forward copies of *all* such communications, including submission letters and routine correspondence. A complete file of such communications is especially useful if and when there is a dispute about whether the agent is entitled to a commission on a particular deal even though he no longer represents the author because the agent claims to have been the first one to contact the publisher on behalf of the author.

Agents, on the other hand, tend to be uncomfortable with a contract that flatly requires them to make copies of each and every item of correspondence; they are fearful of inadvertently breaching the contract by neglecting to send an inconsequential communication from the publisher. Or, perhaps, they're uncomfortable about what the author might make of a supposedly "inconsequential" letter!

A specific clause that requires the agent to report to the author is unnecessary if the agent is attentive—and essential if the agent is lackadaisical. The problem, of course, is that the author never knows what kind of agent she's got until it's too late to do anything about it in the contract.

▷ **Recapture of Commission.** An agent's worst nightmare is that a devious author will allow the agent to canvass the market for a publishing contract and then, just before the deal is closed, fire the agent and cut a deal directly with the publisher, thus cutting out the agent's commission. To avoid such a predicament, most written agency agreements include a provision that allows the agent to "recapture" his commission if a sale is made after the agency has expired or is terminated. ➤ *Form 3: Agency Agreement*

To protect both author and agent, it's a good idea to include a clause in the agency agreement that requires the agent to provide a list of submissions to serve as a benchmark to determine whether the agent is entitled to a commission on a subsequent sale to a particular publisher.

▷ **The Agency Clause.** The agency clause is a potent slug of boiler-plate in a publishing contract between an *author* and a *publisher* that bestows upon the *agent* the right to collect royalties directly from the publisher and to keep his commission before passing along the money to the author.

Most agency agreements will specifically authorize the agent to include an agency clause in any contract that the agent secures on behalf of the author. But even if there is no such clause in the agency agreement—or no written agreement at all—most agents will request that the publisher include an "agency clause" in any publishing agreement that the agent may be able to secure for the author's work. Essentially, the agency clause serves as written confirmation of the agent's right to receive commissions, and the clause makes the agent a "third party beneficiary" of the publishing agreement. If an agency clause appears in a publishing agreement signed by the author, the publisher will be very wary of sending royalty checks directly to the author—even if the author terminates the agent and demands that the checks be diverted to the author!

Here is a typical agency clause:

> Author hereby authorizes her Agent, to collect and receive on behalf of Author all sums of money due to Author under this Agreement, and receipt of such monies by Agent shall be a good and valid discharge of Publisher's obligations to make such payments to Author. Agent is authorized and empowered to act on behalf of Author in all matters in any way arising out of this Agreement.

The agency clause confirms a little-noticed fact of life when dealing with an agent—once an agent has earned the right to a commission on the book by selling it to a publisher, the commission is owed on *all* revenues paid to the author under the publishing agreement. If, as every author and publisher hopes, the book is an "evergreen"—a book

---

THE AGENCY CLAUSE FROM HELL. A young writer accomplished what many veteran authors only dream about—he "worked the floor" at the annual convention of the American Booksellers Association and managed to convince a major publishing house to buy his book.

On the advice of a friend, he asked a New York literary agent to represent him in negotiations with the publisher. Whether or not the agent "sweetened" the deal with the publisher is an imponderable, but the author felt comforted to know that the complex legal boilerplate in the contract had been negotiated by a seasoned literary agent.

The author and the agent never signed an agency agreement of any kind, and when the author grew disillusioned with what he saw as the agent's lack of efforts in selling motion picture and television rights in the book, he sent a letter of termination to his agent and took the book to a West Coast attorney who specializes in movie deals.

That's when the agent pointed out a crucial bit of boilerplate buried in the small print of the book contract that he had negotiated with the publisher—an agency clause that gave the agent the right to commissions on any sale of any rights in the book itself (including motion picture and television rights) and the author's next book, too!

that sells season after season, year after year—the agent continues to collect a commission for as long as the author collects royalties.

Some agency clauses instruct the publisher to pay advances and royalties in separate payments to the author and her agent; for instance, the publisher will issue one check equal to 85% of the advance or royalty and send it directly to the author, and the another check in the amount of the commission only will be sent directly to the agent. Other agency clauses actually empower the author to terminate the agent's right to collect advances and royalties on behalf of the author; if the author exercises the right to terminate the agent, then *all* payments go directly to the author. But such clauses are rare indeed, and few agents are comfortable in giving up the right to receive payments directly from the publisher.

What if the book contract also includes a grant of subsidiary rights (such as audiocassette or motion picture rights) to the publisher? The agency clause probably entitles the agent to collect a commission on the sale of subsidiary rights, too. And if the book contact grants the publisher an option on the author's next work, the agency clause may entitle the agent to a commission on that book. If the author intends it to be otherwise, then the agency clause must be carefully drafted to say so.

▷ **"Power coupled with an interest."** Agency agreements and agency clauses often include a phrase that characterizes the relationship of author and agent as "a power coupled with an interest." Here is a typical example:

> Author engages Agent as her sole and exclusive agent, and hereby grants Agent an exclusive and irrevocable agency coupled with an interest, to represent Author and negotiate for the disposition of all rights in and to the works of the Author in all media and throughout the world.

The phrase—"an agency coupled with an interest"—is a bit of legalese that is intended to make the agency relationship irrevocable. Ordinarily, a principal may terminate the agent at will (or at the end of the contract term), and the agency terminates automatically on the death or disability of the principal. But the law protects an agent who also has a legal or financial interest in the work that is being represented by the agent. Under these circumstances, the agent's stake in the work is characterized as "a power coupled with an interest" and the principal may *not* revoke the agency.

Notably, the agent's right to collect a commission is *not* enough to create "a power coupled with an interest." The law holds that the right of an agent to be compensated for his work is merely "incidental" to the agency relationship, and does not make the agency irrevocable. Since most agency deals give the agent *only* the right to a commission—and *not* an interest in the author's work itself—the use of the phrase adds little or nothing to the rights of the agent in most agency agreements.

If, on the other hand, the author grants the agent an ownership interest in the copyright to her work, then the agent is a copyright proprietor with a legal and financial interest in the work itself, and the agency *is* properly characterized as "a power coupled with an interest." However, it is rare for an agent to receive anything more than the right to receive commissions from his client, and thus the whole notion of "a power coupled with an interest" rarely arises in a conventional agency relationship.

▷ **Power of Attorney.** As a technical matter, an agent may be empowered to sign a publishing agreement on behalf of his client, but it's rarely, if ever, actually done in the publishing industry. Most publishers want to see the *author's* signature on the dotted line. What's more, it's almost always in the author's best interest to limit or withhold the agent's authority to sign legal documents; the author herself ought to be the one who puts her signature on the final version of the contract to make sure that she knows with certainty what deals have been made on her behalf.

If, however, the agent and the author agree that the agent will be the one who actually signs the contracts, it will be useful to give the agent a form of written authority called a power of attorney. Once the author has signed a power of attorney, the agent—acting as what is called an "attorney in fact"—is formally empowered to act on behalf of the author in her absence.

Since a power of attorney is defined as a written instrument by which the principal gives her agent the authority to act on her behalf, *any* written agency agreement technically bestows a power of attorney upon the agent. However, a formal power of attorney usually takes the form of a separate document that incorporates some familiar words and phrases that specifically define the agent's authority to sign documents in the name of the author.

A power of attorney may be "special" or "general." A special power of attorney limits the authority of the agent to specific tasks—for example, negotiating and signing agreements for the disposition of rights in a particular work of authorship. A general power of attorney, by contrast, empowers the agent to do *any* act on behalf of the principal.

Powers of attorney can be treacherous. After all, a general power of attorney authorizes the agent to buy and sell property, to enter into contracts, to borrow money, all in the name of the principal! For that reason, a *special* power of attorney is almost always preferable to a general power of attorney, especially in dealings between author and agent. And, once a power of attorney has been signed, it may be difficult to revoke the authority of the agent at a later date.

Except for the author in highly unusual circumstances—an author living abroad, for example, or an author who frequently travels to inaccessible places—it's almost always preferable that the agent *not* be given a power of attorney at all.

▷ **Termination.** As noted above, an oral agency agreement is terminable at will. A written agreement is terminable on the conditions stated in the agreement itself—some agreements will expire automatically at the end of the term, some will "roll over" into a new term *unless* the agent or author give notice of termination. Of course, *any* agreement can be terminated by mutual assent of the parties, even if the agreement provides for a specific term, but the problem always arises when one party wants out and the other does not.

Both author and agent need to pay attention to the terms and provisions of the agency agreement regarding termination. If the agreement provides for a specific period of notice—say, no less than thirty days prior to the expiration of the initial term—then failure to give timely notice may result in an automatic extension of the contract.

Then, too, some agency agreements specify *how* and *to whom* the notice must be given. Again, these procedures are technicalities that can have serious consequences if they are not observed—a notice mailed to the wrong address, or sent by mail when some other form of delivery is required in the contract, will not be effective to terminate the contract.

As discussed above, some obligations remain in effect even after termination of the agency. If the agent has closed a deal for the author prior to termination, then the agent will continue to receive commissions for the life of the contract. And if the agency agreement contains a "recapture" clause, then the agent may be entitled to commissions on a deal that is made by another agent or the author herself after termination.

Finally, even if the agency relationship is strictly oral, it is a good idea to give *written* notice of termination to create hard evidence of when the agency came to an end.

▷ **Arbitration.** Arbitration of disputes between an author and an agent is an especially appealing alternative to a conventional lawsuit since arbitration is generally faster, cheaper, and more confidential than the proceedings of a trial court. But arbitration cannot be imposed by one party on the other party unless an arbitration clause appears in a written contract between author and agent. ➤ *Form 3: Agency Agreement*

Packagers

"Packaging" in book publishing is an amorphous concept that sometimes resembles the function of an agent or—more often—the function of a publiser or co-publisher.

A book packager is an entrepreneur who lines up an author, an illustrator, an editor, a graphic designer (and perhaps others) to create a book project—and then offers the project to a publishing house. Sometimes the packager merely assembles a team of individuals who will create the book under the direction of the publisher; sometimes the packager actually completes the physical tasks of preparing a book for publication—design, typesetting, copy-editing, layout and so on—and then provides camera-ready boards, film or printing plates to the publisher.

LIKE A VIRGIN. At moments, the distinction between a packager and a publisher is fairly subtle—and, sometimes, it disappears altogether. For example, after Madonna's million-copy success with a book titled Sex, a New York-based packager shopped a new Madonna book project to publishers—and the Material Girl was unimpressed with the offers from domestic publishers who seemed to think that her star was no longer in the ascendancy. So it was announced in Publishers Weekly that the packager itself, Callaway Editions, would publish the book under its own imprint.

"I would never ever bet against Madonna," said Nicholas Callaway to PW's Maureen O'Brien, "because she always ends up exceeding everyone's predictions."

Meanwhile, when last seen at the Fahrenheit 451 bookstore in Laguna Beach, a single copy of Madonna's Sex was on display at the front counter—and browsers were offered a chance to crack the book for a buck a shot!

And sometimes the packager actually arranges for printing and binding, too, and delivers finished books to the publisher's warehouse.

Strictly speaking, a packager is *not* an agent. Rather, she owns or controls the elements that she has packaged into a book project. An agent *sells* rights on behalf of the author and collects a commission; a packager, by contrast, *buys* rights from the author and then resells the rights to a publisher. And so, at least in a conventional packaging deal, it is the packager, not the author, who enters into contracts with the publisher, and it is the packager, not the publisher, who pays the author.

The rights that a packager acquires in the elements of a book package, by the way, may be conveyed to the packager either in a grant of rights or a work-for-hire agreement. Since the packager deals with so many elements—not only the author but also a designer, an editor, an illustrator, and so on—it's probably in the best interests of the packager to acquire rights on a work for hire basis. Then the packager will be the "author" of the completed work under copyright law.

➤ *Chapter 2: Co-Authorship and Copyright*

Some book packages resemble what is more accurately called co-publishing. The packager and the publisher go into business together on a book project; they each contribute time, effort and resources to the project, and they share in the profits according to a mutually agreeable split. Under these circumstances, the packager may even be given an imprint of her own that appears on the title page of the book. Here's an example:

GARDENS ALL MISTY WET WITH RAIN:
A Hagiography of Van Morrison
By Jacob Hersch
POSTCARD PRESS
A Paula Packager Book

The fact that the packager is given an imprint of her own, however, does not necessarily mean that the book is co-published. Sometimes the imprint is merely a deal point in an arm's length packaging deal between the packager and the publisher. Indeed, the very notion of a book packager is so ill-defined—and the "custom and practice" of book packaging is so diverse—that line between agent, packager and publisher is often blurry or even wholly illusory. Only a careful analysis of the contracts will allow the participants in a package to know their rights and duties. But it's essential to define the roles carefully—and in writing!—if only to know whom to call when the royalty check is late!

CHAPTER FOUR

The Book Publishing Contract

4.

The contract for my very first novel was an old-fashioned document printed on long sheets of legal-sized paper, dense with boilerplate, and jacketed in the blue sheets that attorneys call "blue-backs." Like most new authors, I was so delighted to be published at all, and so hungry for the advance, that I promptly signed the contract without bothering to read it.

Publishers, too, tend to pay little attention to the familiar boiler-plate in their standard publishing contracts. Indeed, many publishers rely on old and often improvised contract forms that have been passed from generation to generation—and, often enough, passed from hand to hand by publishers who do not want to invest the time and money to draft a contract of their own.

Yet the publishing agreement is the single most important document in a book deal, the Bible and the Constitution of the business dealings between author and publisher, the place where rights and duties (and money!) are allocated, the benchmark against which disputes are measured and decided. And most book contracts will govern the rights of authors and their heirs far into the future and long after the flesh-and-blood author is dead and buried.

And so, although there's always a temptation on the part of both publisher and author to "just *sign* it," the book publishing contract ought to be vigorously negotiated, carefully drafted, and meticulously scrutinized by both parties *before* it is signed.

A Model Book Publishing Agreement

The following section is a clause-by-clause discussion of a model book publishing agreement that generally includes all of the standard provisions encountered in most publishing industry transactions.

The model book contract in *Kirsch's Handbook* is based on the publishing agreement that I use for my own publishing clients, and my form addresses virtually all of the provisions that appear in standard book contracts. The precise wording (and, therefore, the legal effect) of the sample clauses may differ from the contract used by any given publisher in any given deal. And, of course, the author and publisher who enter into negotiations may come up with terms and conditions that are quite different from the ones in the model book contract.

Certain aspects of any book contract are generally identified as "deal points," a phrase that usually refers to terms and conditions with significant economic value. The advance and the royalty rates, for example, are typical deal points. So is the precise definition of the rights that the publisher is acquiring—book rights, foreign rights, subsidiary and secondary rights, and so on. These are the points that an agent will usually negotiate with the greatest attention and vigor.

But a standard publishing contract includes a great many other terms and conditions that may affect the economic value of the deal and, perhaps more importantly, the rights and duties of both author and publisher over the long term. An option clause, for example, will tie up the rights to the author's next book and perhaps even her next several books; a subsidiary rights clause may affect rights in technologies not yet invented! And, since the duration of copyright usually extends beyond the life of the author, a book contract is binding on the author's heirs and successors.

Bear in mind, of course, that *any* contract form, including the ones offered here, must be carefully reviewed and adapted for each publishing transaction. There is no longer any such thing as a "standard" book deal, and even the custom and practice of the publishing industry have changed and diversified over the years. For that reason, each clause ought to be considered in the context of the particular deal that author and publisher intend to make.

Recitals

This Publishing Agreement ("the Agreement") is entered into as of [Insert Date Here] ("the Effective Date") by and between [Insert Name, Address and Legal Capacity of Publisher Here] ("Publisher"), and [Insert Name, Address, Social

Security Number, Date of Birth, and Citizenship of Author Here] ("Author") concerning a work presently titled [Insert Title Here] ("the Work") and described as [Insert Description of Subject Matter, Length, Etc.].

Recitals. A "recital" is the prefatory section of a contract where the contracting parties are identified and the reasons for the contract are set down. Here, the recitals include some important "defined terms," that is, a definition of what the contracting parties mean by certain capitalized words such as "Author," "Publisher," "Work," etc.

Legal Capacity of Parties. It's good practice to identify the legal capacity of the author and publisher with specificity. An author is usually a living person acting in her individual capacity, and so she should be identified as: "Erica Jong, an individual." If the publisher is a corporation, the contract should say so—and the actual corporate name of the publisher, rather than its imprint, should be specified: "Simon & Schuster, Inc., a New York corporation." And if the publisher is actually an individual, a partnership or a joint venture "doing business as" a publishing house or press name, the fact should be specified. For example: "Virgina Woolf and Leonard Woolf, joint venturers doing business as Hogarth Press."

Effective Date. It's a good practice, although not a legal necessity, to specify a date when the contract is effective. This establishes a benchmark date for all the other time-related obligations in the contract, and avoids any ambiguities about when the contract was finally signed. (As a general rule, and in the absence of an agreed-upon "Effective Date," a contract goes into effect when the *last* of the required signatures is placed on the contract.) And, since the contract actually may be signed before or after the "Effective Date," the phrase "effective as of" makes it clear that the parties are agreeing to a single date as the operative date.

Addresses, Birthdates, Citizenship, Etc. For obvious reasons, it makes sense to include the current addresses of the publisher and the author. However, it may be important for the publisher to know the birthdate, place of birth, citizenship, and Social Security number of the author for reasons of copyright registration, tracking down a missing author, or—in the worst case—tracing the assets of an author against whom the publisher has obtained a judgment!

Description of the Work. Most publishing contracts identify the work to be written by the author in summary terms—sometimes only by a title, a thumbnail description, and perhaps a specified word length: "A manuscript of approximately 100,000 words on Van Morrison." But if author and publisher ever find themselves in disagreement about what the book was intended to be, then a more detailed definition will be crucial to avoiding a dispute or even a lawsuit. If necessary, the book proposal itself—or some other more extended description of the book—can be attached to the contract as an exhibit and "incorporated by reference." It's a simple approach to avoiding the problem that often arises when the manuscript is actually delivered, a problem that both author and publish dread: "This is not the book we expected...."

Grant of Rights

Author, on behalf of himself and his heirs, executors, administrators, successors and assigns, exclusively grants, assigns and otherwise transfers to Publisher and its licensees, successors and assigns, all right, title and interest in and to the Work, throughout the world, in perpetuity, and in any and all media and forms of expressions now known or hereafter devised, including but not limited to all copyrights therein (and any and all extensions and renewals thereof) for the full term of such copyrights, and all secondary and subsidiary rights therein.

The all-important "grant of rights" language in a publishing contract defines exactly what rights in a work are being transferred by the author to the publisher. Since copyright consists of a "bundle of rights," it's crucial for both author and publisher to understand and agree to the specific rights that are being granted in the book contract.

Important Note! The sample grant of rights clause set forth above is intended to convey *all* rights in the author's work to the publisher! Rarely is an author willing to grant such sweeping rights in her work, and the more typical book contract will carefully define the rights that the author is assigning to the publisher—and the rights she is reserving for herself. Other approaches to the grant of rights clause may be found below.

With that caution in mind, here are the key words and phrases in a typical grant of rights clause—and some of the approaches to fine tuning the grant of rights to suit a particular deal.

"...*Author, on behalf of himself and his or her heirs, executors, administrators, successors and assigns....* A contract signed by the author will usually bind anyone who acquires rights in the same work from the author at a later date, whether by contract, by will, or by operation of law. The language here simply makes it clear that the author's rights and duties under the contract will also apply to the author's successors. Thus, for example, if the author assigns her publishing agreement to her spouse, he will receive nothing more and nothing less than the author would have received. And the heirs of a deceased author will have the same rights as the author, too. Similarly, the publisher's successors ("...*its licensees, successors and assigns...*") will be bound by the terms of the contract.

"...*grants, assigns, and otherwise transfers...*" The standard publishing agreement is structured as an outright grant of rights by the author to the publisher, rather than a license (which gives permission to the publisher to make use of a copyrighted work for only a limited period of time) or a work-for-hire agreement (which creates the legal fiction that the publisher is, as a matter of law, the author of the work).

➤ *Chapter 2: Co-Authorship and Copyright*

Even under an outright grant of rights, some or all rights may revert (that is, go back) to the author later on, whether under a reversionary clause (see below) or the author's statutory right to terminate the transfer of rights. But the grant of rights language means that the publisher (and *not* the author) is the owner of important rights in the work once the contract is signed. Both author and publisher must carefully consider whether a license or a work-for-hire agreement is preferable to an outright grant of rights.

"...*all right, title and interest in and to the Work, throughout the world, in perpetuity, and in any and all media and forms of expressions now known or hereafter devised, including but not limited to all copyrights therein (and any and all extensions and renewals thereof) for the full term of such copyrights, and all secondary and subsidiary rights therein.*

The author is granting *all* rights in the work to the publisher without any limitations or reservations. In fact, the sample clause extends not only to the copyright in the author's work, which is limited in duration by statute, but other rights that may belong to the publisher indefinitely. For example, the sweeping grant of rights arguably includes rights to ideas, characters, settings, plot lines, and other material as well as titles and other elements that may be protected under trademark law. ➤ *Chapter 1: Idea Protection & Briefs: Trademark and Unfair Competition*

Such a sweeping grant of rights is clearly preferable for the publisher, but authors may be unwilling to give up all rights in her work to a single publisher in a single contract. More commonly, a publishing contract will narrowly define the rights being granted by the author to the publisher. Typically, the author will reserve one or more of the "bundle of rights" under copyright.

Here's an example of a much more limited grant of rights:

> Author, on behalf of himself and his heirs, executors, administrators, successors and assigns, exclusively grants, assigns and otherwise transfers to Publisher and its licensees, successors and assigns, all print publication rights in the Work in the English language, throughout the world, for the full term of copyright in and to the Work (and any and all renewals and extensions thereof). All rights not expressly granted to Publisher are hereby reserved by Author.

This second example of the grant of rights clause makes it clear that the publisher is entitled to exercise only the rights specifically granted by the author, and all other rights still belong to the author.

The "bundle of rights" under copyright may be divided up between author and publisher in an almost infinite number of ways. Here are some of the principal ways to limit a grant of rights by author to publisher.

Primary Rights. The "primary right" in a book publishing contract is the right to print the work in book form. But even the so-called primary rights may be defined and limited according to the deal that the author and publisher have struck with each other. While a book contract will often assign to the publisher all "print publication rights," it's not uncommon to reserve certain print rights to the author. For example, the book contract may specify that the publisher is being granted hardcover rights only, or trade paperback rights only, or mass market paperback rights only.

Since the very concept of primary rights is not well-defined in publishing law, any book contract that grants less than *all* rights to the publisher ought to identify the specific rights that the author and publisher regard as primary. Here are sample clauses from a book contract that define in legal terms some of the "print publication rights" that may be included in the phrase primary rights.

> "Hardcover Rights," including the exclusive right to publish, or authorize others to publish, hardcover editions of the Work distributed primarily through trade channels such as bookstores and libraries.

Hardback editions are still the most prestigious and, often enough, the most profitable format for publication of a book. Still, the sheer costs of production may make hardback editions a much less common form of publication. Even now, many books appear in simultaneous hardback-paperback editions, or—even more often—as paperback originals only. And the growing importance of "new media" may further endanger the hardcover first edition in the publishing industry.

"Softcover Trade Edition Rights," including the exclusive right to publish, or authorize others to publish, "trade paperback" or "quality paperback" editions of the Work distributed primarily through trade channels such as bookstores and libraries.

Generally, a "trade" or "quality" paperback is the same size as a hardback, and may even be printed from the same plates and on the same paper stock, but the publisher is able to save money (and charge the consumer a lower price) by using a "soft" cover and a less expensive binding. Trade paperbacks and hardbacks are sold and promoted through the same channels of distribution, and when a book is published simultaneously in paperback and hardback, the paperback edition will usually be in a trade paperback format.

"Mass Market Reprint Rights," including the exclusive right to publish, or authorize others to publish, softcover editions of the Work to be distributed primarily through independent magazine wholesalers and to direct accounts.

A "mass-market" or "rack-size" paperback is smaller in overall size than a trade paperback, more cheaply printed and bound. Mass market paperbacks are also known as "rack-size" because they are displayed and sold on racks that are found outside the ordinary channels of the book trade—that is, supermarket check-out stands, magazine stands, airports, and so on. (For that reason, mass-market paperbacks are often distributed to these outlets by magazine distributors rather than book distributors.) Mass-market paperbacks are often (but not always) reprints of books that originally appeared as hardback or quality paperback books, and—of course—mass-market paperbacks are priced to be much cheaper than hardbacks or quality paperbacks.

"General Publication Rights," including the exclusive right to publish, or to authorize others to publish, all of the Work, or excerpts, condensations,

> abridgments, or selections of the Work, in anthologies, compilations, digests, newspapers, magazines, syndicates, textbooks, and other works, and/or in Braille, either before or after first publication of the Work in book form.

The model clause broadly defines "general" publication rights to include, among other things, the right of the book publisher to authorize the use of the author's work in magazines, newspapers, anthologies, textbooks, and even Braille editions. Each of these rights may be granted or reserved by the author as a separate right, but most publishers will expect to own and control at least these print-related rights in the author's book.

Other print publications rights that might be separately identified and included in a book contract include "Foreign Rights," "Translation Rights," "Direct-Response Marketing Rights," "Book Club Edition," "Premiums and Special Editions," "Bulk Sales," "Periodical or Serial Rights," "Anthologies and Collections," "School Editions," "Cheap Editions," "Unbound Sheets," "Microfilm and Microfiche," "Photocopying," "Braille and Other Editions for the Handicapped," "Large Print," and "Publicity," all of which are discussed in Chapter 7. ➤ *Chapter 7: Electronic and Other Subsidiary Rights*

Subsidiary Rights. The "bundle of rights" in a book (or other copyrighted work) includes a great many rights that are characterized as "secondary" or "subsidiary," starting with the right to make an audio version of the author's book, for example, and ranging into electronic publishing and even media that does not yet exist!

The subsidiary rights granted by an author to a publisher depend entirely on how the term itself is defined in the contract, and how the subsidiary rights are allocated between author and publisher. Rights that are often characterized as "subsidiary" in a book contract include "Electronic Rights," "Audio Rights," "Dramatic Rights," "Motion Picture Rights," "Television and Radio Rights," and "Merchandising Rights," all of which are discussed in Chapter 7. ➤ *Chapter 7: Electronic and Other Subsidiary Rights*

Some subsidiary rights have taken on new importance as changes take place in the publishing industry itself. For example, the right to make a spoken-word recording of the book on audiocassette, whether abridged or unabridged, is an increasingly valuable subsidiary right. And so the allocation of subsidiary rights is an increasingly crucial "deal point" in most book contract negotiations, and the final version of the contract must accurately reflect the deal itself. Since the "bundle of rights" under copyright can be broken up into an almost infinite number of separate rights, the contract itself must be precise and specific in its wording.

Territory. The rights granted by author, whether primary or secondary, may be further limited by geographical territory. For example, the author may restrict the grant of rights to North America only, or the United States only, or the worldwide English-speaking market only, or some other specific territory that is defined by geography, language, political boundaries, or other factors. The emergence of new and reconfigured markets in Europe and elsewhere around the world makes it all the more important to understand and define where the publisher is entitled to sell the author's work.

Language. Similarly, the rights granted by the author to the publisher may be limited by language. For example, the right to publish the book in the English language may be—and usually is—granted to one publisher, while the right to publish the same book in French or Spanish is granted to a different publisher in a separate contract. Foreign language rights—that is, the right to make a translation of the book from its original language to a foreign language—is a secondary right that may be granted separately for each language.

Term. The duration (or "term") of the book contract must be specifically defined. Generally, the publisher will seek a grant of rights for as long as possible—"*...for the full term of such copyrights, and any renewals and extensions thereof....*" or even "*...in perpetuity...*"—while the author may prefer a shorter term.

Some book contracts, especially for book club rights or foreign rights, provide for the licensing of rights for a limited term of years rather than an outright grant of rights. It's not unusual for such contracts to renew automatically unless cancelled in writing at the end of the term, or to renew automatically if the publisher succeeds in selling a specified number of books.

Regardless of how the term of a book contract is defined—a specified number of years, duration of copyright, or even "in perpetuity"—most book contracts include a reversion clause (see below) by which the rights in the work revert to the author under certain circumstances or after a certain period of time.

Under certain circumstances, United States copyright law allows an author to *terminate* a transfer of rights after a certain number of years *no matter what term is prescribed by the contract*! (**Note:** The right to terminate a transfer is subject to some important restrictions and procedures that must be strictly observed, and it does not apply at all to a work-for-hire.) ➤ *Chapter 8: Remaindering, Reversion and Copyright Termination*

Future Media. The "all-rights" clause set forth above attempts to secure rights in technologies not yet in existence: "*...any and all media and forms of expressions now known or hereafter devised....*" This is a common example of a publisher's effort to anticipate (and acquire the rights in) what will come next in the accelerating technological revolution in publishing.

The author, of course, will prefer to reserve such rights, especially because recent experience shows us that new products (spoken-word books on audiocassette, for example) and new technologies (such as CD-ROM and "interactive" media) are turning out to be increasingly profitable.

The use of a "future media" clause is treacherous precisely because of the velocity of technological change. Attorneys have been drafting "future media" clauses since the 1930s, when "talkies" replaced silent movies, but such clauses are not always enforceable. Indeed, some courts have ruled that the rights in an entirely new and unknown medium are *not* conveyed to the publisher simply because a contract includes a "future media" clause. That's why a clause that seeks rights in new media should be as specific as possible.
➤ *Chapter 7: Electronic and Other Subsidiary Rights*

Copyright

Publisher shall, in all versions of the Work published by Publisher under this Agreement, place a notice of copyright in the name of the author in a form and place that Publisher reasonably believes to comply with the requirements of the United States copyright law, and shall apply for registration of such copyright(s) in the name of Author in the United States Copyright Office.

Publisher shall have the right, but not the obligation, to apply for registration of copyright(s) in the Work published by Publisher elsewhere in the world.

Author shall execute and deliver to Publisher any and all documents which Publisher deems necessary or appropriate to evidence or effectuate the rights granted in this Agreement, including but not limited to the Instrument of Recordation attached hereto as an Exhibit to this Agreement.

Nothing contained in this Section shall be construed as limiting, modifying or otherwise affecting any of the rights granted to Publisher under this Agreement.

"...Publisher shall...place a notice of copyright...." The publisher is usually given the responsibility of taking care of copyright formalities in the books that it publishes, and so it's up to the publisher to understand the technical requirements of copyright law. For example, under recent changes in United States copyright law, it is no longer mandatory to place a copyright notice in published works, although it is still advantageous to do so. ➤ *Chapter 6: Copyright Formalities*

"...in the name of the author...." The whole point of the book contract, of course, is to transfer rights from the *author* to the *publisher*—but it is a well-established tradition (and a kind of common courtesy) in the publishing industry to give the copyright notice in the name of the *author*. As a legal matter, the copyright notice may be given in the name of the publisher if the publisher has acquired all rights in the author's work, and some publishers reserve the right to do so. ➤ *Chapter 6: Copyright Formalities*

"...apply for registration of such copyright(s) in the name of Author in the United States Copyright Office..." Formal registration of copyright is not mandatory to establish the existence of a copyright. But registration still bestows so many important legal advantages on the copyright proprietor that *every* work of authorship ought to be promptly and automatically registered. The burden of registering the copyright usually falls on the publisher—but it's very much in the author's interest to make sure that the copyright *has* been registered properly, and if the publisher has failed to do so, the author ought to do it herself. ➤ *Chapter 6: Copyright Formalities*

"...Publisher shall have the right, but not the obligation, to apply for registration...elsewhere in the world...." Because of the complexities and expense of foreign copyright registration, most publishers do not obligate themselves to apply for copyright registration outside of the United States. If the U.S. publisher owns the right to publish abroad, it will usually license the right to foreign publishers, and delegate the responsibility for copyright registration to the foreign publisher. Some foreign countries do not offer copyright registration formalities at all. But, when registration is available, it is usually in the best interest of all concerned—the author, the U.S. publisher, and the foreign publisher—to observe the formalities of copyright protection.

"...Author shall execute...any and all documents which Publisher deems necessary...including but not limited to the Instrument of Recordation...." Ordinarily, the book contract itself should be sufficient for the publisher to prove its ownership of rights in the work of

an author. Many book contracts, however, oblige the author to sign additional documents that may be used in a lawsuit or for other legal purposes to provide further evidence of copyright ownership.

One specific example of an additional document that the author may be asked to sign is an "Instrument of Recordation." It's a short summary of the book contract itself—or a "short form," as it is sometimes called—that can be recorded in the United States Copyright Office as a public record. Since author and publisher may be hesitant to put their entire deal on the public record, the short form allows them to summarize the rights that have been granted or licensed to the publisher without disclosing the advance, the royalty rates, and other "deal points."

The book contract set forth here makes the Instrument of Recordation an exhibit to the contract itself, and thus the short form will be signed at the same time as the book contract. The publisher will then be able to send the short form to the United States Copyright Office and complete the registration and recordation at the same time.

➤ *Chapter 5: Instrument of Recordation*

Recordation bestows some important legal benefits on the publisher, especially if the publisher later decides to file an action for copyright infringement. Bear in mind, however, that *recordation* is not equivalent to *registration*, and both formalities ought to be observed.

➤ *Chapter 6: Copyright Formalities*

"*Nothing contained in this Section shall be construed as limiting...the rights granted to Publisher....*" The fact that the copyright notice may be given in the name of the author does not detract from the publisher's legal rights under the contract, and the boilerplate says so.

Manuscript

Author agrees to deliver to Publisher, not later than [Insert Delivery Date.], two (2) double-spaced complete copies of the computer-generated manuscript of the Work in the English language ("Manuscript"), which Manuscript shall be of the length set forth in the Recitals and shall otherwise be acceptable to Publisher in form, content and substance.

On a date to be designated by Publisher, Author shall also deliver the Manuscript as otherwise described above on computer disk(s) in a size, format and word-processing program language acceptable to Publisher. Author agrees to make and keep at least one (1) complete copy of the Manuscript and such disk(s).

The book contract ought to set forth the specific details of the publishing process so that both author and publisher know in advance what is expected of each party to the contract. No detail is too mundane to be treated in a contract—and, if a particular obligation is deemed to be important by either author or publisher, then it ought to be spelled out in language that both parties can understand.

"Author agrees to deliver to Publisher, not later than [Insert delivery date here]..." The delivery date is the very first of a series of benchmark dates that may appear in a book contract (see below). Some contracts will spell out the consequences for late delivery of a manuscript, including the right of the publisher to simply cancel the contract and call back the advance! Even if the contract is silent, however, the failure to perform an obligation by a specified date is a breach of contract, and both author and publisher need to be mindful of the important dates.

"...two (2) double-spaced complete copies of the computer-generated manuscript of the Work...." Nowadays, many publishers prefer to receive a manuscript in the form of computer disks (*"...on computer disk(s) in a size, format and word-processing program language acceptable to Publisher..."*). But if the publisher also wants to see a "hard copy" of the manuscript, the contract needs to say so.

"Manuscript shall be... acceptable to Publisher in form, content and substance...." These few words, which appear in virtually every book contract, are freighted with the heaviest legal and practical consequences—the publisher is entitled to reject a manuscript (and, in most cases, to terminate the contract) if the author fails to deliver what was promised or expected.

> **A Day Late, A Dollar Short.** "A writer is never more creative," said food-and-wine critic Colman Andrews, "than when thinking of reasons <u>not</u> to write." That's why the manuscript delivery date was once a clause that authors and publishers did not take very seriously. Nowadays, however, publishers tend to be more demanding about deadlines, and some publishers are perfectly willing to simply terminate a book contract if the manuscript is late. This is especially true when the author's <u>last</u> book was remaindered six months after publication—or when the original acquiring editor is long gone, and the new editor can't figure out what his predecessor found so compelling. So it's a good practice for the tardy author to ask in advance for an extension of the delivery date—and to confirm in writing any extension that the publisher may be willing to give to the author.

That's why it is in the best interest of the author to make sure that the description of the book project in the contract itself is detailed enough in specifications of length, content, approach, and style to provide a benchmark for the exercise of the publisher's right to accept or reject. Sometimes, the project is only described in terms of its working title and word length; sometimes, the publisher adds a one-line description of the theme or subject matter of the book. But, if the description is too spare, the author can never argue that she delivered what the publisher had asked for.

Sometimes a contract will qualify the right of the publisher to reject a manuscript. An even-handed contract, for example, will oblige the publisher to specify what's wrong with the manuscript and afford the author an opportunity to fix it (see below) before rejecting the manuscript. Sometimes, the contract will specify that the publisher must act "reasonably" in rejecting a manuscript—but sometimes the publisher is entitled to accept or reject the work "in its sole discretion."

An emerging body of law appears to impose on the book publisher some minimum requirements of "good faith and fair dealing" in accepting or rejecting a manuscript. But the "implied" duties of a publisher can only be enforced in a lawsuit. A more practical approach—and a preventative one—is to take care in the book contract itself to define what the author has

THE DUTY TO PUBLISH IN GOOD FAITH. One of the curiosities of American contract law is the fact that certain duties that appear nowhere in the contract itself are imposed by law on contracting parties. Generally, these duties are known as "the implied duty of good faith and fair dealing," and they apply to <u>all</u> contracts. Using the same doctrine, some courts have imposed specific duties on book publishers that go far beyond the "four corners" of the book contracts or even the custom and practice of the publishing industry.

▷ <u>I'd Rather Be Right Than Published</u>. When Harcourt Brace Jovanovich signed up Barry Goldwater and ghostwriter Stephen Shadegg for an autobiography of America's most famous conservative politician, the contract included the customary boilerplate provision that the manuscript must be "satisfactory to the publisher in form and content." But when HBJ rejected the manuscript, Goldwater complained that his publisher breached its duty of good faith by failing to explain <u>why</u> the manuscript was unsatisfactory and by refusing to give the authors a chance to rewrite it. The court in <u>Harcourt Brace Jovanovich v. Goldwater</u> agreed with Goldwater—HBJ had "breached its contract with Shadegg and Goldwater by wilfully failing to engage in any rudimentary editorial work or effort."

▷ <u>And Just What Did You Expect—War and Peace?</u> Julia Whedon sold a novel to Dell on the basis of a twelve-page outline, and when she submitted the first half of the manuscript to her editor, he expressed satisfaction with the work and issued the next installment of the advance. Later, when she delivered the entire manuscript, the publisher told the author that the manuscript "isn't what ➜

➔ we expected," cancelled the contract, and demanded the return of the entire advance. Whedon later sold the book to Doubleday, Dell's parent company, but Dell sued to recover the advance. The court in Dell Publishing Co. v. Whedon ruled in favor of Whedon on surprising grounds: Dell had an implied obligation "to offer Whedon the opportunity to revise the manuscript, with Dell's editorial assistance, to bring it up to publishable standards." When Dell failed to do so, it was the publisher—and not the author—that breached the contract.

▷ How Many Review Copies Are Enough? Even when a manuscript is accepted and published, the duty of the publisher does not end. Gerard Colby Zilg sued his publisher, Prentice-Hall, on the grounds that the publisher had failed to adequately promote his book about the duPont family. Even though Zilg's contract allowed the publisher alone to determine "the method and means of advertising, publicizing and selling the work," the court in Zilg v. Prentice-Hall found that the publisher was still obliged to make "a good faith effort to promote the book including a first printing and advertising budget adequate to give the book a reasonable chance of achieving market success." Once a publisher has satisfied its basic obligations, however, any further efforts to promote a book are up to the publisher: "[A]ll that is required is a good faith business judgment." And the court decided that Prentice-Hall had, in fact, discharged its obligations, and a trial verdict in favor of the author was reversed on appeal.

agreed to deliver and what the publisher has agreed to accept.

➤ *The Duty to Publish in Good Faith–Above*

"*Author agrees to make and keep at least one (1) complete copy of the Manuscript and such disk(s).*" What happens if the publisher manages to lose the hard copy of the manuscript, or the computer disks, or both? A back-up copy in the author's possession is simply a good precaution. And the cautious publisher will *oblige* the author to keep copies in order to discourage the author from suing for damages if the publisher manages to misplace the manuscript.

Artwork, Permissions, Index, and Other Materials.

Author shall deliver to Publisher, not later than the Initial Delivery Date unless otherwise designated by Publisher, each of the following materials:

Original art, illustrations and/or photographs (collectively "Artwork"), in a form suitable for reproduction. Subject to the mutual agreement of Author and Publisher, Publisher may acquire and/or prepare and include in the Work additional art, illustrations, photographs, charts, maps, drawings or other materials, and the expense for such additional materials shall be allocated between Author and Publisher according to their mutual agreement.

> Author shall deliver to Publisher, at Author's sole expense, written authorizations and permissions for the use of any copyrighted or other proprietary materials (including but not limited to art, illustrations and photographs) owned by any third party which appear in the Work and written releases or consents by any person or entity described, quoted or depicted in the Work (collectively "Permissions"). If Author does not deliver the Permissions, Publisher shall have the right, but not the obligation, to obtain such Permissions on its own initiative, and Author shall reimburse Publisher for all expenses incurred by Publisher in obtaining such Permissions.
>
> Author shall prepare and submit, on a date to be designated by Publisher, an index, bibliography, table of contents, foreword, introduction, preface or similar matter ("Frontmatter" and "Backmatter") as Publisher may deem necessary for inclusion in the Work, and if Author shall fail or refuse to do so, then Publisher shall have the right, but not the obligation, to acquire or prepare such Frontmatter and/or Backmatter, or to engage a skilled person to do so, and Author shall reimburse Publisher for the costs of such acquisition or preparation.
>
> Author acknowledges and confirms that Publisher shall have no liability of any kind for the loss or destruction of the Manuscript, Artwork, Frontmatter, Backmatter, or any other documents or materials provided by Author to Publisher, and agrees to make and maintain copies of all such documents and materials for use in the event of such loss or destruction.

A book as actually published, whether it's a spare novella or a multi-volume encyclopedia, consists of more than the words set down on paper or word-processor by the author. Artwork may be an important element, for example, and the text is often dressed up with the miscellany of a well-prepared and well-presented book, ranging from a preface and a table of contents to an index and a bibliography.

Most book contracts will place the burden on the author to both secure and pay for these various other elements, although the publisher will generally reserve the right to acquire what is needed (*"...to acquire or prepare such [material], or to engage a skilled person to do so..."*), and then charge the author for the expense (*"..and Author shall reimburse Publisher for the costs of such acquisition or preparation...."*)

Author and publisher, of course, can negotiate a different allocation of both the burden and expense of securing additional materials for the finished work: *"...The expense for such additional materials shall be allocated between Author and Publisher according to their mutual agreement....*" But, if the burden and expense *are* reallocated, it's important to set down the specific responsibilities of author and publisher in writing, either as a part of the contract itself or in a rider or amendment to the contract.

"Author shall deliver to Publisher, at Author's sole expense, written authorizations and permissions..."

Generally, the publisher looks to the author to provide *"authorizations and permissions"* that are required for the use of any copyrighted work that the author herself did not create, including photographs, illustrations, charts, maps, and similar artwork, as well as prefaces and other text. ➤ *Chapter 2: Co-Authorship and Copyright*

Indeed, a prudent publisher will seek formal permission to use quoted text from a copyrighted work, even if the quotations might be considered "fair use" under the copyright law. Other "proprietary" material, such as the trademarks or trade secrets of a third party, may also require clearance of rights. And some publishers will go even further by asking the author to secure formal permission even from third parties who are merely *"described, quoted or depicted in the Work."* ➤ *Chapter 5: Preparing the Manuscript*

While the clause set forth here places the burden and expense of securing all permissions squarely on the author, it can be negotiated and redrafted to provide for a different allocation of the burden. But it is crucial for *someone* to bear the primary responsibility for securing third party permissions.

"...Publisher shall have no liability of any kind for the loss or destruction of the Manuscript, Artwork... or any other documents or materials provided by Author to Publisher...." The cautious author will always make copies of what she sends to her publisher—and the cautious publisher will include a clause that prevents the author from bringing a claim for damages if the publisher manages to misplace it!

Just Sign on the Dotted Line. When a book contract requires the author to secure the permission of a source who has been interviewed and then quoted or described—or a third party whose copyrighted work is quoted—then it's a good idea for author and publisher to agree in advance on a standard form for securing such releases and permissions. Then the contract itself ought to provide for the use of the standard form: "Publisher acknowledges and agrees the requirements of this Agreement for securing third-party permissions will be satisfied by use of the Permissions Form attached as an exhibit to this Agreement." ➤ *Form 4: Interview Release & Form 5: Permissions Agreement*

Revisions and Corrections

If Publisher, in its sole discretion, deems the Manuscript, Artwork, Frontmatter and/or Backmatter, Permissions and/or any other materials delivered by Author to be unacceptable in form and substance, then Publisher shall so advise Author by written notice, and Author shall cure any defects and generally revise and correct the Manuscript, Artwork, Frontmatter and/or Backmatter, Permissions and/or other materials to the satisfaction of Publisher, and deliver fully revised and corrected Manuscript, Artwork, Frontmatter and/or Backmatter, Permissions and/or other materials no later than thirty (30) days after receipt of Publisher's notice.

Although the revision clause set forth here may strike some authors as fierce and even punitive, it is actually a rather kind and gentle approach to the problematic manuscript. Rather than reserving the right to flatly reject an unsatisfactory manuscript, the publisher agrees to inform the author in writing of any supposed defects in the manuscript—and agrees to allow the author an opportunity to "cure" the defects by revising and rewriting the manuscript.

Indeed, if an author is presented with a book contract that does *not* entitle her to revise and rewrite the manuscript in order to solve any problems that the publisher claims to find, the author ought to ask that precisely such a clause be inserted in the contract.

The procedures described here also protect the publisher from a claim that the publisher acted in bad faith in rejecting a manuscript. By taking the trouble to specify the problems to be solved—and then affording the author a chance to solve them—the publisher has probably discharged its duties of "good faith and fair dealing." If the manuscript is *still* unpublishable, then the publisher is less at risk of a lawsuit from a disgruntled author if the manuscript is finally rejected.

Termination for Non-Delivery

If Author fails to deliver the Manuscript, Artwork, Frontmatter and/or Backmatter, Permissions or other materials required under this Agreement, and/or any revisions and corrections thereof as requested by Publisher, on the dates designated by Publisher, or if Author fails to do so in a form and substance satisfactory to Publisher, then Publisher shall have the right to terminate this Agreement by so informing Author by letter sent by traceable mail to the address of Author set forth above. Upon termination by Publisher, Author shall, without prejudice to any other right or remedy of Publisher, immediately repay Publisher any sums previously paid to Author, and upon such repayment, all rights granted to Publisher under this Agreement shall revert to Author.

Virtually all book contracts bestow upon the publisher the right to reject a manuscript, but it's also necessary to specify when and how the publisher is entitled to exercise its right of rejection—and, most important, exactly what happens if the publisher actually rejects the manuscript. Otherwise, the rights of both author and publisher may be left in limbo.

"Publisher shall have the right to terminate this Agreement...." The publisher is not only entitled to reject the manuscript but to terminate the book contract under at least four circumstances: for non-delivery of the manuscript (or other materials to be provided by the author, including artwork, permissions, and so on) (*"If Author fails to deliver the Manuscript...or other materials...."*); for late delivery of the manuscript or other materials, that is, for delivery at any time after *"...the dates designated by Publisher...;"* for non-delivery of *"...any revisions and corrections...as requested by Publisher...;"* and for failure to deliver the manuscript, revisions, corrections, and other materials *"...in a form and substance satisfactory to Publisher...."*

Since every contract must be read as whole, the right to terminate for these and other reasons may be subject to conditions set forth elsewhere in the contract. For example, the sample contract does *not* allow the publisher to terminate on the grounds that the manuscript is unsatisfactory unless the author is first given an opportunity to revise and rewrite ➤ *Revisions and Corrections—Above*

"....by informing Author by letter sent by traceable mail to the address of Author...." If the publisher elects to terminate the contract, the publisher must send a written notice, by traceable mail such as Federal Express, to the author's address as set forth in the Recitals. Other methods may be described in a contract, but *some* specific mechanism ought to be prescribed in order to establish exactly when and how the contract comes to an end.

"Upon termination..., Author shall...immediately repay Publisher any sums previously paid to Author...." Typically, the publisher may demand the repayment of the advance (or any other money) that the author has already received from the publisher under the contract. The author, of course, will prefer a clause that allows her to keep the advance if the publisher elects to terminate the contract. But not every author has enough clout to demand—and not every publisher is rich enough or generous enough to agree—that the advance be character-ized as "non-refundable" in whole or part. ➤ *Advance Against Royalties—Below*

Editing and Publication Format

Publisher shall have the right to edit and revise the Work for any and all uses contemplated under this Agreement, provided that the meaning of the Work is not materially altered, and shall have the right to manufacture, distribute, advertise, promote and publish the Work in a style and manner which Publisher deems appropriate, including typesetting, paper, printing, binding, cover and/or jacket design, imprint, title and price. Notwithstanding any editorial changes or revisions by Publisher, Author's warranties and indemnities under this Agreement shall remain in full force and effect.

Unless otherwise specified in the book contract, the publisher generally reserves the right to make *all* fundamental publishing decisions, ranging from the title of the work to the number of review copies, all of which is generally described as the "style and manner" of publication.

"Publisher shall have the right to edit and revise the Work for any and all uses..." Most book contracts bestow upon the publisher the unfettered right to edit and revise the manuscript. The only stated restriction in the sample clause is that the editorial changes may not be so extensive

First Proceeds. Some publishers are willing to soften the blow of a cancelled book project by waiting until the author has succeeded in reselling the work to another publisher before demanding repayment of the advance. Under a so-called "first proceeds" clause, the author is obliged to repay the first publisher's advance out of the first monies actually received from the second publisher as an advance and royalties. Here's an example of a typical first proceeds clause: "Upon termination by Publisher, Author shall repay Publisher any sums previously paid to Author out of the first proceeds of any sale or other disposition of rights to the Work."

OU SONT LES NOMS DE PLUME D'ANTANS? Any aspiring writer of romance novels will quickly discover that she is expected to write under a pseudonym—and she will discover, too, that the author does not own her own nom de plume! Publishers of "bodice-rippers" understand that the author's byline can become a marketable commodity in itself, and the publishers generally reserve all rights in the pseudonym that the author may use. And so the publisher is free to hire any number of authors to create new works that will appear under a particularly popular pen name.

The same issue may arise if the author's work is published as part of a series of related books—a travel guide series, for example, or a collection of cookbooks. So the watchful author may ask the publisher to clarify who owns and controls the title of the book itself, the series title, the logo and graphic design, and other features of the author's book as actually published. ➤ *Briefs: Trademark and Unfair Competition* that *"...the meaning of the Work is ... materially altered...,"* a concept so vague that most publishers do not feel very inhibited (and most authors do not feel very protected).

Sometimes the publisher may agree to "reasonably consult" with the author before making changes, but the ultimate right to decide usually remains with the publisher. Only rarely is the publisher willing to modify the contract in order to give the author an equal role (*"...No changes or revisions shall be made in the Work without the mutual consent of Author and Publisher..."*).

"...and [Publisher] shall have the right to manufacture, distribute, advertise, promote and publish the Work in a style and manner which Publisher deems appropriate...." Typically, the right to make virtually all of the crucial marketing decisions are reserved to the publisher alone: whether or not there will be an author tour or other promotional efforts; how much money, if any, will be spent on advertising; how many review copies will be sent out, and to whom, and so on.

What's more, the publisher will decide all the particulars of publication, including *"...typesetting, paper, printing, binding, cover and/or jacket design, imprint, title and price...."* Thus, the size and configuration of the book, the kind and quality of the binding, the choice of imprint, the suggested retail price, and even the title are subject to the *publisher's* final say in most book contracts.

Sometimes the publisher will agree in advance to certain specifications and certain promotional efforts. Even more often, the publisher will agree that the title of the book will be determined by mutual consent of author and publisher. Indeed, all of these terms are negotiable, at least in theory. But the cautious author will ask that all such promises be inserted into the contract itself; thanks to the so-called merger clause that appears in most contracts, any promise that

---

WHERE HAVE YOU GONE, MAX PERKINS?
Among the bells and whistles that are sometimes found in book contracts is the so-called "editor's clause"—an escape clause that allows the author to terminate his contract with a publisher if his favorite editor leaves the publishing house. Nowadays, thanks to the turmoil and turnover in the publishing industry, the clause may be difficult for all but the hottest-selling authors to obtain. But John Irving (The World According to Garp, The Hotel New Hampshire, etc.) managed to put one in his contract with William Morrow—and when his editor at Morrow retired, Irving used the clause to make a jump to Random House only months before his next book (A Son of the Circus) was to be published by Morrow.

---

is *not* written down is probably *not* enforceable! ➤ *Entire Agreement—Below*

"*Notwithstanding any editorial changes..., Author's warranties and .indemnities...shall remain in full force and effect....*" Every book contract includes solemn and weighty guarantees (*"warranties and indemnities"*) by the author that the book will not expose the publisher to a lawsuit for copyright infringement, defamation, invasion of privacy, or other claims. ➤ *Author's Indemnity of Publisher—Below*

The sample clause specifies that the guarantees apply to the edited and revised version of the author's work, and not merely the unedited version that the author delivers to the publisher in the first place. In other words, the clause seeks to impose liability on the author for changes and insertions made during the editing process.

The author, of course, may object to taking responsibility for material that the *publisher* inserts into her work in the process of editing, revising and illustrating the book. For that reason, many publishers are willing to exclude such additional material from the scope of the warranties and indemnities by adding a phrase here: "*Author's warranties and indemnities shall remain in full force and effect except as to new matter inserted in the Work by Publisher.*"

Proofs

Publisher shall furnish Author with a proof of the Work. Author agrees to read, correct and return all proof sheets within seven (7) calendar days after receipt thereof. If any changes in the proof or the printing plates (other than corrections of printer's errors) are made at Author's request or with Author's consent, then the cost of such changes in excess of 5% of the cost of typesetting (exclusive of the cost of setting corrections) shall be paid by Author. If Author fails to return the corrected proof sheets within the time set forth above, Publisher may publish the Work without Author's approval of proof sheets.

"*Publisher shall furnish Author with a proof of the Work.*" The last chance—and, sometimes, the *only* chance—of the author to see how her book has been edited, revised and corrected is when the publisher provides proof sheets, galleys or some other preliminary form of the author's book shortly before publication. That's why the author ought to insist on a clause that specifies exactly when and how she will be afforded an opportunity to review and correct proofs *before* the book goes to press.

Note that the standard clause does *not* specify that the author will be given an opportunity to review the cover art. Since the right to design the cover is usually reserved to the publisher alone (see above), the author may find that she is sent a proof of the cover so late in the publishing process that it is too late to make any changes. If the author has bargained for the right to review and approve the cover or any aspect of the book other than the text, the book contract ought to specify what materials she is entitled to review, and when and how she will exercise these rights.

"Author agrees to read, correct and return all proof sheets within seven (7) calendar days...." The time allowed for correction of proofs by the author is rarely shorter than seven days or longer than thirty days, but there is no standard practice—it's up to the author and the publisher to work out a mutually acceptable period.

As a practical matter, however, the proofs are usually provided very late in the production process, and the publisher is usually anxious to get back the corrected proofs as early as possible. That's why the sample clause includes a kind of "fail-safe" provision that allows the publisher to simply go to press *without* the author's corrections *"...[i]f Author fails to return the corrected proof sheets within the time [allowed]...."*

Authors are notorious for "rewriting on galleys"—that is, making changes in style and content on the proof sheets rather than merely correcting typographical errors (or *"...printer's errors...,"* as the sample clause puts it). For that reason, the correction-of-proof clause in a standard book contract requires the *author* to pay for the cost of making any changes other than the correction of typographical errors. The sample clause, like most standard correction-of-proof clauses, allows the author to make a certain number of purely stylistic changes at the publisher's expense, but thereafter it is the author who pays.

Time of Publication

Publisher agrees that the Work, if published, shall be published within eighteen (18) months of the Final Delivery Date, except as the date of publication may be extended by forces beyond Publisher's control. The date of publication as designated by Publisher, but not later than the date of first delivery of bound volumes, shall be the "Publication Date" for all purposes under this Agreement.

Typically, the publisher promises that the author's work will be published within a specified period of time. The 18-month "window" in the sample clause represents a mid-range in the custom and practice of the publishing industry, but the period is rarely less than twelve months after signing of the contract.

"*...except as the date of publication may be extended by forces beyond Publisher's control....*" The obligation of the publisher to actually publish the author's work—and, generally, *any* obligation under contract that is time-related—may be subject to what is called a "force majeure" clause, that is, a mechanism that extends the period in which the publisher must publish in case of unavoidable delays such as a strike, a natural disaster or some other "act of God."

"*The date of publication...[shall be] not later than the date of first delivery of bound volumes....*" The publisher will usually designate an arbitrary date as the "Pub Date" of a book, which is usually (but not always) the date when the book is placed into commercial distribution. The sample clause, however, establishes a benchmark date as the *latest* publication date in the absence of a formal announcement by the publisher.

The sample clause does not define what happens if the publisher fails to publish within the time allowed in the contract. Unquestionably, the publisher will be in breach of the contract—but what other consequences will follow from tardy publication, or, for that matter, no publication at all?

The cautious author will ask for an additional provision to provide for specified consequences—an automatic reversion of rights, for example, and the right to keep the advances paid to date. Here's an example of such a provision:

> Without limiting any other remedy of Author at law or equity, if Publisher fails to publish the Work within the time allowed, then all rights in and to the Work shall revert fully and wholly to Author, automatically and without notice, and Author shall be entitled to retain any and all advances and other amounts paid to date.

The publisher may not be eager to spell out the author's rights and remedies in the time-of-publication clause. The disadvantage to both author and publisher, however, is that it may take a lawsuit to determine the precise consequences of late publication or non-publication.

Author's Copies

> Publisher shall provide Author with ten (10) copies, free of charge, of each edition of the Work published by Publisher. Author shall be permitted to purchase

additional copies of the Work, for personal use only and not for resale, at the
normal dealer discount, to be paid upon receipt of Publisher's invoice.

The publisher is obliged to give the author free copies of her
book—not only ten copies of the first edition but also ten copies of any
future edition of the same work that the publisher may publish. Some
publishers are more generous with free copies, of course, and authors
are almost always eager to get as many free copies as they can. Indeed,
the number of author's copies is often a surprisingly contentious issue
in the negotiation of a book deal!

The sample clause offers the author the right to buy additional
copies *"...at the normal dealer discount...,"* but the term is intentionally vague. The "standard" wholesale discount, at least according to
tradition, is 40% off the suggested retail price—but much deeper
discounts are routinely given to book and discount chains. So the
author may wish to demand the right to buy copies at a specified
discount or *"...at the best available discount...."*

> **I CAN'T GET IT FOR YOU WHOLESALE.**
> One of my clients was an author whose
> children's book had been in print so long
> that her current readers were the grand-
> children of her original readers. And her
> contract, which dated back to an earlier
> era in book publishing, entitled her to buy
> author's copies at a "standard" discount of
> 40% off the cover price. But she no longer
> bothered to buy her own books from the
> publisher. Thanks to the deep discounts
> that her publisher offered the discount
> chains, she told me, "I can get them
> cheaper off the shelf at the Price Club."

The sample clause prohibits
the author from reselling her
author's copies. This is an especially uncomfortable provision
for authors who make personal
appearances, work the lecture
circuit, offer their services as
consultants, or teach classes. All
of these are opportunities for the
author to make direct sales
of her books, and many authors
keep their books in print almost
entirely on the strength of direct
sales.

If the author is unable to persuade a publisher to simply drop the
prohibition against resale of author's copies, some publishers are
willing to permit resale so long as the initial sale of copies by the
publisher to the author is royalty-free. In other words, the publisher
does not pay a royalty to the author when she buys a copy of her own
book, but the author is permitted to resell the copy and keep the
difference between the wholesale price and the retail price. Under most

book contracts, the spread is so much greater than the royalty that the author makes more money on each sale!

The sample clause requires the publisher to send an invoice to the author—and requires the author to write a check directly to the publisher. Thus, if the author is not earning sufficient royalties against which to deduct the cost of author's copies, she is still required to pay the publisher. The author, on the other hand, may wish to demand that the purchase price of author's copies *"...be deducted from royalties otherwise payable to Author, if any...."* ➤ *Author's Royalties—Below*

Advance Against Royalties

Publisher shall pay to Author, as an advance against royalties and any other amounts owing by Publisher to Author under this Agreement, the sum of [Insert Amount Here] to be paid as follows: One-third upon signing of this Agreement, one-third upon delivery and acceptance of the complete Manuscript, and one-third upon publication of the Work in the firstt Publisher's edition.

How the heart races, how the imagination soars, at the very thought of the advance! "A five figure advance," is the shorthand phrase that every author expects to hear from the agent, but the magic phrase is richer yet: "Six figures!" And the author's enthusiasm and interest regarding the advance is well-justified: the sad fact is that most books never earn back the initial advance, and—sadder yet—most authors never see another dime after they've spent the advance.

An advance, of course, is essentially nothing more or less than an interest-free loan to the author from the publisher, and the publisher simply pays itself back out of any royalties or other compensation that the fortunate author may earn on the sales of her book. Only after the publisher has recouped the advance will the author begin to receive additional payments of royalties on sales or a share of subsidiary rights sales. ➤ *Author's Royalties—Below*

The advance is the essential "deal point" in any book contract, and so the advance clause will differ in amount, terms, and other particulars from contract to contract. The advance is a measurement of the publisher's opinion of the commercial value of a book, and so it is the allure of the book and the author—rather than the "clout" or negotiating skills of the agent—that will determine how big the advance will be and on what terms it will be paid. And, as some authors discover, many book publishers pay only a modest advance or no advance at all!

A GOOD DEAL IF YOU CAN GET IT. A "most-favored-nation clause" is a promise by the publisher that the author will be given at least as good a deal as the very best deal offered to anyone else. While they're common enough in the motion picture industry, only the most successful authors are able to command such treatment from book publishers. When I negotiated a new contract with a publisher on behalf of a pair of authors whose successful series of books were the publisher's "cash cow," the publisher was willing to make the following promise:

"Publisher acknowledges and agrees that Author shall be paid advances and royalties no less than advantageous than those offered to any other author whose work is now or hereafter published by Publisher, and in the event that Publisher shall later enter into a contract with one or more authors on more advantageous terms than those set forth here, then this Agreement shall be modified and amended to provide that any such more advantageous terms shall be paid to Author under this and any other agreement between Author and Publisher."

"*Publisher shall pay to Author....*" The advance is characterized as a payment in the sample clause (and most book contracts), but it is really only a loan secured by the author's future royalties—"*...an advance against royalties...,*" as the advance clause typically puts it. The publisher may be entitled to demand repayment of the advance if the manuscript is late or unacceptable. And the publisher is entitled to retain *all* royalties and other payments that would otherwise go to the author until the full amount of the advance is repaid. ➤ *Author's Termination for Non-Delivery—Above & Accounting—Below*

"*...to be paid as follows: One-third upon signing of this Agreement [etc.]....*" The amount and the timing of payment of the advance will vary from contract to contract, but the advance is almost always paid in installments that are carefully calculated to keep the author hard at work and on schedule!

The sample clause, for example, provides for only one-third of the advance to be paid on signing. Another third will be paid only when the manuscript is not only delivered by the author but *accepted* by the publisher. Thus, the publisher is entitled to hold back the second installment of the advance until the author has completed any revisions that the publisher may require. And only when the book is actually published will the author receive the final installment.

Another typical approach is to divide up the advance into more and smaller installments—a certain amount on signing of the agreement, and additional installments when the first half of the manuscript is delivered, when the complete manuscript is delivered, when rewrites and revisions are delivered, and so on. And some of the headline-making "seven figure" advances are actually based on a complicated series of contingencies. For example, the advance may include a so-called bestseller bonus—an additional advance paid if the author's work appears on a specified bestseller list.

Royalty on Publisher's Editions
(A Model Royalty Clause Based on Retail Price)
For each Edition of the Work published by the Publisher under this Agreement, Publisher shall credit Author's account with the following royalty on Net Copies Sold:

(i) ____% of the Invoice Price on the first 5,000 Net Copies Sold of any Edition;

(ii) ____% of the Invoice Price on the next 5,000 Net Copies Sold of any Edition; and

(iii) ____% of the Invoice Price on sales in excess of 10,000 Net Copies Sold of any Edition.

On bulk, premium, deep discount, and other sales at discounts of greater than 40%, and on direct-response sales, and other sales out-side of the conventional channels of distribution in the book industry, Publisher shall pay one-half (1/2) of the royalty rate set forth above.

"Invoice Price," as the term is used in this Agreement, means the price shown on Publisher's invoices to its wholesaler and retailer customers from which the Publisher's whole-saler and retailer discounts are calculated. The difference between the Invoice Price and the suggested retail price or cover price as such price may be printed on the dust

AND THE REST OF THE ADVANCE IS DONE WITH MIRRORS. Authors who are forced to content themselves with advances expressed in mere thousands of dollars are understandably eaten up with envy when they read of multi-million-dollar book deals. But the fact is that the biggest advances often include big chunks of money that are based on contingencies which may not happen at all.

For example, the author may have to wait until paperback rights or foreign rights or movie rights are sold before the full advance is paid. Some portion of the advance may be payable only if the book reaches the bestseller lists. And some-times a payment is triggered by some fairly remote and unpredictable events.

Consider, for example, the foreign rights deal that was struck by St. Martin's Press, the American publisher of LouAnne Johnson's novel, My Posse Don't Do Homework. According to Paul Nathan in Publishers Weekly, a German publisher agreed to pay an initial advance of $40,000 for the right to publish a German-language edition of the book.

The German publisher, mindful of the fact that a film version of the novel star-ring Michelle Pfeiffer was being planned, promised an additional $10,000 advance if the movie is screened in 100 movie theaters in Germany, $15,000 if the film shows up on 150 screens, and $20,000 for any number of bookings in excess of 150. (Given the uncertainties of the movie industry, the author is best advised not to spend her share of the extra $20,000 advance until she sees it!)

jacket or cover of the Work shall not exceed 5% without Author's consent.

"Net Copies Sold," as used in this Agreement, means the sale less returns of any and all copies sold by Publisher through conventional channels of distribution in the book trade, and does not include promotional and review copies, author's copies (whether free or purchased by author), or copies for which a royalty rate is otherwise set forth in this Agreement.

"Edition," as used in this Agreement, refers to the Work as published in any particular content, length, and format. If the Work is materially revised or redesigned in any manner, or expanded in length or content, then the Work as revised shall be considered a new "Edition" for purposes of this Section.

Royalties are the most common form of payment by a publisher to an author. A royalty, of course, is usually a payment of money based on the sales of the author's book. In theory—and, for example, in certain kinds of licensing arrangements—the royalty can be expressed as a fixed amount that is paid on the sale of each copy.

More often, author's royalty is expressed as a percentage of the suggested cover price, or a percentage of the net revenues received by the publisher, or a percentage of some other amount of money as defined in the book contract.

"Standard" royalties, back in the good old days of book publishing, were routinely expressed as a series of escalating percentages based on the sales: 10% of retail price on the first 5,000 copies, 12 1/2% on the next 5000 copies, and 15% on sales in excess of 10,000 copies. And some of the larger publishers still pay the same royalty rates on hardback editions. But the publishing industry is so unsettled, so diverse, and so dependent on "deep" discounts to wholesalers and chain stores, that publishers no longer feel obliged to honor these old traditions. Nowadays, royalty rates are a "deal point" that will be vigorously negotiated by the publisher, and a variety of royalty mechanisms are in use.

> Royalty Free. Royalties are the conventional method of paying an author for the rights granted to the publisher in a book contract— but royalties are not the only method of compensating an author. If, for instance, a writer is an employee of the publisher, she may be paid a salary for the work she creates; if she is an independent contractor working under a work-for-hire agreement, she may be paid a flat fee; if she is a joint venturer or partner in the publishing business, she may be paid a share of the profits. Indeed, as long as an author receives some form of "consideration"—that is, something of value—the book contract will be binding.

Two basic approaches to author's royalties are described here. The first one, as illustrated in the sample clause set forth above, is based on suggested retail price. The second one, which is based on net revenues, is illustrated in an alternative sample clause set forth below. These are not the only royalty mechanisms in publishing contracts, but they are the two most common ones.

"...*Publisher shall credit Author's account....*" In a conventional book deal, the publisher will open and maintain an "account" to keep track of the money owed by the publisher to the author for sales of her work—*and* the money, if any, owed by the author to the publisher. From time to time, the publisher will render statements of account and pay any amounts then owing to the author. ➤ *Accounting—Below*

The credits are fairly simple and straightforward. If the publisher sells a copy of the author's book, then the publisher will credit the account with the royalty on that sale. Other amounts may be credited to the author's account for the sale of secondary and subsidiary rights, if such rights are granted to the publisher. But debits to the author's account tend to be more complex—and, unhappily for many authors, more common—than credits. ➤ *Secondary and Subsidiary Rights—Below*

For example, the author's account will be debited for "returns," a curious and vexing practice that is especially common in the book publishing industry. The sale of books by the publisher to a retail bookstore is generally made on a "returnable" basis—that is, the retail bookstore orders a copy of the author's book, places the book on the shelf, and then, if no one has purchased the book or if the book is damaged, the retailer is entitled to return the unsold book to the publisher for full credit on the purchase of another book from the publisher.

When the retailer orders a copy of the author's book, the transaction is posted on the publisher's books as a sale. And so the author's account is *credited* with a royalty on the sale of the book. But there is always a risk—and, often enough, a likelihood—that the book will be returned by the bookstore. So the author's account will be *debited* in the same amount if and when the book is returned.

The author's account may also be debited for other amounts owed to the publisher under the book contract. The most common example, of course, is the debt for any advances the publisher may have paid to the author prior to publication. The account will be debited for any costs that the author is obliged to pay; for example, if the author makes corrections on proofs in excess of a certain permitted number of corrections. And the account may be debited if the publisher is obliged to defend a lawsuit. ➤ *Advances—Above; Proofs—Above; & Author's Indemnity of Publisher—Below*

"*...the following royalty on Net Copies Sold...*" As discussed above, the royalty is paid only when a book has actually been sold. The sample clause defines exactly what is meant by "*...Net Copies Sold...*"—that is, no royalty is paid on books that are ordered and then later returned by bookstores, on copies that are sent to book reviewers or used for other promotional purposes, or on copies that the publisher sells to the author. Other definitions may be used, however, and the author may ask the publisher to limit the number of royalty-free promotional copies, for example, or to pay royalties on copies purchased by the author. ➤ *Author's Copies—Below*

"*...[a royalty of]* ____% *of the Invoice Price....*" Royalties are usually stated as a percentage rather than a flat amount per copy. But two basic questions arise in every royalty clause: What percentage? And to what figure is the percentage applied to determine the actual royalty?

Royalty Rates. The royalty *rates* are strictly a "deal point," and it's up to the author (or her agent or attorney) and the publisher to strike a deal that both find acceptable. Bear in mind that the economic value of a specified royalty rate depends on whether the royalty is paid on the retail price, net amounts actually received by the publisher, or some other figure. The stated royalty rate in a book contract may be as low as 5% or 6% on a mass-market paperback, or as high as 15% on a hardback book, and it's not unusual to see a variety of royalty rates in a single contract.

For example, a recent contract issued by HarperCollins states a separate and different royalty rate for hardcover copies, "trade-size" (or "quality") paperback copies, rack-size (or "mass-market") paperback copies, and large-print copies. The royalty rates for each category of book also vary according to such factors as the discount at which the book is sold, whether the book is sold in the United States or abroad, and whether the books are sold in "ordinary channels of trade" or through some other outlet—including, for example, "book fairs"!

Calculation of Royalties. Of course, it's not enough to know the royalty *rate* in order to measure the economic value of a book contract. What also matters is the number to which the royalty rate is applied.

For example, the sample royalties clause obliges the publisher to pay the royalty as a percentage of "*...invoice price....*" Other (and more traditional) royalty clauses use the term "suggested customer's price" or "cover price" or "retail price" as the basis for calculating royalties. Yet another approach, which is described in greater detail below, is the calculation of royalties as a percentage of "net amounts actually received by publisher."

The sample clause uses a well-established definition of "invoice price" as the basis for calculating royalties. The invoice price differs from the "retail price" or "cover price" in an important way—the "invoice price" does *not* include the so-called "Freight Pass Through" charge that is sometimes used in setting the suggested retail price printed on the dust jacket of the book. Thus, the invoice price is *lower* than the retail price, and a royalty calculated on the invoice price will be less than a royalty calculated on the retail price!

("Freight Pass Through" is an amount of money that is included in the retail price of a book to compensate the bookseller for the cost of shipping books back and forth between the publisher's warehouse and the bookstore. If the suggested retail price of a book is $10.00, for example, 50 cents of the price may be earmarked as Freight Pass Through. Thus, the invoice price is actually $9.50, and the publisher will use $9.50 as the base price when applying the discount to determine the wholesale price of the book. And the publisher will use $9.50, too, when calculating the author's royalties under the sample royalties clause. But the customer is asked to pay $10.00 for the book.)

Payment of royalties on the cover price—or even the invoice price, which may be *lower* than the cover price—generally favors the author, since the publisher does not actually receive the retail price in payment for a book (unless the book is sold directly to the consumer by mail order). Rather, the publisher receives only the wholesale price of the book, which reflects a discount that is seldom less than 40% off the retail price or invoice price, and sometimes much more. Sales at "deep discounts" of 50% or more are increasingly common in the publishing industry, and publishers are sometimes reluctant to pay a royalty based on the retail price when they are actually selling the books at such drastic discounts.

"If the Work is materially revised..., then the Work as revised shall be considered a new "Edition"...." The sample clause carefully defines what is meant by "Edition" because the author's royalty rate depends on how many copies of any specific edition are sold.

For example, if more than 10,000 copies of a particular edition of the author's book are sold, then the sample clause provides that the author will receive the maximum royalty rate on all subsequent sales. But if the publisher decides that the book ought to be *"...materially revised or redesigned in any manner, or expanded in length or content...,"* then the author is paid at the *minimum* royalty rate because the revised book is defined as a new and different edition, and the calculation of total sales starts at zero with the new edition!

The Hard-Soft Dilemma. Once upon a time, the first edition of a book was usually in hardcover, and the right to print a paperback reprint was a potentially valuable "subsidiary" right that was sold off to a paperback publisher. Nowadays, because of the trend toward mergers and acquisitions in the publishing industry, the larger publishing houses may issue both hardcover <u>and</u> paperback books through various divisions, and thus the publisher will seek to acquire <u>both</u> hardcover and paperback rights at the same time in what is known as a "hard-soft deal." That's why, for example, a typical "hard-soft" contract used by HarperCollins will state a different royalty rate for hardcover copies, "trade-size" (or "quality") paperbacks, and "rack-sized" (or "mass-market") paperback editions, all of which will be published by one of the divisions or sister companies of the conglomerate. So the so-called paperback auction, once a source of big money for authors, is now becoming a rarity.

"On...sales at discounts of greater than 40%..., and on ...other sales outside of the conventional channels of distribution in the book industry,...Publisher shall pay one-half (1/2) of the royalty rate set forth

above...." Typically, the royalties clause permits the publisher to pay a reduced royalty on certain categories of sale where *"...discounts of greater than 40%..."* are given by the publisher, and where the sales take place *"...outside of the conventional channels of distribution...."* Generally, the publisher will realize a reduced profit on these categories of sale, and so the author is expected to accept a reduced royalty.

Some of these reduced-royalty categories of sale are specified in the sample clause. *"Bulk"* and *"premium"* sales, for example, are transactions where a corporation, for example, or an institution buys a large number of the author's book at a volume discount for use as in-house textbooks, promotional gifts, or some other special purpose. A premium sale might also include a special edition imprinted with an advertising or promotional message from the buyer, and a bulk sale might also include the sale of a large number of copies on a non-returnable basis to a discount chain. Since the premium or bulk purchaser is able to demand a deep discount, the publisher claims the right to pay a discounted royalty to the author.

The reduced royalty rate also applies to *"direct-response sales,"* such as single-copy sales by mail order directly from the publisher. Generally, direct-response sales are generated by direct mail, radio or television advertising, or other forms of advertising and promotion; for that reason, publishers find that single-copy sales by direct mail tend to be less profitable than sales through a retail bookstore, and a reduced royalty rate is applied. The same reduced rate would apply, for example, on sales through a gift shop or a specialty catalogue, which are generally considered to be *"...outside the conventional channels of distribution...."*

The sample clause attempts to deal with reduced-rate royalties in a single all-inclusive paragraph and a single reduced royalty that is 50% less than the standard royalty, but many book contracts set a specific royalty rate for each category of sale. For example, the standard Random House contract for a hardback book prescribes a reduced royalty rate—sometimes calculated as a percentage of the retail price and sometimes as a percentage of the amounts actually received by the publisher—for each of the following categories:

Sales at a discount of greater than 48% from the retail price; sales of less than 400 copies in a six-month period (which are sometimes called "slow sales" in some book contracts); sales "directly to the consumer;" premium and "subscription" sales; sales of copies as college textbooks or "school editions;" sales of copies in a Modern

Library edition (which is equivalent to what is sometimes called "cheap edition," that is, a lower-priced hardback edition); sales of any lower-priced edition which may be "sold for export;" sales of copies "outside normal wholesale and retail channels;" copies printed by a "government agency" using the publisher's plates; book club editions; foreign language editions; anthologies, newspapers, magazines and digests in which all or a portion of the author's work appears; and Xerox and microfilm reproduction of all or a portion of the author's work.

Royalties Based on Net Revenue. Another basic approach to royalties is based on *net revenues* rather than *retail price.*

Because of the prevalence of deep discounts, and the increasingly treacherous economics of book publishing in general, more and more book publishers are inclined to pay royalties on *net revenues*—that is, the money actually received by the publisher on the sale of a copy of the author's book—rather than the retail price or the invoice price.

Here is another sample royalties clause that disregards the retail price altogether, and uses *"...Net Revenue..."* as the basis for calculating royalties.

<u>Royalty on Publisher's Editions</u>
(Another Form of Royalty Clause Based on Net Revenues)
For each Edition of the Work published by the Publisher under this Agreement, Publisher shall credit Author's account with the following royalty:
___% of Net Revenues from the sale of any and all net copies sold.

"Net Revenues," as used in this Agreement, refers to money actually received by Publisher, for the sale of copies of the Work, net of returns, after deduction of shipping, customs, insurance, fees and commissions, currency exchange discounts, and costs of collection.

A royalty based on net revenue ignores the complexities of the suggested retail price, cover price, or invoice price. Rather, the publisher pays a royalty calculated on the money that actually ends up in the publisher's bank account after a book is sold. Thus, *"Net Revenues,"* as the term is defined in the sample clause, is the money actually received by the publisher on sales *"...net of returns..."* after the deduction of certain specified costs and expenses: *"...shipping, customs, insurance, fees and commissions, currency exchange discounts, and costs of collection...."*

The sample clause states the royalty rate as a flat percentage of net revenues. If the author and the publisher agree, of course, the publisher may establish an escalating royalty rate based on the volume of sales—after all, the publisher's profit margin usually increases as the number of copies sold increases, since going back to press for additional copies is less costly than preparing a book for publication in the first place. Then, too, the cost per copy drops enormously as the press run increases.

The use of net revenues as the basis for royalties tends to favor the publisher, since the publisher only pays a royalty on the money that has been actually collected, rather than the purely theoretical figure of the retail price. It's also a much simpler and more straightforward method of royalty calculation than a sliding-scale royalty based on the invoice price and the wholesale discount. But the author is understandably wary of a royalty based on net revenues since the royalty per copy will appear to be drastically less than a retail price royalty.

Subsidiary and Secondary Rights

Except as otherwise provided below, Publisher shall credit Author's account with a royalty equal to 50% of all Net Revenues actually received by Publisher for the exploitation or disposition of Secondary and Subsidiary Rights in the Work.

Generally, the author and the publisher share the proceeds from the exploitation of secondary and subsidiary rights in specified percentages. Of course, the specific secondary rights, if any, which are shared between author and publisher—and the specific percentages in which they are shared—are important deal points that will vary according to the deal itself. ➤ *Grant of Rights—Above and Chapter 7: Electronic & Other Subsidiary Rights*

The sample clause presumes that the publisher has acquired *all* rights in the author's work, and specifies a fifty-fifty split on *all* revenues from the exploitation of such rights. Of course, if the publisher acquires *no* secondary and subsidiary rights, then the book contract will not contain such a clause at all. And even if the publisher acquires some or all secondary rights, the author's share of revenues for any specific right may be as much as 90%, although most publishers will ask for a split of no less than fifty-fifty on most subsidiary rights.

The split of revenues from the exploitation of subsidiary rights is a hotly-negotiated deal point. The first phase of the negotiation, of course, is whether the publisher is acquiring *any* subsidiary rights. And then the author and publisher must resolve what percentage of the proceeds will be paid to the author. As with most aspects of book negotiation, the real issue is how badly the publisher wants the book, and how much the publisher is willing to pay to get it. ➤ *Grant of Rights—Above*

Typically, the publisher is most generous in sharing the proceeds from the least valuable rights. The author will usually be given 90% of periodical rights, that is, the right to publish an excerpt of the author's book in a magazine or newspaper, whether before the book is published ("First Serial Rights") or after the book is published ("Second Serial Rights"). But the publisher will hold out for a bigger share of the most valuable rights, including audio rights, electronic rights, or motion picture and television rights. ➤ *Chapter 7: Electronic and Other Subsidiary Rights*

"Publisher shall credit Author's account..." The author's share of revenues from secondary and subsidiary rights is not paid outright. Rather, it is *"...credit[ed] to the Author's account...,"* and the publisher is entitled to deduct the unearned portion of the advance and other amounts owing to the publisher before paying over what's left to the author. ➤ *Accounting—Below*

"...all Net Revenues actually received by Publisher...." Unlike royalties on the publisher's editions of the author's work, which are sometimes calculated as a percentage of the cover price, the author's compensation for the sale or exploitation of secondary rights is almost always expressed as a percentage of money *"...actually received..."* by the publisher. The sample clause, by using the defined term "Net Revenues," makes it clear that the author's percentage is applied to the amount of money that remains *"...after deduction of shipping, customs, insurance, fees and commissions, currency exchange discounts, and costs of collection...."*

Licensing of Secondary Rights to a Related Company. A special concern arises when the book publisher is selling or licensing secondary rights to a related company. Nowadays, for example, many hardback publishers are part of a corporate structure that includes a mass-market paperback publisher, an audio publisher, or even a motion picture studio. Under these circumstances, the author may be justifiably concerned that the hardback publisher will sell secondary rights in the author's work to a "sister" company at an unrealistically low price or on disadvantageous terms.

The cautious author will ask for an additional clause that requires the author's consent to transactions between the publisher and a related company, or a clause that requires any such transaction to be "on terms and conditions no less advantageous to Author than an arm's length transaction with a third party."

Agency Clause

Author hereby irrevocably appoints [Name and Address of Agent] ("Agent") as Author's sole and exclusive agent with respect to the Work which is the subject of this Agreement, and authorizes and directs Publisher to pay to Agent all amounts owing to Author under this Agreement, and to render to Agent all statements of account required under this Agreement. In consideration of services rendered by Agent, Author hereby authorizes Agent to receive, deduct and retain 15% of gross monies paid to Author under this Agreement. Any sums payable to Author and paid to the Agent pursuant to this Section shall constitute a full and valid discharge of Publisher's obligation to Author with respect to such sums.

The agency clause is usually inserted into a book contract by the author's *agent* as a means of assuring that the agent's commission will be paid. Essentially, the clause makes the agent a "third party beneficiary" of the book contract, and directs the publisher to pay royalties and advances to the agent rather than the author.

"Author hereby irrevocably appoints...Agent...as Author's sole and exclusive agent...." The sample clause confirms that the author has engaged the agent on the terms set forth in the agency clause, and thus often takes the place of a formal agency agreement between the author and the agent. ➤ *Chapter 2: Agents and Packagers*

"...with respect to the Work which is the subject of this Agreement...." The sample agency clause generally authorizes the agent to handle *all* rights in the work that is being sold to publisher, since it makes no distinction between primary and secondary rights in *"...the Work which is the subject of this Agreement...."* If the author wishes to restrict the scope of the agency, then the agency clause must be carefully drafted (or modified) to make it clear exactly which rights in the author's work are exclusively represented by the agent.

"...authorizes and directs Publisher to pay to Agent all amounts owing to Author under this Agreement, and to render to Agent all statements of account required under this Agreement...." The essential function of the agency clause, as far as the agent is concerned, is to direct the publisher to make payments and render statements to the *agent* rather than the *author*. The agent is authorized *"...to receive, deduct and retain..."* his commission out of the money paid by the publisher. Only then is the agent required to pass along

what's left to the author.

"Any sums ...paid to the Agent...shall constitute a full and valid discharge of Publisher's obligation to Author...." The sample clause also reassures the *publisher* that payment of advances and royalties to the *agent* will satisfy its obligation to the *author* under the book contract. In other words, if the publisher pays the agent, but the agent fails to pay the author, the publisher need not worry about a lawsuit from the author—rather, the author must pursue her own agent for what is owed to her.

Pulling the Plug on an Agent. What happens if the author terminates her relationship with an agent after signing a contract with an agency clause? Most book contracts do not permit the author to cut off the agent. But the contract form used by St. Martin's Press includes an agency clause with an escape mechanism for the author: "The Publisher may pay all sums hereunder to the said agent...[u]ntil the Publisher shall have received written notice from the Author of the termination of such agency. Upon receipt of such notice, the Publisher shall pay all further sums...directly to the Author or to such other persons as the Author shall direct in writing."

Author's Representations and Warranties.

Author represents and warrants to Publisher that: (i) the Work is not in the public domain; (ii) Author is the sole proprietor of the Work and has full power and authority, free of any rights of any nature whatsoever by any other person, to enter into this Agreement and to grant the rights which are granted to Publisher in this Agreement; (iii) the Work has not heretofore been published, in whole or in part, in any form; (iv) the Work does not, and if published will not, infringe upon any copyright or any proprietary right at common law; (v) the Work contains no matter whatsoever that is obscene, libelous, violative of any third party's right of privacy or publicity, or otherwise in contravention of law or the right of any third party; (vi) all statements of fact in the Work are true and are based on diligent research; (vii) all advice and instruction in the Work is safe and sound, and is not negligent or defective in any manner; (viii) the Work, if biographical or "as told to" Author, is authentic and accurate; and (ix) Author will not hereafter enter into any agreement or understanding with any person or entity which might conflict with the rights granted to Publisher under this Agreement.

The representations and warranties of the author, which are standard terms in virtually every book contract, amount to a series of guarantees by the author to the publisher. A "representation" is simply a statement of fact, and a "warranty" is a promise that the statement of fact is true.

Thus, the author's representations and warranties amount to a guarantee that the author is entitled to sell the rights in her work and that the work will not expose the publisher to the risk of liability for copyright infringement, defamation, or any other legal claim. And, as set forth below in the section on indemnification, the author promises to bear the consequences if any of the warranties or representations turn out to be false or inaccurate.

Authors tend to regard warranties and representations as an unfair demand by the publisher. How is the typical author to know with absolute certainty, for example, that her work is *not* "in contravention of law or the right of any third party"? And isn't the publisher, who is usually richer and better served by attorneys, in a better position than the author to make such a judgment?

The publisher, however, regards the author as the one who best knows whether there are flaws in the author's work. It's the author, after all, who knows whether she has cribbed from the copyrighted work of another author, or if the facts in her work have been verified with credible sources, or if rights in the work have already been sold to another publisher.

So the publisher turns to the author and demands a series of warranties and representations that amount to a kind of money-back guarantee. As we will see, the obligation of the author to back up her guarantee is one that cannot be treated lightly or ignored. It's a dollar-and-cents commitment by the author, and so the author needs to understand exactly what promises she is making to her publisher in this particularly weighty hunk of legal boilerplate.

"*...the Work is not in the public domain....*" The author guarantees that her work is subject to protection under the laws of copyright. (A work that is *not* protected under copyright is generally characterized as being in the "public domain.") Otherwise, of course, the publisher need not enter into the contract at all—a work that is in the public domain may be freely published by anyone.

"*...Author is the sole proprietor of the Work and has full power and authority...to enter into this Agreement and to grant the rights...to Publisher....*" The author guarantees that she alone owns and controls the rights that she is purporting to grant to the publisher; if she did not control these rights, of course, the book contract would be meaningless to the publisher.

And she guarantees, too, that she has not already granted the same rights to another publisher: The work is warranted to be "*...free of any* *rights of any nature whatsoever by any other person...."*

If the author is *not* the sole owner of copyright, of course, then she must advise the publisher *before* she signs the contract. If, for example, the author is the joint owner of the work along with a co-author or collaborator, then all of the joint owners ought to sign the contract. And, if a third party claims to own the rights that are being granted by the author—but the author disputes the claim—the publisher may be willing to modify the warranties and representations to reflect the rights are in dispute. But it's very much in the author's interest to address such issues at the outset of her dealings with the publisher.

➤ *Chapter 2: Co-Authorship and Copyright*

"...the Work has not heretofore been published, in whole or in part, in any form...." The standard book contract presumes that the author's work is original and previously unpublished. Of course, the facts may be different for any given work of authorship—the author may be selling reprint rights or foreign language rights in a work that has already been published, or the author's book project may be based on a magazine article or perhaps a portion of an earlier book. If so, the representation ought to be modified to reflect the actual history of the project.

"...the Work does not, and if published will not, infringe upon any copyright or any proprietary right at common law...."

The author is promising that she did not copy any portion of her work from someone else's copyrighted work. But the promise really goes much farther by ruling out *any* copyright defect, even an innocent or inadvertent one.

Suppose, for example, the author quotes a passage from a copyrighted work in the honest belief that she is entitled to do so under the doctrine of "fair use," a principle of copyright law that permits some limited use of copyrighted material without the consent of the copyright owner. Later, the author and publisher are sued, and it turns out that the judge or jury decides that the fair use doctrine does *not* apply. Under these circumstances, the author has breached her warranties and representations, even though she acted in good faith and even if she relied on an attorney's advice! ➤ *Chapter 5: Preparing the Manuscript*

The guarantee that the work does not infringe "any proprietary right" is a much broader concept that is intended to rule out any claim by a third party that the author has infringed a trademark, or misappropriated an idea or a trade secret, or invaded rights that were previously granted by the author to someone else.

"...the Work contains no matter whatsoever that is obscene, libelous, violative of any third party's right of privacy or publicity, or otherwise in contravention of law or the right of any third party...." The author guarantees that her book, whether fiction or nonfiction, is not defamatory and does not invade the privacy of the people she writes about. Aside from copyright infringement, a lawsuit for libel or invasion of privacy is probably the most likely risk of publication, and so the guarantee needs to be taken seriously by both author and publisher in screening the manuscript. ➤ *Chapter 5: Preparing the Manuscript*

The author also guarantees that the book does not infringe upon another person's "right of publicity," a legal doctrine that arises from the law of privacy but protects a very different interest—the right of an individual to use his "name, image or likeness" in advertising, product endorsements and merchandising. Again, the risk of a lawsuit for invasion of privacy may be minimized by a careful "vetting" of the manuscript, but "right of publicity" claims can also arise in the advertising and promotion of the book itself. So author and publisher need to pay attention to dust jacket design, blurbs, press releases, and other aspects of book promotion where an endorsement may be claimed or implied without the consent of the endorser. ➤ *Chapter 5: Preparing the Manuscript*

The author also guarantees that the book is not obscene, a circumstance that theoretically exposes both author and publisher to criminal sanctions. And, nowadays, a new generation of would-be censors are crusading to extend civil liability to authors, publishers and others whose work supposedly inspires crimes of violence. Although obscenity prosecutions are far less common than they once were, the obscenity laws are *not* a dead letter in the United States—and, in fact, the risk of both civil and criminal liability under various kinds of obscenity laws is a real risk in publishing. ➤ *Chapter 5: Preparing the Manuscript*

"...all statements of fact in the Work are true and are based on diligent research...." The guarantee of truthfulness, accuracy and *"...diligent research..."* is primarily intended to reassure the publisher that the author's work does not contain false and unfounded assertions of fact that may expose author and publisher to a claim for libel. Accuracy and reliability in the author's research and writing also reduce the risk that some reader will claim to have been injured by bad advice or faulty instruction in a nonfiction book. ➤ *Chapter 5: Preparing the Manuscript*

"...all advice and instruction in the Work is safe and sound, and is not negligent or defective in any manner...." The author guarantees that her work is not *"...defective..."* in the concrete sense that a reader will not be injured if he follows the *"...advice and instruction..."* in the book. A claim of negligence may arise in connection with a book of legal, medical, psychological or financial advice, a how-to book, even a travel book. Although the author and publisher ought to consider the appropriate use of a disclaimer to limit such claims, the publisher will ultimately rely on the author to make sure that the book does *not* contain matter that is injurious to the health of the reader, whether mental, physical or economic. ➤ *Chapter 5: Preparing the Manuscript & Form 6: Warning and Disclaimer*

"...the Work, if biographical or "as told to" Author, is authentic and accurate...." The author of a biography—and, especially, the professional writer who is engaged to write a celebrity autobiography—guarantees the factual accuracy of her work. The guarantee is slightly redundant, since the author has already assured the publisher that her work is not libelous and that *"...all statements of fact in the Work are true and are based on diligent research...."* However, the publisher may wish to emphasize the responsibilities of the author in the two instances that are implied in the guarantee itself.

If the work *is* a biography of a living person, the risk of a claim of libel or invasion of privacy is heightened because the very subject matter of the book consists of facts that the subject may find sensitive or objectionable. Then, too, if the author is working closely with a celebrity, a criminal or a crime victim, or a "subject matter expert" on an "as told to" autobiography, the publisher is forced to rely on the author to make sure that the story is told accurately.

"... Author will not hereafter enter into any agreement or understanding with any person...which might conflict with the rights granted to Publisher...." The author has already guaranteed that she has not previously granted rights in her work to a third party—and now she guarantees that she will not do so in the future. As a technical matter, any such grant of rights by the author at a later date will probably be ineffective—but the publisher asks for a specific guarantee as a reminder to the author and as a legal basis for bringing a claim against the author if a conflicting grant of rights forces the publisher to bring or defend a lawsuit. ➤ *Author's Indemnity of Publisher—Below*

<u>Author's Indemnity of Publisher</u>

Author shall indemnify, defend and hold harmless Publisher, its subsidiaries and affiliates, and their respective shareholders, officers, directors, employees, partners, associates, affiliates, joint venturers, agents and representatives, from any and all claims, debts, demands, suits, actions, proceedings, and/or prosecutions ("Claims") based on allegations which, if true, would constitute a breach of any of the foregoing warranties, and any and all liabilities, losses, damages, and expenses (including attorneys' fees and costs) in consequence thereof.

Each party to this Agreement shall give prompt notice in writing to the other party of any Claims.

No compromise or settlement of any Claims shall be made or entered into without the prior written approval of Publisher and Author.

In the event of any Claims, Publisher shall have the right to suspend payments otherwise due to Author under the terms of this Agreement as security for Author's obligations under this Section.

Author's representations, warranties and indemnities as set forth above and this Section shall extend to any person or entity against whom any Claims are asserted by reason of the exploitation of the rights granted by Author in this Agreement, as if such representations, warranties and indemnities were originally made to such third parties. All such warranties, representations and indemnities shall survive the termination or expiration of this Agreement.

Perhaps no single clause in a standard book contract is more startling and even shocking to the new author than the indemnity clause—a solemn promise that the poor struggling *author* will pay the costs of defending the rich corporate *publisher*. "Shouldn't it be the other way around?" is the author's plaintive cry.

And yet no clause in a standard book contract is more sacrosanct in the publisher's eyes. Publishers are often asked to delete the indemnity clause, but I have not yet encountered the publisher who is willing to do so. The reason is simple: The indemnity clause puts teeth in the warranties and representations of the author, and—by putting the author at risk if a lawsuit is filed—the clause gives the author a powerful incentive to present a united front with the publisher in defending the lawsuit.

Some publishers may be willing to cushion the blow of the indemnity clause by adding the author to its insurance policy, if any, or by

THE PUBLISHER MADE ME DO IT! The whole point of an indemnity clause is to prevent the publisher's worst nightmare: A lawsuit is filed, and the author agrees to cooperate with the plaintiff in exchange for an agreement that the plaintiff will pursue only the "deep-pocket" publisher and not the poor author. The nightmare came true for one magazine publisher when a libel suit was filed against the publisher and a freelance contributor who wrote a controversial story for the magazine. Magazine freelancers rarely sign contracts—and when they do, the contracts rarely include indemnity provisions—and so the author felt free to make a deal with the plaintiff. The writer agreed to testify in favor of the plaintiff, and the plaintiff agreed not to execute any judgment against the assets of the writer. The publisher was left to defend the lawsuit without the assistance of a key witness—the writer who actually did the research and wrote the story!

limiting the duty to indemnify to a dollar amount equal to what the author receives in advances and royalties, or by sharing the expense of defending and settling claims. But it's unlikely that the author will be able to negotiate her way out of the indemnity clause. ➤ *Insurance Rider—Below & Briefs: Insurance*

"*...Author shall indemnify, defend and hold harmless Publisher....*" The basic obligation of the author is to "*hold [the publisher] harmless,*" which means that the author will pay the legal costs of defending a lawsuit, the entire amount of any settlement, and—if no settlement is achieved—the entire amount of any judgment that may be entered against the publisher. Although the precise phrasing of an indemnity clause may limit the obligations of the author in subtle and technical ways, the phrase "indemnify, defend and hold harmless" imposes a sweeping and comprehensive duty on the author. And the sample clause extends the scope of the indemnity not only to the publisher but also to "*...its subsidiaries and affiliates, and their respective shareholders, officers, directors, employees, [etc.]....*"

"*...any and all claims, debts, demands, suits, actions, proceedings, and/or prosecutions ("Claims")....*" The duty to indemnify extends not only to lawsuits, but to virtually *any* claim or demand that might be brought against the publisher as a result of the contents of the author's work. Thus, the author's duty to defend arguably include, for example, an obscenity prosecution or a proceeding to impound royalties under a so-called "Son of Sam" law. ➤ *Chapter 5: Preparing the Manuscript*

"*...based on allegations which, if true, would constitute a breach of any of the foregoing warranties....*" Here is the cutting edge of the indemnity clause: The author's duty to indemnify the publisher is fundamentally defined in terms of the "representations and warranties" that appear in the previous section of the book contract. The author has "warranted" (or guaranteed) that various representations about her work are true and accurate. If any of the author's representations turn out to be false or inaccurate, then the author is on the hook to the publisher under the indemnity clause.

For example, the warranties and representations clause includes a promise by the author that her work does not *"...infringe upon any copyright..."* and that the work *"...contains no matter...that is...libelous...."* So any claim by a third party that the author has defamed him or infringed his copyright raises the risk that the author's representations were wrong, and she is now responsible for backing up her warranties with the money to pay the costs of defense, settlement or judgment in the lawsuit for libel or copyright infringement.

Note, too, that the *claim* of wrongful conduct is enough to invoke the author's duty to indemnify the publisher. It is *not* necessary for the publisher to wait until the plaintiff in a lawsuit has actually *won* his case. As long the claim of wrongful conduct, *if* true, would amount to a breach of the author's warranties, the publisher's right of indemnity is enforceable against the author!

"...any and all liabilities, losses, damages, expenses (including attorneys' fees and costs)...." Under the indemnity clause, the author is liable to the publisher for *all* costs of defense, settlement and judgment, including not only the money that may be paid to a claimant but also the fees charged by the publisher's attorneys in defending the claim.

Some indemnity clauses are more generous toward the author. For example, some publishers are willing to share the cost of defense, especially in a case where the claim is ultimately shown to be without merit. Unless author and publisher specify some allocation of expense, however, the standard indemnity clause is likely to put the burden entirely on the author.

"Each party...shall give prompt notice in writing to the other party of any Claims...." Whether it is the author or the publisher who first learns of a claim against the author's work, the other party must be notified in writing. The requirement of giving notice of a claim does not appear in every indemnity clause, but it affords some benefits to both the publisher (who may be entitled to suspend royalty payments until the claim is settled or resolved) *and* the author (who will want to participate in the decision to defend or settle a claim, especially since *she* is the one who will pay!).

"No compromise or settlement of any Claims shall be made... without the prior written approval of Publisher and Author...." The decision to defend or settle a claim is subject to the joint approval of the author and the publisher. Many standard indemnity clauses, however, reserve the decision to the publisher alone—after all, the author may be ultimately liable to her publisher for the costs of defending and settling a claim, but it is usually the publisher who lays out the money to hire lawyers and pay for settlements.

The right to determine when and how a claim is settled may be the subject of some controversy between the author and the publisher. An author may be justifiably concerned that the publisher will settle too quickly or too generously, and then recoup the cost of settlement out of the author's royalties (see below). The publisher, on the other hand, may worry that an author will stand on principle as long as she is not actually paying the costs of defense out of her own pocket.

"...Publisher shall have the right to suspend payments otherwise due...as security for Author's obligations...."

The publisher usually assumes that the author cannot really afford to reimburse the publisher for the sometimes huge costs of defending and settling a lawsuit, even if the indemnity clause obliges her to do so, and thus the publisher will want to keep the royalties and advances as a kind of collateral for the author's obligation.

The author, of course, is likely to regard the suspension of royalties as a financial catastrophe and a punitive gesture,

---

THE DEBIT THAT DEVOURS ROYALTIES. An author once learned the hard way how treacherous an indemnity clause can be. After many years of research and writing, the author's work was finally published—but when her first royalty statement arrived, she noticed an unexplained $20,000 charge against royalties. When she inquired about the mysterious charge, she was told that another publisher had claimed that certain technical aspects of her book amounted to trademark infringement—and her publisher had promptly agreed to pay $20,000 in settlement of the claim without consulting or even informing her. Under the indemnity clause, the publisher simply charged the settlement to her royalty account. At the author's request, I called the publisher to protest—we both believed that the claim was spurious and should have been vigorously defended. Later, she discovered that another $75 had been debited on her royalty statement—it was a quarter-hour of time charged by the publisher's lawyer for talking on the telephone to me. And that's why the author ought to negotiate for a provision in the indemnity clause that obliges the publisher to inform the author of any claims—and to consult with the author before settling a claim.

especially if the claim appears to be frivolous. But only rarely will a publisher give up the comfort of keeping the author's royalties in the bank as security for the author's duty to indemnify.

"...Author's representations, warranties and indemnities...shall extend to any person...against whom any Claims are asserted by reason of the exploitation of the rights granted by Author...." The author's duty to indemnify is not limited to the publisher alone. If the book contract entitles the publisher to sell or license rights in the author's work to third parties—and if a claim is made against the third party who has purchased such rights—then the author is obliged to "indemnify and defend" the third party, too.

Suppose, for example, that the book contract conveys audio rights as well as print rights to the publisher. Later, the publisher licenses the right to create a spoken-word version of the author's book to an audio publisher. If someone sues the audio publisher for libel on the basis of the spoken-word version of the author's work, then the indemnity clause *in the book contract* requires the author to indemnify the audio publisher. *"All such warranties, representations and indemnities shall survive the termination or expiration of this Agreement..."* The author is not relieved of her obligation to indemnify the publisher simply because the book contract itself has expired. If a claim is made against the publisher at *any* time, even long after the book is out of print and the rights have reverted to the author, the author's obligations to indemnify the publisher remain in effect. As a practical matter, however, the risk of a lawsuit will diminish over the years as potential claims for copyright infringement, libel, and other causes of action are barred by the various applicable statutes of limitation.

Advertising and Promotion

Publisher shall have the right to use, and to license others to use, Author's name, image, likeness and biographical material for advertising, promotion, and other exploitation of the Work and the other rights granted under this Agreement.

Publisher shall have the right to determine the time, place, method and manner of advertising, promotion and other exploitation of the Work, except as Author and Publisher may set forth in a writing signed by both parties.

The right to use an author's name to promote an author's book is, of course, so fundamental that it is probably *implied* in the other terms and conditions of the book contract. But the sample clause makes it explicit—the author is bestowing upon the publisher what is called the "right of publicity," that is, the right of an individual to decide how and when her name is used to endorse a product. ➤ *Chapter 5: Preparing the Manuscript*

"*Publisher shall have the right to determine the time, place, method and manner of advertising [and] promotion....*" The publisher usually makes no promises about the advertising and promotion efforts that will be undertaken in support of the author's book. Although *some* basic effort to promote the author's book is imposed on the publisher by law, it's rare for the publisher to make any detailed commitments to the author in writing. ➤ *The Duty to Publish in Good Faith—Above*

Thus, if the author has been promised *any* specific advertising or publicity efforts by the publisher in the course of negotiations—an author tour, for example, or an advertising budget—then the publisher's promise must be set down in "*...a writing signed by both parties....*" Otherwise, the publisher is only bound by what the contract specifically obliges the publisher to do.

Author's Non-Competition

During the duration of this Agreement, Author has not prepared or published, and shall not prepare or publish, or participate in the preparation or publication of, any competing work that is substantially similar to the Work, or which is likely to injure the sales of the Work.

The non-competition clause says out loud what is arguably implicit in every book contract under the law of both contract and copyright. Once she has granted exclusive rights in her work to a publisher, the author may not write another book that injures the sales of the work. And if she writes another book that is "substantially similar" to the first book, then she may be infringing the very rights that she granted to the publisher! A non-competition clause is a good way to define what the author may and may not write and publish after the book contract is signed.

Option

Publisher shall have the right to acquire Author's next book-length work on the same terms and conditions set forth in this Agreement. Author shall submit a detailed outline and sample chapter of such to Publisher before submitting the work to any other publisher, and Publisher shall have a period of 30 days in which to review the submission and determine whether or not to exercise the option. The 30-day period described above shall not begin to run earlier than

> 60 days after the publication of the Work. If Publisher declines to exercise its option, then Author may submit the work to other publishers or otherwise dispose of the work.

The option clause is designed to allow the publisher to participate in the success of the author's work by bestowing upon the publisher the right to publish the author's *next* book, too. Since the publisher has taken a chance on the author, or so the publisher will argue, it's only fair that the publisher should reap some benefit if the publication of the author's first book creates a readership that is anxiously awaiting the next book.

Authors, on the other hand, tend to regard option clauses as a kind of indentured servitude, especially if the clause eliminates the right to negotiate a better deal on the second book than the publisher was willing to give on the first book. And authors are especially wary of an option clause that extends to more than one book or an option that remains in effect from book to book.

For that reason, option clauses are often vigorously negotiated, and a number of alternative approaches to the standard option clause—some even more restrictive, some less restrictive—are discussed below.

"*...the right to acquire Author's next book-length work on the same terms and conditions...*" The sample clause gives the publisher what is sometimes known as a "right of first refusal," that is, a firm option that allows the publisher to pick up the author's next work on the same terms that appear in the book contract for the author's initial work. The publisher need not negotiate with the author on any of the terms, and the author is not permitted to offer the book to other publishers.

> THE BOOK OF J. One of the best-loved tales about an author at war with a publisher over an option is told about publisher Lyle Stuart, a true renegade of the book industry, and the author who wrote a couple of runaway bestsellers, The Sensuous Woman and The Sensuous Man, under the pseudonym "J". Under the option clause in the author's contract, Lyle Stuart was entitled to publish J's next book on the same terms that applied to the first two books. Of course, "J" wanted a richer deal for her third book, but the publisher stood on his rights. So "J" decided that her next book would be a guide to the golf courses of Florida—and she satisfied her obligations under the option clause by delivering the yawner to Lyle Stuart, thus freeing herself to make a deal with a publisher who was willing to pay bigger bucks for a book with a bigger bang.

By the way, since *all* terms and conditions of the initial book contract are applied to the author's next work, the option clause will apply, too. As a result, the author's work will be continue to be subject to an option in favor of the publisher for as long as the publisher exercises its option on each of the author's books! Only when the publisher *declines* to pick up the author's next book is the chain of options broken, and only then will the author be free to negotiate elsewhere.

Right of First Negotiation. Of course, if the author's initial book has been a commercial success, then the author will wish to negotiate a better deal on the next book, and an option clause that eliminates the prospect of negotiation will be highly distasteful to the author. For that reason, the author may demand—and the publisher may be willing to accept—an option clause that allows the author to negotiate with the publisher on advances, royalty rates, and other terms of publication, or, even better, to shop the book around to see if a better offer is available.

A common form of option is one that allows the publisher to take a "first look" at the author's next work and to enter into negotiations for a new deal—but one that does not require the author to agree in advance to the terms and conditions that appear in the initial agreement. Strictly speaking, such a clause gives the publisher a "right of first negotiation," not an option, and allows the author to go elsewhere if she cannot reach a deal with the publisher. Note, however, that the author is allowed to enter into a deal with another publisher only if the terms are better than the deal offered by the current publisher. Here is a sample clause that establishes a right of first negotiation:

> Author shall submit a detailed outline and sample chapter of Author's next book-length work to Publisher before submitting the work to any other publisher, and Author and Publisher shall engage in exclusive good-faith negotiations for publication of such work for a period of not less than 30 days after such submission. If the parties are unable to reach a mutually acceptable agreement for publication of such work within the period of exclusive negotiation, then Author shall be free to enter into negotiations with other publishers or otherwise dispose of the work, except that Author shall not enter into an agreement with another publisher on terms less favorable than those offered by Publisher.

Right of Last Refusal. Yet another variant of the option clause gives the publisher what is called "capping rights" or the right of "last refusal"—that is, one last chance to make a deal with the author by matching the best offer made by another publisher. (Such a clause protects the publisher from an author who takes an unreasonable position during the period of exclusive negotiation—and then proceeds to make a deal with another publisher on terms no better than the publisher's last offer. By *adding* the following sentence to the clause set forth above, the publisher will enjoy both the right of first negotiation and the right of last refusal:

> If Author and Publisher do not reach an agreement on Author's next work, and Author submits such work to other publishers, then Publisher shall have the right to acquire the Author's next work on terms and conditions substantially equivalent to the best bona fide offer in writing from another publisher.

"...a detailed outline and sample chapter of such to Publisher before submitting the work to any other publisher..."
The sample clause requires the author to make a formal written submission (*"...a detailed outline and sample chapter..."*) to the current publisher before submitting her next work to another publisher, and to afford the current publisher a specified period (*"...not less than 30 days..."*) in which to make up its mind. Some option clauses, however, are even more demanding and require the submission of the *completed manuscript* of the author's next work.

"...[The] period...shall not begin to run [until] after the publication of the Work..." Typically, the option clause will allow the publisher to wait until after publication of the author's initial book before deciding whether to exercise an option on the author's next book. The publisher, of course, wants to see how the first book is received by critics and, especially, the marketplace before deciding whether to buy the second book! Authors and agents, however, prefer an option clause that allows the submission of the author's next work *before* the publication of the first work.

Review by Publisher's Counsel

Notwithstanding any other provision of the Agreement, Publisher shall have the right, but not the obligation, to submit the Work for review by counsel of its choice to determine if the Work contains material which is or may be unlawful, violate the rights of third parties, or violate the promises, warranties and representations of Author set forth in this Agreement. If, in the sole opinion of Publisher or its counsel, there appears to be a risk of legal action or liability on account of any aspect of the Work, then Publisher may, at its sole option, (i) require the Author to make such additions, deletions, modifications, substantiation of facts, or other changes to avoid the risk of legal action or liability; or (ii) terminate this Agreement without further obligation, and Author shall be obligated to repay all amounts advanced by Publisher. Upon such repayment by Author, all rights granted to Publisher shall revert to Author. Nothing contained in this Agreement shall be deemed to impose on Publisher any obligation to review or verify the contents of the Work, or to affect in any way the warranties and representations of Author and/or the duty of indemnification of Author.

Not every publisher actually engages an attorney to "vet" a manuscript before publication. (Vetting is a shorthand phrase for carefully reviewing a manuscript to determine that it is factually accurate and legally sound.) But some publishers prefer the comfort of a clause that assures them the right (but *not* the duty) to do so—and one that describes what happens if the lawyer declares the manuscript to be legally problematic. ➤ *Chapter 5: Preparing the Manuscript*

In the event the publisher's attorney spots a problem in the manuscript, the fundamental right of the publisher under the sample clause is simply not to publish the author's work at all. If the publisher elects to terminate the contract, then the author gets back the rights to her work, and the publisher gets back any advance that may have been paid. Or, the publisher may decide to compel the author to make any changes that its attorney deems necessary to remedy the legal problems or reduce the risk of a lawsuit.

The vetting of the manuscript, however, is strictly at the option of the publisher—and whether or not the publisher chooses to incur the expense of paying a lawyer to vet the author's work, *the author remains obliged to the publisher under the warranties, representations and indemnities if a lawsuit is later filed!*

Copyright Infringement

If, at any time during the effective term of this Agreement, a claim shall arise for infringement or unfair competition as to any of the rights which are the subject of this Agreement, the parties may proceed jointly or separately to prosecute an action based on such claims. If the parties proceed jointly, the expenses (including attorneys' fees) and recovery, if any, shall be shared equally by the parties. If the parties do not proceed jointly, each party shall have the right to proceed separately, and if so, such party shall bear the costs of litigation and shall own and retain any and all recovery resulting from such litigation. If the party proceeding separately does not hold the record title of the copyright at issue, the other party hereby consents that the action be brought in his, her or its name. Notwithstanding the foregoing, Publisher has no obligation to initiate litigation on such claims, and shall not be liable for any failure to do so.

A publisher is entitled to sue for infringement of copyright and trademark interests in the author's work even without a specific infringement clause, but the sample clause sets up some procedures that clarify how the costs and benefits, if any, of an infringement suit will be allocated between the author and the publisher.

"*...the parties may proceed jointly or separately to prosecute an action...*" Either the author or the publisher may initiate a lawsuit for infringement without the consent of the other—or, if they agree to do so, the author and the publisher may file a joint lawsuit. But the author can never *require* the publisher to do so: "*...Publisher has no obligation to initiate litigation....*"

"*If the parties proceed jointly, the expenses (including attorneys' fees) and recovery, if any, shall be shared equally by the parties....*" The sample clause states a simple rule of thumb: If expenses are shared equally, so is "*...the recovery...,*", whether in the form of a settlement or a judgment.

"*... [The] party [proceeding separately] shall bear the costs...shall own and retain any and all recovery....*" On the other hand, if either the author or the publisher declines to join in the lawsuit, then the other party is free to go to court on its own initiative *and* on its own resources. And, if so, the party who pays the costs is entitled to keep whatever recovery is obtained against the infringer.

"*... the other party hereby consents that the action be brought in his, her or its name....*" What if one party decides not to join in a copyright infringement suit against an infringer, but the other party still wants to pursue the claim in court? As a general rule, a copyright infringement suit must be brought in the name of the person who owns or controls the rights that have been infringed. If, for example, the author has retained foreign language rights but the U.S. publisher wants to sue over a pirated foreign edition of the author's book, then the clause allows the publisher to file a lawsuit against the infringer "*...in [the] name [of]...*" the author. But the publisher would still pay all the costs—and keep all the recovery—even though the lawsuit was filed under the author's name.

Accounting

Publisher shall render to Author a statement of account on the sales of the Work in all Publisher's editions, any other exploitation and disposition of rights to the Work, and other credits and debits relating to the Work and the rights granted in this Agreement, and pay Author any amount(s) then owing, as follows: (i) On or before September 30 for the previous six-month period from January 1 through June 30; and (ii) On or before March 31 for the previous six-month period from July 1 to December 31.

Publisher shall have the right to debit the account of Author for any overpayment of royalties, any and all costs, charges or expenses which Author is required to pay or reimburse Publisher under this Agreement, and any amounts owing Publisher under any other agreement between Publisher and Author.

Publisher shall have the right to allow for a 20% reserve against returns. If royalties have been paid on copies that are thereafter returned, then Publisher shall have the right to deduct the amount of such royalties on such returned copies from any future payments under this or any other Agreement.

As set forth in the Indemnity Clause above, in the event that any Claims are asserted against Author or Publisher, Publisher shall have the right to withhold royalties and other payments otherwise payable under this Agreement (or any other agreement between Author and Publisher) as a reserve pending a final determination thereof. Publisher shall have the right to apply any of such withheld royalties and other payments then or thereafter accruing to the reduction, satisfaction or settlement of such Claims.

Author shall have the right, upon reasonable notice and during usual business hours but not more than once each year, to engage a certified public accountant to examine the books and records of Publisher relating to the Work at the place where such records are regularly maintained. Any such examination shall be at the sole cost of the Author, and may not be made by any person acting on a contingent fee basis (other than the Author's literary agent during the course of the agent's regular and customary representation of Author). Statements rendered under this Agreement shall be final and binding upon Author unless Author sets forth the specific objections in writing and the basis for such objections within six (6) months after the date the statement was rendered.

Royalty statements are the single most important—and, sometimes, the *only*—communication between the publisher and the author once the book itself is actually published. It's a formal mechanism for calculating and reporting the money that one party may owe the other party, and the ultimate expression of the commercial success or failure of the book.

The royalty statement will be organized to reflect the particulars of the deal that the publisher and the author have made with each other.

For that reason, it is impossible to generalize on what specific information the author will find in the royalty statement of any given publisher. Indeed, one of the frequent topics of debate in the publishing industry focuses on what information ought to be disclosed by the publisher to the author, and how to disclose the information in a way that is intelligible to the author.

The sample accounting clause is typical of standard book contracts in its general terms, but the author and publisher may choose to flesh it out to reflect the specific royalty structure that applies to a particular book deal.

"Publisher shall render to Author a statement of account on the sales of the Work in all Publisher's editions..." The basic function of *every* royalty statement is to report on the sales of the author's book by the publisher. Thus, at a minimum, the royalty statement ought to include (i) the number and price of copies sold; (ii) the number of copies returned; (iii) the royalty rate applicable to each sale; and (iv) the royalty, if any, owed by the publisher to the author.

But seldom is the royalty statement quite so straightforward. For example, some book contracts call for a different royalty rate in each of several categories—one rate for ordinary sales through the book trade, another rate for "deep discount" sales, and yet another rate for direct sales to the consumer. If the book is published in simultaneous hardback and paperback editions, a different royalty will probably apply to each edition of the book. And if the royalty rate increases as greater numbers of copies are sold, then it's possible that sales of a single book will be covered by two or more royalty rates. Thus, the statement may very well include separate calculations of royalties in each of the several categories of sales. ➤ *The Hard-Soft Dilemma—Above*

Other information that the author might want to see in her royalty statement includes the number of copies printed; the number of copies damaged or destroyed; the number of copies sold at each discount rate offered by the publisher; the number of copies given away as review copies or promotional copies; the number of copies sold to the author; and other information that may be necessary for the author to satisfy herself that the proper royalties and other payments have been made by the publisher.

"...any other exploitation and disposition of rights to the Work...." If the publisher has acquired any secondary or subsidiary rights in the author's work—audio rights, for example, or foreign rights—then the statement should also include a report of any transactions for the sale

or license of these rights. If the publisher is obliged to pay the author a specified percentage of amounts actually received by the publisher, then the statement need only report the payment by a third party to a publisher, and then apply the author's percentage to determine what the publisher is obliged to pay the author. More complicated calculations will be required if, for example, the contract entitles the publisher to deduct its expenses in making the sale, such as agent's commissions, or if the author's participation in the sale of subsidiary rights takes the form of a royalty. ➤ *Secondary and Subsidiary Rights Clause—Above*

Royalties, of course, are the most common example of a credit that appears on the author's account. However, there are other amounts that the publisher may owe the author, and the sample clause obliges the publisher to show *"...other credits and debits ..."* on the statement.

For example, if an additional advance is payable under the terms of the contract, or if the publisher has agreed to reimburse the author for some or all of her expenses, then the publisher may be obliged to pay the author something more than royalties on sales of the book. All such amounts are credited to the author's account along with the royalties, if any.

The publisher is also entitled, however, to *debit* the author's account for any amounts of money that the *author* may owe the *publisher*, including recoupment of the advance. And the publisher is only obliged to pay the *net* amount, if any, that may be owing to the author after all credits and debits are calculated.

Unhappily for the author, debits are far more common than credits on a typical royalty statement.

▷ **Recoupment of Advance.** The publisher will deduct (or "recoup") the full amount of the author's advance against earned royalties. ➤ *Advance—Above*

▷ **Returns.** If the publisher has previously credited the author's account with royalties on sales of books that have been returned by the bookseller, the royalties on the returns will be deducted. And the publisher is entitled to hold back a portion of the royalties as a "reserve against returns," since the publisher anticipates that some of the books will be returned in the future. ➤ *Author's Royalties—Above*

Some standard book contracts allow the publisher to maintain a "reasonable" reserve against returns, an intentionally vague term that does not impose any specific limits on the publisher. Other contracts specify a reserve as a percentage of the gross amount of royalties otherwise payable to the author—5% is at the low end of the range, and 25% is at the high end.

Some authors are able to secure a restriction on the reserve against returns by requiring the publisher to pay the earned royalties if no returns are received within a specific period of time. Thus, for example, the accounting clause might state that "Publisher may hold a reserve against returns for no longer than one accounting period." Such a restriction calls for some fairly complex accounting, but it prevents the publisher from holding back royalties for an unlimited period or aggregating the reserve over an extended period.

▷ **Other Costs and Expenses.** The publisher is entitled to debit the author's account for *"...all costs...which Author is required to pay...."* For example, if the author is obliged to acquire artwork or prepare an index but declines to do so, the publisher may be entitled to hire an artist or an indexer, and then deduct the costs from the royalties otherwise payable to the author. Or, if the author has purchased copies of her own book, the publisher may deduct the wholesale cost of the books from the royalties. ➤ *Artwork, Permissions, Index, and Other Materials and Author's Copies—Above*

▷ **Cross-Collateralization.** The publisher is also entitled to debit the author's accounts for *"...any amounts owing Publisher under any other agreement between Publisher and Author."* The mechanism is commonly called "cross-collateralization," and it is intended to give the publisher the right to set off any money owed by the author, whether under the current contract or any other contract.

The most common example of cross-collateralization is an author who has signed two book contracts with the same publisher. Suppose, for instance, that the author received an advance on her first book— but the first book was not a commercial success, and the publisher was unable to recoup the first advance. Then the author and publisher enter into a second contract for a second book, and a new advance is paid. The sample clause now entitles the publisher to recoup the unearned advance on the *first* book out of royalties otherwise paid on the *second* book!

Note, by the way, that the sample clause specifically permits the publisher to deduct royalties paid to the author on books that are later returned *"....from any future payments under this or any other*

Agreement." Thus, the principle of cross-collateralization applies not only to unearned advances but also to overpayment of royalties on returned books.

Authors and their agents frequently ask publishers to strike out cross-collateralization clauses because they fear that the unrecouped advance on an unsucccessful book will soak up the royalties otherwise payable on the sales of a successful one!

▷ **Indemnity.** The publisher is also entitled to hold back money otherwise payable to the author as a reserve against the cost of defending, settling or paying for *"...any Claims...asserted against Author or Publisher..."* under the indemnity clause. The sample clause entitles the publisher to hold *all* royalties and other payments *"...pending a final determination..."* of the claim. And the publisher is entitled to apply the royalties and other payments *"...to the reduction, satisfaction or settlement of such Claims...."* In other words, the royalties and other payments that the publisher owes to the author under *"...this or any other agreement"* are essentially characterized as security for the author's obligations to "indemnify and defend" the publisher under the indemnity clause. ➤ *Author's Indemnity of Publisher—Above*

"...[o]n or before September 30 for the previous six-month period from January 1 through June 30...." The sample accounting clause calls for statements to be rendered twice a year, and allows the publisher a period of 90 days after the close of each six-month reporting period to assemble the sales data, prepare the statement, and pay the author whatever is owed.

Some publishers oblige themselves to render statements on a quarterly basis, and the rare publisher may prefer to report to the author only once a year. It is not unusual for the publisher to oblige itself to render accounts within 30 or 60 days after the end of each quarter. Whatever the accounting period, however, authors will find that the accounting routines and programs of a publisher are so well-established that the publisher will be reluctant to agree to a more frequent reporting schedule.

"Author shall have the right... to examine the books and records of Publisher relating to the Work...." The author enjoys a right to audit the publisher's books and records to satisfy herself that the statements of account rendered by the publisher are accurate, complete and honest. But the sample clause, like most standard book contracts, imposes various restrictions on the audit rights—some designed to

reduce the expense and inconvenience to the publisher, and some designed to discourage the author from exercising her audit rights at all!

▷ **Time, Place and Manner of Audit.** The restrictions on the author's right to audit focus on the timing of the audit (*"...upon reasonable notice and during usual business hours..."*), the frequency of audits (*"...not more than once each year..."*), the person who will be allowed to actually inspect the books and records of the publisher (*"...a certified public accountant..."*), and even the location of the audit (*"...the place where such records are regularly maintained..."*).

▷ **Cost of Audit.** The sample clause is intended to shift the cost of the audit to the author alone. Indeed, the clause even prohibits the author from hiring an accountant to conduct an audit on a contingency fee basis. The author, of course, may regard such a restriction as unfair and even punitive; the publisher, on the other hand, argues that an accountant who is paid only if he finds an error in the author's favor is essentially on a fishing expedition. Like most standard accounting clauses, however, the contingency fee restriction does *not* prevent the author's agent from "inspecting the publisher's books and records *"...during the course of the agent's regular and customary representation of Author....*"

Some accounting clauses provide that the cost of the audit will be shifted to the *publisher "if the audit reveals errors in favor of the author in excess of 5% [or some other specified percentage] of the amounts owed by publisher to author."*

▷ **Finality of Statements.** The sample clause purports to impose a time limit on the author's right to challenge the accuracy of the publisher's statements of account, a kind of private statute of limitations. Unless the author objects *"...in writing..."* within a specified period of time after the statement is rendered—the sample clause uses a six-month cut-off—the statements will be *"...final and binding upon the Author...."* It's arguable whether such a clause will, in fact, preclude a lawsuit by the author against the publisher for a breach of contract or an act of fraud, but the prudent author may choose to negotiate for a period of time in which to challenge a royalty statement that is equivalent to the statute of limitations for breach of a written contract, which is four years in most (*but not all*) states.

<u>Revisions</u>

Author agrees to revise the Work as Publisher may deem appropriate during the effective term of this Agreement. The provisions of this Agreement shall apply to each revision of the Work by Author, which shall be considered a separate work, except that the manuscript of each such revision shall be delivered to Publisher within a reasonable time after Publisher's request for such revision.

Author may decline the Publisher's request to revise the Work, but if Author so declines, or if Author provides the manuscript of a revision of the Work which is unacceptable to Publisher, or should the Author be deceased or disabled, then Publisher shall have the right, but not the obligation, to make such revisions, or engage a skilled person to make such revisions, and Author (or, as appropriate, Author's estate) shall reimburse Publisher for all its actual costs of making such revisions. If Publisher engages one or more persons to make such revisions, then Publisher, in its sole discretion, may afford appropriate credit (including authorship or co-authorship credit) to such person(s).

If the author's work remains in print long enough to justify a revised edition, the publisher enjoys the right to require the author *"...to revise the Work as Publisher may deem appropriate...."* Of course, the author may not be happy about the prospect of investing more time and effort in revising her book. But the clause is intended to keep the book in print for as long as possible, and—at least in theory—both the author and the publisher will enjoy the benefits.

As a general proposition, the basic terms and conditions of the original contract—the grant of rights, the royalty rates, and so on—will apply to the revised edition as if it were a new work. The only stated exception in the sample clause itself is the delivery date for the revised manuscript, which is defined as a date *"...within a reasonable time after Publisher's request...."*

Bear in mind, by the way, that the revisions contemplated in the sample clause are *not* related to the revisions to the original manuscript. And, even though some novelists are tempted to rewrite even their most successful work, the sample revision clause does *not* belong in a contract for a work of fiction! ➤ *Revisions and Corrections—Above*

"...each revision of the Work by Author...shall be considered a separate work...." The revised edition of the author's work is deemed to be a new and separate work, which may have several practical implications for the author and the publisher. For example, the term of copyright protection for the revised materials will start anew on

publication of the revised edition. And, if the author's royalties are based on incremental sales of each edition, the royalty rate may be adjusted downward on the new edition. ➤ *Author's Royalties—Above*

"*Publisher shall have the right, but not the obligation, to make such revisions, or engage a skilled person to make such revisions....*" The author is not in breach of contract if she declines to make revisions as requested by the publisher; rather, the publisher is entitled to make the revisions itself, or hire a new author to make the revisions. Similarly, if the author *does* revise the work but her revisions are deemed unacceptable by the publisher—or if the author is dead or disabled—the publisher may make revisions on its own initiative.

If the publisher elects to make revisions on its own initiative, however, "*...the actual costs of making such revisions...*" are chargeable to the author under the sample clause. Thus, as a practical matter, the author may decide that it is in her best interest to work on the revision after all, both to avoid the burden of paying someone else to do it, and to preserve her editorial control over the contents of the work (see below).

"*Publisher, in its sole discretion, may afford appropriate credit (including authorship or co-authorship credit) to such person(s).*" If the author does not revise the work at all—or if the author's revisions are unsatisfactory to the publisher—the publisher is empowered to credit the individuals who are engaged to revise the author's work. The precise wording of the sample clause suggests that the original author's name may even be deleted from the revised work, since the clause distinguishes between "*...authorship...*" and "*...co-authorship...*" credit.

The revision clause is often a troublesome point of negotiation, since authors tend to see it as a form of involuntary servitude *and* as a potential attack on the integrity of their works of authorship. The publisher, on the other hand, may insist on a mechanism for making sure that a successful book does not grow stale or even obsolete. Only rarely is a book contract entirely silent on the point of revisions.

Reversion of Rights

If the Work goes out of print in all Publisher's editions, Author shall have the right to request that Publisher reprint or cause a licensee to reprint the Work. Publisher shall have Twelve (12) months after receipt of any such written request from Author to comply, unless prevented from doing so by circumstances beyond Publisher's control. If Publisher declines to reprint the Work as described above, or if Publisher agrees to reprint the Work but fails to do so within the time allowed, then Author may terminate this Agreement upon sixty (60) days' notice in writing. Upon such termination, all rights granted under this Agreement, except the rights to dispose of existing stock, shall revert to Author, subject to all rights which may have been granted by Publisher to third parties under this Agreement, and Publisher shall have no further obligations or liabilities to Author except that Author's earned royalties shall be paid when and as due. The Work shall not be deemed out of print within the meaning of this Section so long as the Work is available for sale either from stock in Publisher's, distributor's or licensee's warehouse, or in regular sales channels.

Typically, a reversion of rights clause establishes a mechanism by which the author may reclaim some or all of the rights originally granted to the publisher in the book contract prior to the termination date, if any, of the contract itself. But the rights do not revert unless and until the author has satisfied a number of conditions, and the publisher is given plenty of opportunity to keep the rights in the author's work by complying with these conditions.

(Bear in mind, by the way, that the reversion clause is an altogether *different* mechanism from the author's right to terminate the transfer of copyright.) ➤ *Chapter 8: Remaindering, Reversion and Copyright Termination*

"*If the Work goes out of print in all Publisher's editions...*" The triggering event in the sample reversion clause, as in most book contracts, is the failure of the publisher to keep the author's work "in print." But the author's book is *not* "out of print" "*...so long as the Work is available for sale either from stock in Publisher's, distributor's or licensee's warehouse, or in regular sales channels....*" Thus, at least in theory, the author cannot reclaim the rights in her work as long as a single copy of her book is still in the warehouse!

"*Author shall have the right to request that Publisher reprint....*" If the author believes that her work is, in fact, out of print, she has the initial right to demand *in writing* that the publisher either reprint the work or "*...cause a licensee to reprint the Work....*" Thus, the publisher can satisfy the author's demand—and keep the rights to the author's book—by going back to press with its own edition, or by arranging for an edition to be published by another publishing house.

What's more, the publisher is allowed up to "*...twelve months...*" to put the author's book back into print—and even the one-year period may be further extended "*...by circumstances beyond Publisher's control...*" Thus, for example, if the printing plant is damaged by fire or a flood, the publisher is given additional opportunity to go back to press.

"If Publisher declines to reprint the Work...or if Publisher agrees to reprint the Work but fails to do so within the time allowed...." After giving written notice to the publisher, the author must still wait to see what the publisher elects to do within the one-year period. If the publisher simply states that it will *not* reprint the work, then the author may proceed to the next step in the reversion process. If, however, the publisher states its intention to reprint, then the author must wait up to twelve months to see if the publisher, in fact, goes back to press.

"...then Author may terminate this Agreement upon sixty (60) days' notice in writing...." The author's right to terminate the book contract and reclaim her rights only arises if and when the publisher declines or fails to put her book back into print within one year. Then the author must give yet another written notice to the publisher that the book contract will terminate—and the notice of termination is not effective for *another* 60-day period.

(Some book contracts, by the way, provide that *no* rights will revert to the author "if the Author is indebted to the Publisher for any sum owing to it under the Agreement." If, for example, the author's original advance has not been recouped by the publisher out of royalties—not an uncommon circumstance in an out-of-print book—the reversion clause would not apply at all! This language does not appear in the sample clause.)

Upon termination of the book contract, the publisher's obligations to the author come to an end, *"...except that Author's earned royalties shall be paid when and as due...."* (Of course, it's unlikely that the publisher will owe the author any royalties if the book has been out of print for a year.) And, as discussed below, several of the *author's* obligations to the *publisher* do not come to an end. ➤ *Rights Surviving Termination—Below*

"...all rights granted under this Agreement...shall revert to Author...." Upon termination of the book contract, the author will once again own and control *"...all rights..."* previously granted to the publisher in the book contract—but with two major exceptions.

> **Now Hear This!** The author (or, for that matter, the publisher) may choose to record formal notice of reversion in the Copyright Office to confirm that the book contract is no longer in effect and some or all rights have reverted to the author. By making the reversion of rights a matter of public record, the author will reduce the likelihood of confusion over who owns her book if she later resells the rights to a new publisher. ➤ *Chapter 6: Copyright Formalities & Form 7: Notice of Reversion*

First, if the publisher still has copies of the author's book on hand, the publisher is entitled to "...dispose of existing stock...," a process that is described in greater detail below. (Of course, a reversion of rights under the sample clause usually occurs when the publisher has *no* stock of the author's book. But the clause also applies when the publisher simply declares its intention to stop selling the author's book, a decision that may have been prompted by the fact that the publisher has plenty of unsold books on hand!)➤ *Remainders—Below*

Second, any rights "...*which may have been granted by Publisher to third parties*..." will remain in effect even after the reversion of rights to the author. Thus, for example, if the hardback publisher has licensed the motion picture rights in the author's book to a studio or a network, the purchaser of the movie rights is still permitted to make a film based on the book even after the other rights have reverted to the author.

Remainders

If the Publisher shall determine that there is not sufficient demand for the Work to enable it to continue its publication and sale profitably, the Publisher may dispose of the copies remaining on hand as it deems best. In such event, Author shall have the right, within two (2) weeks of the giving of written notice by Publisher, to a single purchase of some or all of such copies at the best available price, and the purchase of film and plates at Publisher's actual cost of manufacture. If Author declines to purchase such copies, Publisher may dispose of such copies, and shall pay Author a sum equal to 5% of the amounts actually received by Publisher in excess of the costs of manufacture.

If a book is deemed commercially unsuccessful, the publisher will take the book out of distribution and sell off existing inventory at the "...*best available price*...," a process known as "remaindering." Remaindered books are often sold in bulk at rock-bottom prices to specialty distributors and publishers known as "remainder houses," and remaindered books usually end up in catalogues and on "sale" tables in bookstores. As a practical matter, remaindering usually takes place when the book is declared out of print, and thus the reversion clause and the remainder clause are often combined in standard book contracts.➤ *Chapter 8: Remaindering, Reversion and Copyright Termination*

"*Author shall have the right.... to purchase...such copies at the best available price....*" The author is given an opportunity to buy remaindered copies of her own work at the best price offered to the publisher by a remainder house or other buyer. The sample clause also allows the author to buy "...*film and plates at Publisher's actual cost of manufac-*

ture...," which the author may find useful if she places the book with another publisher or decides to publish it herself.

"*Publisher...shall pay Author a sum equal to 5% of the amounts actually received by Publisher in excess of the costs of manufacture....*" If the author does not elect to buy all of the remaindered copies of her book, the publisher is free to sell what's left. The sample clause obliges the publisher to pay the author a sharply reduced royalty that is calculated on the "*...amounts actually received...*" by the publisher and only applies to the difference between the "*...costs of manufacture...*" of the books and the remainder price. The royalties on remainders vary widely in the book industry, but the author often receives nothing at all when her book is remaindered.

Rights Surviving Termination

Upon the expiration or termination of this Agreement, any rights reverting to Author shall be subject to all licenses and other grants of rights made by Publisher to third parties pursuant to this Agreement. Any and all rights of Publisher under such licenses and grants of rights, and all representations, warranties and indemnities of Author, shall survive the expiration or termination of this Agreement.

As stated elsewhere in the contract, certain provisions "*...survive...*" even after the contract itself has been terminated and the rights have reverted to the author.

First, any contracts between the publisher and third parties for the sale or license of rights in the author's work will remain in effect. Second, the publisher is entitled to rely upon "*...all representations, warranties and indemnities...*" of the author even after the book is out of print and the contract has been terminated. Thus, if the publisher is later sued by a third party, the author is still obligated to "*...indemnify and defend...*" the publisher. ➤ *Reversion of Rights, Author's Warranties and Representations & Author's Indemnity of Publisher—Above*

Bankruptcy

If a petition in bankruptcy or a petition for reorganization is filed by or against Publisher, or if Publisher makes an assignment for the benefit of creditors, or if Publisher liquidates its business for any cause whatsoever, Author may terminate this agreement by written notice within sixty (60) days after any of the foregoing events, and all rights granted by Author to Publisher shall thereupon revert to Author.

Publishers often make a gracious effort to prevent the author's rights from disappearing into the maw of the bankruptcy courts if the publisher itself declares bankruptcy. The sample clause purports to give the author the right *"...to terminate this Agreement..."* and reclaim *"...all rights granted by Author to Publisher..."* if the publisher suffers certain kinds of financial distress, including the filing of bankruptcy proceedings.

The author's predicament in the event of the publisher's bankruptcy, of course, is that she is unlikely to receive royalties from an insolvent publisher—or at least not *all* of her royalties—and yet she cannot readily sell her rights elsewhere if the book contract is considered an asset of the bankrupt publisher. And it can take years—and a small fortune in attorneys' fees—to sort out the legal problems of a publisher in bankruptcy.

The sample bankruptcy clause is a fairly simple version of a clause that often appears in book contracts in a more extensive and complex form. Such clauses, however, may be of dubious value to the author, since the question of whether or not a book contract may be terminated in the event of the publisher's bankruptcy is usually decided by the bankruptcy court itself. In other words, it's unlikely that the author will avoid entanglement in the bankruptcy proceedings even if a bankruptcy clause appears in the book contract.

Applicable Law

Regardless of the place of its physical execution, this Agreement shall be interpreted, construed and governed in all respects by the laws of the State of [Insert Name of State].

The so-called "choice of law" clause specifies what body of law will apply to a legal dispute between the author and the publisher. Usually, the publisher will insist on the law of *its* state, since it's always cheaper and easier to a hire a local lawyer who does not have go to the law library to figure out what the law of another state actually provides! Some publishing lawyers, however, prefer the law of the State of New York since much of the case law regarding publishing industry disputes has been decided in New York courts. (Bear in mind that the choice-of-law clause does not determine *where* a lawsuit must be filed—the "jurisdiction" and "venue" of a lawsuit are determined by a number of factors and, as a general matter, cannot be chosen by the parties.) ➤ *Arbitration—Below*

Modification and Waiver

This Agreement may not be modified or altered except by a written instrument signed by the party to be charged. No waiver of any term or condition of this Agreement, or of any breach of this Agreement or any portion thereof, shall be deemed a waiver of any other term, condition or breach of this Agreement or any portion thereof.

Any change in the terms of the book contract must be written down and signed by the *"...the party to be charged..."*—that is, the party against whom the new terms are to be enforced. Under the sample clause, *oral* modifications are not effective at all.

Thus, by way of example, if the author rings up her editor and asks for more time to deliver the manuscript—and her editor agrees to a new deadline over the telephone—the contract is *not* modified and, under most circumstances, the publisher can still hold her to the original deadline. That's why a confirming letter, *signed by the publisher*, is necessary to extend the deadline.

What's more, if the author or the publisher agrees to "waive" a term of the book contract—that is, disregard the requirements of a certain clause, or forgive a breach of contract by the other party—then the fact that one term has been waived is *not "...a waiver of any other term, condition or breach...."* For example, if the editor agrees to accept late delivery of the first half of the manuscript, thus "waiving" the original contract deadline, it does not mean that he is obliged to accept late delivery of the second half of the manuscript.

Notices

Any written notice or delivery under any of the provisions of this Agreement shall be deemed to have been properly made by delivery in person to Author, or by mailing via traceable mail to the address(es) set forth in the Recitals and General Provisions above, except as the address(es) may be changed by notice in writing. Author and Publisher agree to accept service of process by mailing in the same manner.

A formal procedure is prescribed for giving notices and delivering materials—delivery of a notice to the author *by hand* is always proper, but any other notice or delivery by one party to the other party must be *"...by traceable mail...,"* such as Express Mail, Federal Express, or some other form of mail where a proof of receipt is provided to the sender. Other book contracts may establish different forms of notice, and some contracts still provide that mailing of a notice "by the United

States mail, postage prepaid" is sufficient. But *some* mechanism ought to be prescribed, thus avoiding any future dispute over when (and whether) a notice was properly delivered.

"*...to the address(es) set forth in the Recitals and General Provisions....*" The addresses to be used are those set forth at the very beginning of the contract, "*...except as the address(es) may be changed by notice in writing....*" Since a book contract may remain in effect for a lifetime, the author and publisher need to be mindful of letting the other party know of changes in address.

The same, of course, applies to the author's agent, since it is not uncommon for the agent to insert *his* address as the proper address for giving notice to the author! And, for that matter, the author may wish to provide that notices be given to *both* the author and the agent, although publishers are often reluctant to oblige themselves to give duplicate notices.

"*...to accept service of process at such addresses....*" In the event of a lawsuit between the author and the publisher, the sample clause authorizes one party to serve legal papers on the other party by the same mechanism. Thus, one party will be entitled to claim that a lawsuit has been properly served merely by *mailing* the legal papers to the address of the other party by some form of traceable mail. Otherwise, as a general rule, it will be necessary to *personally* serve the lawsuit on the other party or the party's designated agent.

Right to Withdraw Offer

Publisher shall have the right to withdraw its offer of agreement at any time prior to delivery of this Agreement to and execution of this Agreement by Publisher.

What if the publisher sends out a contract for signature and then changes its mind? The sample clause allows the publisher to back out of the deal at any time prior to the signing of the book contract "*...by the Publisher....*" As a general rule, a contract is not effective until it has been signed by *both* parties, and so many publishers accomplish the very same result by mailing out unsigned contracts and asking the author to sign first. Thus, the contract does not go into effect until the author has returned a signed contract to the publisher—and the *publisher* signs it. The sample clause simply reinforces the right of the publisher to do so, and makes it abundantly clear that no contract is made until the publisher's signature appears on the book contract.

Headings and Footers

Headings and footers are for convenience only and are not to be deemed part of this Agreement.

Here's a bit of hypercautious boilerplate that instructs any future judge who may be asked to interpret the contract to disregard the headings, subheadings and even the "footers" at the bottom of the page, and focus *only* on the text itself. But the clause does *not* oblige the judge (or, for that matter, the parties) to ignore insertions, deletions, marginal notes, and other words and phrases that may have been added or taken out. Indeed, under the conventional rules of contract interpretation, anything that is added to a contract form during the negotiation process—whether by hand or by typewriter—is entitled to great weight, since it reflects the real back-and-forth of negotiation and *not* just boilerplate!

Binding on Successors

This Agreement shall be binding on the heirs, executors, administrators, successors or assigns of Author, and the successors, assigns and licensees of Publisher, but no assignment by Author shall be made without prior written consent of Publisher.

Initial Here, Please. Nowadays, thanks to the wonders of word processing, it's easy to modify a standard contract on computer and then print out the customized version for signing. But it's a tradition in book publishing—and a sensible one—to use a hard copy of the standard book contract and make all changes by striking out the clauses to be deleted, and writing in the new clauses between the lines or in the margins. The additions and deletions can be handwritten or typed in, but every addition and deletion should be initialed by both author and publisher to confirm that it's part of the deal. The result is a document that can be quickly and easily scanned to determine what changes, if any, have been made in the standard contract form.

As a general matter, anyone who is assigned the rights of another person under a contract simply "steps into the shoes" of the assignor. Thus, the sample clause merely restates the conventional rule—the book contract is binding on anyone who steps into the shoes of the author or publisher, whether by an assignment of the contract, a license of rights under the contract, or by succession to the author's heirs upon the death of the author.

As a practical example, if the publisher owns or controls the audio rights in the author's book, and the publisher licenses the rights to an audio publisher, then the audio publisher is subject to the terms and conditions of the original book contract—the audio publisher gets nothing more from the book publisher than the book publisher got from the author.

However, the sample clause makes it clear that the *author's* right to assign the contract to another person is sharply limited—she cannot do so without *"...the prior written consent of Publisher...."* The publisher seeks to restrict the assignment of the contract, of course, because it is the author's talent and experience that prompt the publisher to offer the contract in the first place; the publisher does not want to find itself in a deal with a new author! And some publishers may be reluctant to approve an assignment of royalties only, since the publisher may worry that an author who is not looking forward to the royalty check may be less motivated to write well and on time!

Arbitration

If any dispute shall arise between Author and Publisher regarding this Agreement, such disputes shall be referred to binding private arbitration in the City of [Insert location of arbitration] in accordance with the Rules of the American Arbitration Association, and any arbitration award may be entered and shall be fully enforceable as a judgment in any court of competent jurisdiction. Notwithstanding the foregoing, the parties shall have the right to conduct discovery and the right to seek injunctive relief in any court of competent jurisdiction.

Arbitration is an increasingly popular form of "alternative dispute resolution" that permits the parties to a contract to avoid the time, trouble, and expense of a lawsuit if they find themselves in a dispute. Arbitration, as a general matter, is simpler, faster, cheaper, and more confidential than a conventional lawsuit—the parties submit their dispute to an agreed-upon decision-maker, known as an arbitrator, in an informal hearing (rather than a full-scale trial), and the arbitrator (rather than the judge or jury) decides who will prevail in the dispute.

Precisely because arbitration is cheaper and faster than litigation, however, some publishers tend to disfavor arbitration clauses. The publisher is usually the more affluent and sophisticated party—and, therefore, the party better able to afford a conventional lawsuit. Why then, the publisher may figure, should we make it easier for the author to enter into a dispute with the publisher by giving her the right to arbitrate instead of litigate?

Unless an arbitration clause appears in a contract, neither party can *compel* the other party to arbitrate a dispute, although some state courts will encourage (or, in some instances, require) a form of court-supervised arbitration. And if the parties take the trouble to negotiate an arbitration clause in advance, then many of the particulars can be agreed upon in the contract itself, thus simplifying the procedures that will be apply to the dispute if and when arbitration becomes necessary.

"...such disputes shall be referred to binding private arbitration..." An arbitration clause also allows the parties to choose in advance where—and under what rules—the arbitration will take place. The sample clause provides that arbitration will be confidential, that it will be conducted under the rules of a private arbitration service called the American Arbitration Association, and that the arbitration award may be entered and enforced in *any* *"...court of competent jurisdiction...,"* thus giving the prevailing party the right to satisfy the judgment by taking the property of the losing party as if the whole dispute had been decided in court in the first place.

"...the parties shall have the right to conduct discovery and the right to seek injunctive relief...." One of the *disadvantages* of arbitration is the fact that it limits or eliminates the right of the parties to gather evidence (*"...discovery..."*) and to restrain the other party from objectionable conduct while the lawsuit is in progress (*"...injunctive relief..."*). The sample clause provides that these rights are still available to the author and the publisher even though the dispute itself will be arbitrated.

Attorneys' Fees

In any action on this Agreement, including litigation and arbitration, the losing party shall pay all attorneys' fees and costs incurred by the prevailing party.

Unless the recovery of attorneys' fees is specifically allowed in a contract or by a statute, such as the Copyright Act, each party to a lawsuit is responsible for paying its own attorneys. The sample clause is intended to allow the *"...prevailing party..."* in any dispute to recover *"...all attorneys' fees and costs..."* from the *"...losing party...."*

The conventional wisdom is that an attorneys' fees clause will encourage a poor but aggrieved litigant to file a lawsuit if she has confidence in the merits of her claim, since she knows that she will recover some or all of the fees that she has paid to her lawyers if she wins. And, as a practical matter, it may be easier to find a lawyer to take the case—even if the attorney will not accept the case on a contingency fee basis, he or she may decide that the prospect of recovering fees *and* damages make the case more attractive.

At the same time, an attorneys' fees clause may *discourage* the filing of a spurious claim, since the plaintiff has something more to lose if she does not prevail in the legal dispute—the defendant who vigorously and successfully defends the case will be able entitled to recover attorneys' fees from the plaintiff. Still, publishers tend to disfavor attorneys' fees clauses on the reasoning that the publisher is better able than the author to hire and pay lawyers, and thus the *absence* of an attorneys' fees clause will discourage the unhappy author from filing a lawsuit in the first place.

Multiple Authors

Whenever the term "Author" refers to more than one person, such persons will be jointly and severally responsible for all duties, obligations and covenants under this Agreement, and shall share equally in all royalties and other amounts to be paid under this Agreement, unless otherwise specified in a writing signed by all parties.

If the book is to be written by more than one author, the contract must specify what share of the work each author will undertake, and what share of the revenues each author will be entitled to receive. The sample clause assumes that all of the co-authors will be equally obliged to perform the work, and will *"...share equally in all royalties..."* unless some other arrangement is *"...specified in a writing signed by all the parties...."* If there *is* a collaboration agreement between the co-authors that allocates the burdens and benefits of the contract in some other manner, it ought to be attached to the book contract as an exhibit. ➤ *Chapter 2: Co-Authorship and Copyright & Form 1: Collaboration Agreement*

Entire Agreement

Publisher and Author acknowledge that they have communicated with each other by letter, telephone and/or in person in negotiating this Agreement. However, Author acknowledges and agrees that this Agreement supersedes and replaces all other communications between Author and Publisher, and represents the complete and entire agreement of Author and Publisher regarding the Work.

The sample clause, which is known as a "merger" or "integration" clause, is intended to simply erase any legal effect of the promises that may have been made during the negotiations between the author (or her agent) and the publisher, and any other "side deals" that may have been made prior to the date of signing the book contract. Accordingly, the book contract itself is *"...the complete and entire agreement of Author and Publisher...,"* and neither the author nor the publisher is entitled to rely on anything else but the contract to define their rights and duties. Even if a "merger" clause appears in the contract, however, the terms of the contract still may be modified by *"...a writing signed by the party to be charged...,"* but only if the writing is dated *after* the effective date of the contract. ➤ *Modification and Waiver—Above*

Advice of Counsel

Author acknowledges that Publisher has explained that he or she is entitled to seek the advice and counsel of an attorney or other counselor of Author's choice before agreeing to the terms set forth in this Agreement, and Publisher has encouraged Author to do so. Author acknowledges that, in the event Author signs this Agreement without seeking the advice of an attorney or other counselor, it is because Author has decided to forego such advice and counsel.

Publishers are more likely than authors to consult an attorney during the negotiation and drafting of a book contract. The sample clause is intended to prevent the author from later arguing that the contract is unfair because the publisher was represented by an attorney but the author was not. As a practical matter, it will always be difficult for the author to extricate herself from a contract on *any* theory, including the lack of representation by an attorney, but the sample clause is intended to make it even harder!

Riders and Exhibits

This Agreement consists of Section 1 through [Insert number of final paragraph or section] and the following additional Exhibits and Riders, if any: [Insert description of Exhibits and Rider].

Since many books contracts are loaded up with schedules, riders and exhibits, the sample clause is a "housekeeping" tool to make it clear exactly what is included in the book contract. If any additional documents have been attached, then these they should be identified in the body of the contract itself.

<u>Signatures</u>
IN WITNESS WHEREOF, Author and Publisher have executed this Agreement as of the day and year written above.

The signature blocks on a book contract should clearly identify the parties to the contract in a manner that is consistent with the usage at the very beginning of the document. Thus, for example, if the publisher is an individual "doing business as" a publishing house, then the signature block should indicate both the individual's name and the name of the company. If the publisher is a corporation, then the signature block should identify the name and the specific corporate title (i.e., "President," "Vice President," "Secretary," or so on) of the person signing the document on behalf of the publisher. And if multiple authors are entering into the contract, then each one of them should sign the book contract. ➤ *General Provisions and Recitals—Above*

<u>Insurance Rider</u>
Publisher agrees to include Author as an additional insured under any policy of insurance which Publisher may now or hereafter secure in connection with media liability, and to pay any and all premiums for such policies. Author will be an additional insured only in respect to the Work. Author acknowledges that his liability to Publisher under the Indemnification Clause of this Agreement in any amount in excess of the policy limits shall not be affected.

Authors will frequently ask to be relieved of their obligations under the indemnification clause, and publishers almost invariably refuse to do so. However, if the publisher has secured insurance, the publisher may be willing to add the author to its insurance policy. Such policies, which are variously known as "Publisher's Errors and Omissions," "Media Risks," "Media Perils," or "Media Liability," generally cover libel, invasion of privacy, infringement of the right of publicity, trademark or copyright infringement, and similar claims. ➤ *Author's Indemnity of Publisher—Above & Briefs: Insurance*

The insurance rider is usually phrased carefully to make it clear that the publisher is *not* required to actually maintain such insurance in effect. Rather, it's up to the publisher to decide if insurance is to be purchased—and only if the publisher actually decides to buy insurance is the author entitled to coverage.

An insurance rider may also limit the author's responsibility for the deductible, if any, that the publisher is required to pay under the insurance policy. Suppose, for example, the policy includes a deductible of $50,000; the publisher may specify that *"Author and Publisher shall each pay 50% of the first $25,000 of the deductible, and Publisher shall pay the balance of the deductible."*

Under other circumstances, the Publisher may impose the entire burden of the deductible on the Author: *"In the event that an adverse judgment is entered on a claim for copyright infringement, then the entire deductible will be paid by Author."*

Unless the insurance rider says so, the insurance coverage does *not* relieve the author from liability under the indemnification clause. Thus, for example, if a judgment for copyright infringement is entered against author and publisher in an amount in excess of policy limits, then the publisher will still look to the author to pay the excess portion of the judgment: *"Author remains liable to Publisher for any amount in excess of coverage."*

If the author has been promised coverage on the publisher's policy, it is prudent to ask for some proof of coverage, which usually takes the form of a "Certificate of Insurance" issued by the insurance company: *"Publisher shall obtain and provide to Author a Certificate of Insurance which confirms the coverage of the Author as an Additional Insured in conformity with this Insurance Rider."*

And Now the Book!

Once the book contract has been negotiated, drafted, marked up, and signed by both author and publisher, the document usually disappears into a file drawer.

Of course, the signed original—or, at least, a complete copy—ought to be safely stored where it can be found again. If a dispute between author and publisher arises at any time in the future, even after the death of the author or the dissolution of the publishing company, it is the original book contract that will usually decide who wins and who loses.

Safe storage of the signed contract in a place where it can be found again is a less obvious task than most authors and publishers may think. More than a few authors have sheepishly admitted to me that they simply cannot find a copy of a signed contract—and, more than once, it turns out that neither the author nor the publisher has a copy!

The reason that contracts are misplaced and forgotten is easy enough to understand. Much *angst* and energy and sometimes anger go into the tug-of-war of a negotiation and the parsing out of words and phrases in the contract itself, but it is only when the contract is signed, sealed and delivered that the real work of author and publisher begins!

5.
Preparing the Manuscript

CHAPTER FIVE

When the First Amendment decrees that Congress shall make no law abridging the freedom of speech, said Supreme Court Justice and free speech purist Hugo Black, it means *no law*. And so we are tempted to comfort ourselves with the notion that the First Amendment is something almost sacred, a first principle of American constitutional law that allows us to write, speak and publish exactly what we want to say.

The reality, however, is that the First Amendment is not quite so straightforward and all-encompassing. In fact, while the First Amendment defines a kind of safe haven for free expression, it is hedged on all sides by laws that have been approved as perfectly legal incursions on the right of free speech.

The laws of copyright, trademark, libel, slander, obscenity and negligence—as well as the right of privacy and the right of publicity— are all exceptions to the right of free speech, and both author and publisher expose themselves to the risk of a lawsuit when they wander into these minefields.

To minimize the risk of a lawsuit, the author and publisher must be watchful throughout the publication process—when the author is gathering information, when the author is actually writing the manuscript, when artwork and other supplementary materials are being acquired, even when the jacket is being designed and the catalogue copy is being written. And, ideally, the author and publisher will carefully review and evaluate the entire project for potential risks—a process known as "vetting."

The vetting process itself, however, is best conducted by an experienced publishing lawyer. The body of publishing law changes so quickly, and sometimes so fundamentally, that the legal review of a manuscript can only be effective if undertaken by someone who is fully up-to-date on the latest cases and statutes.

For that reason, the summaries and checklists of legal hazards set forth in this chapter are not foolproof, and even the most meticulous review of a manuscript by an editor or author cannot take the place of a formal vetting process by a qualified attorney. Indeed, the use of checklists should be seen as no more than a distant early warning system to help identify the problems that only an attorney can solve. Once a potential legal problem has been identified, it may require expert advice to figure out if and how it can be fixed.

> **Whose Responsibility? Whose Liability?** The vetting of a manuscript is usually done by an attorney retained by the **publisher** (or sometimes, the publisher's insuranc carrier). But it is the **author** who is primarily liable to the publisher for any legal defects in her work under the warranties, representations and indemnifications that appear in virtually every book contract. What's more, although both author and publisher may be liable for copyright infringement, defamation, and other claims, the author may be more at risk than the publisher under certain legal theories. So it is in the best interests of both author and publisher that the manuscript be properly screened in advance of publication. Indeed, if the publisher does not plan to submit the manuscript for legal review, then the author may wish to hire an attorney of her own to do the vetting! ➤ *Chapter 4: The Book Publishing Contract*

Research and Writing Guidelines

As a basic rule, the author ought to be able to cite the specific source of factual material in a manuscript, especially direct quotations and other attributed materials, and to know in advance if any special restrictions have been placed on the use of such materials. Here are some guidelines to assist the author (and any researchers the author may engage to assist her) to make sure that the task is somewhat easier than finding a needle in haystack.

▷ Keep "hard copies" of all written and printed documents, including books and articles, government records, correspondence, financial and accounting statements, print-outs of research data from databases and other "on-line" computer services, and the like. Make sure that the *source* and *identity* of the document is readily apparent. For instance,

Publish or Perish?: Risk Analysis in the Vetting Process. Vetting is essentially a process of spotting the potential legal risks in a manuscript. The problem of what to do about the risk is quite another question. Often enough, the risk of a lawsuit can be reduced but not eliminated. So every problem that arises in the vetting process must be analyzed according to a simple question: How much risk, if any, are author and publisher willing to accept?

Suppose, by way of example, the publisher identifies a quoted passage from a copyrighted work in the manuscript that the author submits. The doctrine of fair use allows an author or publisher to use a portion of a copyrighted work without the permission of the copyright owner under certain limited circumstances. But the publisher cannot know with certainty whether any particular use of copyrighted work is fair use unless and until he is sued for copyright infringement and a judge or a jury decides whether he guessed right. So the decision that must be made during the vetting process is based on an assessment of risk. Here's how the hypothetical risk in the example plays out. ➤ *Fair Use—Below*

▷ No risk: The author and publisher may be able to eliminate all risk by either obtaining written permission from the copyright owner to use the passage, or else by dropping the quoted passage altogether.

▷ Moderate risk: The author and publisher may reduce (but not eliminate) the risk of a lawsuit by extensively rewriting the problematic passage in order to reduce the similarities to the original work.

▷ High risk: The publisher may go through the exercise of applying the fair use tests to the passage in question and come to the conclusion that no changes need be made and no permission is necessary under ➜

if the author uses a photocopied article from a published book, it's a good practice to make a photocopy of the title page and the copyright notice page, too. Or if a source has provided a confidential document such as a tax return or a financial statement, the document should be clearly marked to indicate where, when and under what circumstances the document was provided to the author.

▷ Clearly label all notes and tape recordings to indicate the identity of the source or interview subject, and the date, time and place of the interview or research.

▷ When taking notes from published sources, be sure to carefully identify the words and phrases that are directly quoted to make sure that they do not find their way into the manuscript. Make note of the author, publisher, copyright owner (if different), and date of publication.

▷ It's useful to cross-reference the manuscript to the source materials to the greatest extent possible. Many word-processing programs allow the author to create footnotes and endnotes quickly and easily as she writes; one copy of the manuscript can be saved with the notes intact, and the notes can be deleted from the final draft of the manuscript or saved at the end of the manuscript as endnotes. A carefully footnoted draft will be an indispensable resource if and when the manuscript is vetted or fact-checked—and it may spare the author, editor and attorney

---

THE GHOST IN THE MACHINE. One author of my acquaintance sent galleys of his book to a number of experts in his field in order to solicit jacket blurbs. Among the recipients of the bound galleys was an influential colleague whose response was not a glowing endorsement but the threat of a lawsuit for copyright infringement—the expert found several dozen passages in the author's manuscript that were quoted without attribution from <u>his</u> books!

The author was aghast—and baffled, since he had certainly not knowingly plagiarized the expert's famous books. When the author set about rewriting the offending passages, he realized what had happened. In the early stages of his work, as he entered his research into his word-processor, he was not careful enough in distinguishing between raw notes, passages quoted from published works, and his own sketches and drafts. As a result, he inadvertently used words, phrases and even paragraphs that he had found in the work of other authors.

The lesson to every author: Be sure to identify the nature and source of research materials, and make sure that the data is clearly earmarked in notes or word-processing entries for later reference during the writing process!

→ the fair use doctrine.

The same risk analysis applies in every instance where the vetting process identifies the risk of a lawsuit. For instance, if a passage in the manuscript reveals an especially intimate detail about a living person, the author and publisher may be concerned about a claim for invasion of privacy. So they may eliminate the risk of a lawsuit by either dropping the passage altogether or obtaining formal consent to publication from the person who is described in the passage. They may choose to rewrite the passage to play down or remove the potentially offending matter. Or they may decide that the passage is legally defensible and decide to publish it without modification. ➤ *Invasion of Privacy—Below*

And so the dilemma faced by the decision-maker often reduces to a simple question: Do you feel lucky today?

---

hundreds of anxious hours of archival research!

▷ The author ought to keep a detailed record of the names, addresses, telephone numbers, and other pertinent information regarding each of her sources in case it is necessary to contact a source for fact-checking or to obtain a release.

▷ The cautious author will keep a duplicate set of tapes, computer disks, and documents (and, of course, the manuscript itself!) in a different site as a precaution against loss or destruction of research materials.

Tape Recording. The use of tape recording in interviews can be a useful and reliable method of research, especially because a tape-recorded interview allows the author and publisher to show exactly what the subject actually said in an interview. But tape recording also raises some potential legal problems that can usually be avoided by taking the following precautions:

If a tape-recorded interview is ever used for legal purposes, it may be necessary to "authenticate" the recording, that is, to prove the identity of the voices on the tape, and the purpose of the recording. For that reason, it's good practice for the interviewer to make an identifying statement at the beginning of each segment of a taped interview. A statement along the following lines is probably sufficient:

> SEX, LIES AND AUDIOTAPE. When New Yorker contributor Janet Malcolm profiled psychoanalyst Jeffrey Masson, she quoted him as calling himself an "intellectual gigolo" who intended to turn the Sigmund Freud archives into "a place of sex, women, fun." Masson denied that he had ever said such things, and sued Malcolm and her publishers for libel. And Malcom, who had tape-recorded many of the interviews and claimed to have taken notes of other conversations, was unable to come up with a tape to verify the quotations. The Supreme Court in Masson v. New Yorker Magazine ruled that the fabrication of embarassing quotes, if they are embarrassing enough, can be defamatory. "A fabricated quotation may injure reputation," the Supreme Court held, "because the manner of expression or even the fact that the statement was made indicates a negative personal trait or an attitude the speaker does not hold."

> *This is Jake Hersh. Today is Friday, December 19, 1994. I am tape recording an interview with Van Morrison at Cafe Montana in Santa Monica for my book on the music of Van Morrison to be published by the Postcard Press. Are you ready to begin [or: resume] the interview, Mr. Morrison?*

It's important to elicit a *spoken* response from the subject of the interview to make it clear that he knows that he is being tape-recorded, and that the tape recording will be used for a book.

Ideally, the identification will be repeated after every pause in the recording itself and at the beginning of each side of an audio-cassette. In other words, if you turn off the tape recorder for any purpose, the identification ought to be repeated when the machine is turned on again.

Recording the words of another person, whether in person or over the telephone, may be a criminal violation of state and federal law unless the other person *knows* he is being taped and *consents* to the taping. The particulars of such laws, which are designed to prevent wiretapping and electronic eavesdropping, are highly technical, and the legality of unauthorized taping may vary from state to state. However, the use of an identifying introduction as described above is *probably* sufficient to avoid liability under most such laws. Written consent is even more effective, and the use of a formal release with each interview subject is a good practice. ➤ *Form 4: Interview Release*

Confidential Sources

Authors and journalists often find it useful and sometimes essential to enter into agreements with their sources regarding confidentiality. An agreement to maintain the confidentiality of a source, however, can come back to haunt an author if she has not clearly understood what the source actually expects her to do. And a grant of confidentiality can be catastrophic if the author is later sued for libel and cannot prove the truth of her allegedly defamatory statements because she has promised to keep her source a secret.

Understanding the Terms of Confidentiality. Essentially, a grant of confidentiality is a contract—the source agrees to disclose information in exchange for the author's promise to use it only under certain conditions. So the *terms* of the agreement are essential.

Some of the common phrases that are used by journalists in dealing with confidential sources—"Off the record," "Background only," "Not for attribution"—are especially treacherous because these phrases do not have standard and well-understood meanings in all circles. Thus, the author and the source should discuss and agree upon the terms of confidentiality in plain English *before* undertaking an interview

> **Confidentiality Issues in Vetting.** A grant of confidentiality by an author to a source may become a hot issue during the vetting process—and an even hotter one if the author and publisher are sued for libel. Suppose, for example, that a particular statement in the author's work raises concerns about a potential claim for defamation or invasion of privacy. The publisher's attorney—or perhaps the plaintiff's lawyer—asks the author to prove the truthfulness or accuracy of the statement. If the author cannot name her source, then it may be impossible to successfully defend a lawsuit. Indeed, a judge who is forbidden to compel the disclosure of a confidential source under the "shield" laws may simply decree that, as a matter of law, the author did not have any such source. And so the publisher may insist on eliminating the problematic statement if the author cannot convince the confidential source to "go public." ➤ *Reporter Shield Laws—Below*

or moving into confidential subject matter during an interview.

The agreement of the author and the source regarding a grant of confidentiality—including specific terms and conditions of confidentiality—should then be recorded in some form. Ideally, the cautious author would ask the source to sign a written agreement regarding the terms of confidentiality. But, in most cases, the whole deal is usually handled orally.

If the author and the source "talk out" the terms of confidentiality during a tape-recorded interview, then there is at least *some* record of the deal. If, however, the grant of confidentiality appears only in the author's notes, it makes sense to ask the source to initial the notes to indicate that he agrees to the terms.

Reporter Shield Laws. Some states have extended a certain degree of legal protection to a journalist's confidential sources in the form of "shield" laws. Generally, a shield law prevents a judge from citing a reporter for contempt of court if the reporter defies an order to disclose the identity of confidential sources or, in some cases, if the reporter declines to produce the unpublished notes or recordings of an interview with a confidential source.

A serious question arises, however, when the author of a book seeks to invoke the protection of a shield law. Many shield laws, which vary from state to state, appear to apply only to employees of news-gathering organizations such as newspapers and television stations. However, some courts have held that even a freelance magazine writer or the author of a book is entitled to protect her confidential sources.

Bear in mind that shield laws do *not* afford an absolute privilege against disclosure of confidential sources. The judge in a lawsuit may impose sanctions other than a contempt of court citation if the journalist refuses to divulge confidential information. For example, some judges are perfectly willing to enter a default judgment against a journalist who is sued for libel and refuses to disclose his sources— the journalist stays out of jail, of course, but faces a multi-million-dollar verdict!

Vetting the Manuscript

"Vetting" is a shorthand term for the process of reviewing a manu-script prior to publication to determine if the work poses a risk of lia-bility for copyright infringement, trademark infringement, defamation, invasion of privacy, obscenity, or some other legal claim. Ideally, the vetting process will be conducted by an attorney who is experienced in these areas of law. Sometimes, an insurance underwriter will use its own attorneys to perform the same task before issuing a "media perils" insurance policy. Often enough, of course, a manuscript is vetted only by the publisher—or sometimes not at all—but a careful and competent vetting is the best precaution against a lawsuit. ➤ *Briefs: Insurance*

> **The Lady on the Dust Jacket.** It's not enough to vet the manuscript itself. The dust jacket, the catalogue copy, the advertising, and virtually every other word or image that is associated with the work itself must be reviewed for legal risk, too. For example, novelist Oscar Hijuelos and his publisher were once sued for misappropriating the right of publicity of a 40's-era singer whose photograph was used in a collage on the dust jacket of <u>The Mambo King Play Songs of Love</u>. And Geraldine Barr, author of a celebrity biography of her sister, Roseanne Arnold, was once sued for libel on the basis of a few words and phrases that appeared in the publisher's spring catalogue! ➤ *Right of Publicity—Below*

Red Flags in the Vetting Process

The potential legal problems in a manuscript are sometimes so subtle that even an expert eye will overlook them. But certain kinds of content ought to be viewed as "red flags" that always require further inquiry and analysis. And these red flags may appear not only in the author's manuscript but also in virtually any aspect of the book project, including the preface or foreword, illustration and photography, advertisements and press releases, copy in the publisher's or distributor's catalogue, even the dust jacket of the book!

▷ Does the work contain any material that was contributed by someone other than the author? ➤ *Copyright Infringement and Fair Use—Below*

▷ Does the work contain potentially damaging statements about or depictions of a living individual or an existing company? ➤ *Defamation—Below*

▷ Does the work contain potentially embarrassing statements about or depictions of a living individual? ➤ *Invasion of Privacy—Below*

▷ Does the work make use of the business name, trademarks or trade dress of an existing business? ➤ *Trademark and Trade Dress Infringement & Trade Libel—Below*

▷ Does the work make use of the name, image, or likeness of an individual, whether living or dead, for purposes of advertising, promotion, merchandising or implied endorsement? ➤ *Right of Publicity—Below*

▷ Does the work offer instruction or advice that might affect the reader's mental, physical, legal or financial well-being? ➤ *"Negligent Publication" and Disclaimers—Below*

▷ Is the work written by (or does it draw upon the experiences of) a criminal? ➤ *Son of Sam Laws—Below*

▷ Does the work contain explicit sexual content? ➤ *Obscenity—Below*

Copyright Infringement and Fair Use

The risk of a claim for copyright infringement must be considered whenever the author's work includes words and phrases, photographic or illustrated images, even charts and graphs that are derived from another copyrighted work. The risk is greater if passages from the copyrighted work are copied verbatim, but a risk is also present even if the words and phrases are merely paraphrased. Generally, the use of quoted material with proper attribution to the source is safer than unattributed borrowing—but there is no hard and fast rule on how much and under what circumstances an author may "borrow" material from a copyrighted work. Each instance must be evaluated on its own facts and circumstances.

Checklist of Copyright Infringement Issues

The following checklist will assist in measuring the risk of a claim for copyright infringement once it is determined that the author's work has borrowed in some manner from another author's copyrighted work.

(For the sake of clarity, "the author's work" refers to the manuscript that is being vetted, and "the copyrighted work" refers to the work from which the author has copied material.)

▷ **Is the quoted material in the public domain?** By definition, an author or publisher cannot be liable for copyright infringement by copying words or images that are in the public domain. Indeed, the very phrase "public domain" is best defined as words, images and other expressions that are *not* subject to protection under the copyright law.

Some or all of a work of authorship may be in the public domain because the work was *never* subject to the laws of copyright—for example, the works of Shakespeare or the King James Version of the Bible or, for that matter, a work by a federal government employee if the work was created within the course and scope of employment. Some works may be in the public domain because the term of copyright protection has expired—*Huckleberry Finn*, for example, or *Moby Dick*. And some *portions* of a copyrighted work may be in the public domain—an author may copy the text of the Gettysburg Address from newly published biography of Abraham Lincoln, but not necessarily the text that precedes or follows it.

A work that is in the public domain cannot be brought back under the protection of copyright. However, a *new* work that is derived from or incorporates a portion of a work in the public domain may, in fact, be entitled to its own copyright protection. Thus, for example, a new and original English translation of *Candide* may be entitled to copyright protection even if the original French text is in the public domain.

> **What Is In the Public Domain?** Whether or not a particular work is in the public domain in the United States is a question that requires both factual research and legal analysis to answer. The research, which must be conducted in the records of the U.S. Copyright Office, may done by the author or publisher, but it is more common to hire one of several private firms that specialize in copyright research. To interpret and evaluate the copyright records, an attorney with expertise in copyright issues ought to be consulted. ➤ *Briefs: Information Resources and Other Services*

Some elements of a copyrighted work may be in the public domain because they are *never* protected by copyright. For example, copyright protects only the particular expression of ideas and information by an author—and *not* the idea or the information itself. Thus, an author is generally free to copy "mere" ideas or "facts and figures" from a copyrighted work as long as he does not copy the particular words and images in which the ideas, facts and figures are *expressed* by the author of the copyrighted work.

Finally, some elements of a work may not be subject to protection under copyright law because they are so commonplace that they belong to no one. For example, certain words and phrases are considered to be so "hackneyed" that no one can claim ownership under the copyright law. And certain elements of storytelling known in copyright as *scenes a faire*—for example, a barroom brawl in a Western—are considered to be outside the protection of copyright law because they are virtually inevitable in certain kinds of stories.

Sweat of the Brow Copyright. Although copyright does not protect ideas or information, there is at least some scant protection for the author or publisher who goes to the trouble of gathering information, then organizes and presents the information in an original way—a doctrine that is sometimes called "sweat of the brow" copyright. For example, an ordinary telephone directory that consists of alphabetical listings of all subscribers to a telephone system is <u>not</u> protected and, as a general matter, may be freely copied. But a directory that presents the same information in an unusual manner—for example, a directory of Chinese-speaking businesses organized under specific topical headings—may be protected under copyright law. But only the selection and arrangement of the listings—and not the information in the listings themselves—are within the scope of copyright protection.

▷ **Is the material in the author's work "substantially similar" to the copyrighted work?** The essential test of copyright infringement is whether the allegedly infringing work is "substantially similar" to the copyrighted work. Unfortunately, the phrase itself is merely a legal conclusion, and it's up to a judge or a jury to decide whether one work *is* substantially similar to another work. And the law of copyright offers very little intelligent guidance in determining in advance whether one work is similar enough to another work to raise a concern over copyright infringement.

Indeed, one famous copyright case declared that substantial similarity is to be measured by comparing the "total concept and feel" of the two works, a standard so amorphous and so subjective that it is virtually impossible to predict how a court will decide a given case. As a rule of thumb for purposes of vetting, however, the author and publisher must simply assume that the more one work resembles another work, the greater the risk of a claim for copyright infringement—and the greater the need for a careful analysis of the two works by an expert in copyright law.

▷ **Does the copying of the copyrighted work fall within the doctrine of "fair use"?** Under the proper circumstances, the so-called "fair use" doctrine permits the copying of a limited amount of a copyrighted work without permission of the copyright owner. Technically, fair use is a *defense* to an action for copyright infringement, and thus the author and publisher will not find out with certainty whether a particular use *is* fair use until they have been sued and the case goes to a verdict. But the fair use doctrine may offer some guidelines during the vetting process to determine the degree of risk posed by a particular use of a copyrighted work.

Whether or not the fair use doctrine applies at all is determined by a series of tests that are set forth in the Copyright Act. No single test is determinative, and it is impossible to predict with certainty how a particular case will be decided. But the attorney who vets a manuscript will be guided by these factors.

Purpose and Character of Use. What was the author's purpose in copying a portion of the copyrighted work? The fair use statute itself approves such use for purposes of "criticism, comment, news reporting, teaching..., scholarship, or research." Parody and satire may be entitled to protection as fair use if the work directly comments upon or criticizes the original work. And the statute makes a distinction between use for "commercial" and "nonprofit educational" purposes. A commercial use is less likely—and a nonprofit use is more likely—to be fair use, but the fact that the author's book is published for profit does *not* rule out a finding of fair use.

Nature of the Copyrighted Work. The courts will look at the nature of the copyrighted work in determining whether the copied work is eligible for treatment as fair use. For example, a finding of fair use is less likely when the copyrighted work is a work of "fiction or fantasy" rather than a work of fact or scholarship, or when the copyrighted work is intended for the educational market. Then, too, fair use is less likely to be found (although it is *not* ruled out) when the copyrighted work is an unpublished manuscript or a private letter.

Amount and Substantiality. The fair use statute requires a comparison of "the amount and substantiality of the portion used" and "the copyrighted work as a whole." In other words, if the author has copied a great deal of the copyrighted work, then the copying is less likely to be fair use; and if he has copied a very small portion, then it is more likely to be fair use. Some courts have applied the

PERMISSION GRANTED. Publishers often comfort themselves by printing stern warnings in their books to caution readers against illegal copying. A particularly well-drafted example appears on the copyright notice page of the McGraw Hill edition of Golden Days by Carolyn See: "Except as permitted under the Copyright Act of 1976, no part of this publication may be reproduced or distributed in any form or by any means or stored in a data base or retrieval system, without the prior written permission of the publisher." But the crucial language here is: "Except as permitted under the Copyright Act," since the doctrine of fair use allows critics, scholars, biographers, and others to quote selectively from copyrighted works even without the permission of the author or publisher.

same test to the author's work—that is, if the author's work is largely made up of material copied from the copyrighted work, then it is unlikely to be fair use. Still, the copyright law recognizes that even a very small amount of copying may not be entitled to treatment as fair use if the copied material is the "heart" of the copyrighted work.

Effect on the Potential Market. The fair use statute asks whether the use of the copied material in the author's work will hurt the sales or otherwise diminish the market value of the copyrighted work. Thus, for example, if the reader is less likely to buy a copy of the copyrighted work because the essence of the work is available in the author's work, then the author's work is unlikely to be fair use. On the other hand, if the author's use of the copied material is minor in quantity and merely incidental to her work—or if an attributed quotation is likely to generate sales for the copyrighted work— then it is more likely to be fair use.

> THE MYTH OF THE 300-WORD RULE. The folklore of book publishing holds that a quotation of 300 words or less is <u>always</u> fair use—but the folklore is simply wrong. No specific word-count can be reliably characterized as fair use. <u>All</u> of the fair use factors must be applied and considered in each case, and the "amount and substantiality" of the copied material is merely one of several factors. The 300-word rule probably originates with the hoary old custom of sending out review copies with the familiar admonition: "Permission is granted to quote passages of 300 words or less for purposes of a published book review." And, in fact, when <u>Nation</u> magazine published a short article that quoted between 300 and 400 words from a 7,500-word excerpt of Gerald Ford's as-yet-unpublished autobiography, the magazine was found to be liable for copyright infringement.

▷ **Who is the owner of the copyrighted work?** Once it is determined that the author's work contains a passage that is copied or derived from someone else's copyrighted work, then the question arises: *Who is the owner of copyright in the quoted work?* Only the owner of copyright is entitled to give permission for the use of his copyrighted work—and so the identity of the copyright owner is essential if the author and publisher decide to seek formal permission. (Of course, a copyrighted work may have more than one owner if it is jointly authored or if the author has granted some but not all rights in her work to a publisher, a movie producer, or so on.) Then, too, only the owner of copyright is entitled to sue for copyright infringement—and sometimes the identity of the copyright owner will give some indication of the likelihood of a

TAKING OUT THE KINKS. Under certain limited circumstances, the Copyright Act permits photocopying of copyrighted works by libraries and archives without the permission of the copyright owner. But another common use of the photocopier—the creation of custom-made classroom anthologies by photocopying, assembling and binding various chapters and articles from other published works—has been condemned as copyright infringement. The photocopiers defended the so-called practice of "Professor Publishing" on the grounds of fair use, but the court disagreed. "A quotation of copyrighted material that merely repackages or republishes the original is unlikely to pass the test," ruled the court in Basic Books, Inc. v. Kinko's Graphics Corporation. Nowadays, any entrepreneurial professor or photocopier who wants to create a photocopied textbook ought to contact the Copyright Clearance Center, a clearinghouse that licenses the right to make photocopies of copyrighted works in exchange for the payment of a royalty fee that is allocated to participating copyright owners. ➤ *Briefs: Information Resources and Other Services*

lawsuit. The identity of the copyright owner can sometimes been determined simply by checking the copyright notice in the published work, although ownership of copyright may have changed since the work was printed. Other works may require research in the Copyright Office, either directly or through a private search service, to discover the current owner of copyright. ➤ *Briefs: Information Resources and Other Services*

▷ **Has the copyrighted work been registered in the Copyright Office?** The likelihood of a lawsuit is greater if the allegedly infringed work has been registered in the United States Copyright Office. First, any copyright owner who goes to the trouble of registering the work is more likely to be vigilant about protecting his rights. Second, the fact that a work has been registered bestows upon the copyright owner some remedies and procedural advantages that may encourage him to file a lawsuit. Thus, it's important to know *when* and *by whom* the work was registered—and it's usually necessary to conduct at least some research in the Copyright office to find out.

➤ *Chapter 6: Copyright Formalities & Briefs: Information Resources and Other Services*

Defamation

A claim for defamation may be brought by an individual (or, under certain circumstances, a company or organization) who seeks to recover damages caused by the publication of spoken or written words that somehow injure the person's reputation. Strictly speaking, *libel* is based on a *written* statement and *slander* is based on an *oral* statement, but the distinctions between these two forms of defamation are no longer very important in an era of electronic mass media.

The essence of defamation is injury to reputation: Does the allegedly defamatory statement "lower him in the estimation of the community or deter third persons from associating or dealing with him"? Some statements are clearly injurious to reputation—the assertion that an accountant is a convicted check forger, for example, is so obviously damaging that it is characterized in the law as "libel

> SPEAKING ILL OF THE DEAD. You cannot libel a dead person, or so goes the conventional wisdom of the publishing industry, and, unlike many other truisms, it's generally true. For example, when they were still alive and kicking, both oil mogul Armand Hammer and publishing czar Robert Maxwell managed to keep "unauthorized" biographies out of the bookstores by threatening to sue the publisher of each book for libel. Within days after each man died, however, the publishers of the offending books began to ship the copies that had been sitting in the warehouse while Hammer and Maxwell were still alive.

per se." But sometimes the defamatory content is more subtle. To describe someone with the greatest sympathy as poor and sick may be defamatory if it is not true. And even the juxtaposition of true statement may be libelous if it prompts the reader to come to a false conclusion.

Only a *living* person (or, under certain circumstances, an existing business) is entitled to bring a lawsuit for defamation, and the person must prove that he or she is identifiable to the reader. But the fact that a person is not actually named or depicted in the author's work is *not* enough to eliminate the threat of a defamation suit. As long as a single reader is able to identify the person by the setting, physical description, or other characteristics, then the person is entitled to sue. (The same is true, by the way, even if the defamatory statement refers to a group, as long

> SMILE WHEN YOU SAY THAT, MISTER. The very question of whether a statement is defamatory is a litmus test of what is politically correct at any given moment in history. In a 1917 case, the misidentification of a white person as black was found to be libelous, but a half-century later it was no longer so. An even more dramatic shift in values is reflected in the use of the term "Communist." "Labelling someone a communist...has been considered first defamatory, then non-defamatory, and next defamatory again, depending largely on United States foreign policy changes," observed the court in Gottschalk v. State.

150

as an individual who is a member of the group can prove that the reader would identify him by the reference.) And so a work of nonfiction that does not "name names"—or even a work of fiction in which the names and characters supposedly exist only in the author's imagination—may raise the risk of a lawsuit for defamation.

HIDE IN PLAIN SIGHT. Even a work of fiction can draw a libel suit, as novelist Gwen Davis Mitchell learned when Doubleday published Touching, her novel about a "crude, aggressive and unprofessional" therapist who conducts nude encounter groups. A real-life therapist named Paul Bindrim, whose nude therapy sessions Davis had actually attended (but promised not to write about), sued for libel on the grounds that the fictional character in Touching was recognizable as Bindrim himself. "The fact that 'Touching' was a novel," the court ruled in Bindrim v. Mitchell, "does not necessarily insulate Mitchell from liability for libel, if all the elements of libel are otherwise present." And it was only necesssary for Bindrim to show that a single reader saw Bindrim and the fictional character as one and the same in order to prevail in a libel suit. To make matters even worse, the publisher promptly sued the author under the indemnity clause in her contract to make her pay the judgment!

Wanted Dead or Alive. Publishers and movie-makers alike have long used a familiar disclaimer in fictional works as a precaution against libel claims. Here is a typical example from the Viking edition of WLT: A Radio Drama by Garrison Keillor: "This is a work of fiction. Names, characters, places, and incidents either are the product of the author's imagination or are used fictitiously, and any resemblance to actual persons, living or dead, events, or locales is entirely coincidental." But even such a well-drafted disclaimer would be ineffective against a libel claimant who is able to convince a judge or jury that even a single reader was able to recognize a living person in the guise of a supposedly fictional character.

Truth as a Defense. The rule in *most* (but not all) states is that truth is an absolute defense in a libel case. (A few states go further and require a showing that the truthful but damaging statement was published without bad motive.) For that reason, the number and quality of sources for an allegedly defamatory statement is the single most important factor in the vetting process. The underlying sources must be reliable, credible, and admissible in court in order to establish truth as a defense. That's why the very best defense to a potential libel action is actually mounted during the research and writing of the book itself!

No Liability Without Fault. Out of deference to the First Amendment, the courts have generally ruled out a finding of liability in defamation cases without a showing of fault. At a minimum, the

Trade Libel. A company or corporation may be entitled to sue for "corporate libel," "trade libel" or "product disparagement" if the author's work contains a false statement that injures the business reputation of a corporation or the sale of a company's products. Generally, the plaintiff will be required to prove that the author or publisher acted with knowledge of falsity and an intent to cause injury—a standard of proof that tends to discourage litigation. Any disparaging comment about a business or product, however, is another red flag that the author and publisher should heed in the vetting process.

plaintiff in a defamation suit must show that the author or the publisher acted <u>negligently</u> before they can be punished for making a false and defamatory statement—that is, the author or publisher failed to meet the "standard of care" that a "reasonable" person would have been expected to meet in researching, writing and publishing the offending work. And some plaintiffs must go beyond a showing of negligence and prove that the author or publisher acted with "actual malice."

Whether the greater burden of proof applies to a particular claim of defamation depends on whether the plaintiff is a public figure and, in some states, whether the plaintiff is seeking "punitive" damages in addition to "compensatory" damages. As a general proposition, if the plaintiff is an elected public official or some other kind of public figure, then he or she must prove that the defendant acted with "actual malice" in publishing a false statement. And even a plaintiff who is *not* a public figure may be required to prove "actual malice" if he seeks *punitive* damages in addition to compensatory damages for an allegedly defamatory statement that is a matter of "public concern."

Like so much else in the law, however, "actual malice" is what lawyers call "a term of art"—that is, "actual malice" does not mean actual malice at all. Rather, it is defined as either *actual knowledge of the falsity of the statement*, or *reckless disregard for the truth or falsity of the statement*. Even though the concept of "actual malice" is one of those hazy legal formulations that don't offer much in the way of concrete guidance, the definition suggests that an author or publisher who can show a workmanlike job of research, writing and fact-checking is entitled to avoid a finding of "actual malice."

Be forewarned: The law of defamation is so subtle and so complex that it is impossible to define exactly what constitutes culpable conduct by an author or a publisher, or to decide with certainty whether a particular manuscript can be successfully defended in a defamation lawsuit. Then, too, the law of libel varies from state to state, and even from month to month, as new cases are decided.

Public Figure or Private Figure. The test of whether a plaintiff is a public official, a public figure, or a private figure is fundamental in the law of defamation. Essentially, there is a sliding scale of fault in defamation cases: A plaintiff who is an elected public official enjoys the least protection against defamation and bears the greatest burden in winning a defamation case, while a strictly private figure enjoys the greatest protection and bears the lightest burden. Somewhere in between are the potential libel plaintiffs whose degree of celebrity must be carefully measured on a case-by-case basis—public figures who do not hold elective office, private figures who never sought publicity (such as the victim of a crime), and various other permutations of celebrity).

Indeed, the question of whether a specific individual is a public figure or a private figure is often a hot issue in a defamation case. Any elected office holder, ranging from the President of the United States to the county sheriff, is clearly a public figure. So is a celebrity whose fame (or notoriety) is "pervasive." But a public figure may also include a government bureaucrat, a private individual who seeks public attention, or even the unwilling victim of a crime who is suddenly thrust into the headlines out of sheer bad luck.

Opinions, Humor, and "Fair Comment". Certain works may be protected from a claim of libel even if they might be otherwise damaging to one's reputation. A "pure" opinion—that is, a purely subjective judgment rather than an assertion of fact—is not actionable under the law of libel. Critical reviews of a book, a movie or a restaurant are generally protected to the extent that the critic is expressing a value judgment rather than a verifiable statement of fact. Humor, parody and satire may be exempt so long as the author makes it clear to the reader that the content of the work is fictional and fanciful. And "fair comment" about a public official or some matter of public concern is strongly protected from a claim of defamation under the First Amendment. Thus, for example, Gore Vidal was unsuccessful in a libel suit against William F. Buckley after the eyebrow-arching conservative dismissed Vidal as "perverted" and *Myra Breckenridge* as "a pornographic potboiler done for money."

But it is not enough to merely characterize a defamatory statement as opinion or satire in order to escape liability. The basic test is whether the allegedly defamatory statement contains an assertion of fact that can be proven to be untrue. Even if the statement is couched in the lan-

I Am Not a Crook. It's still the cherished belief of some authors and publishers that an "opinion" can never be the basis of a defamation claim. But even a statement that is couched in the language of an opinion may be libelous if it is actually a statement of fact. "It is my considered opinion that Richard Nixon is a crook," for example, may appear to be an opinion, but the statement arguably contains a verifiable assertion of fact—and so Richard Nixon would have been entitled to sue for libel during his lifetime, if he had only dared! Only a statement that is truly a subjective expression of belief and thus is not subject to verification at all—"It is my opinion that Richard Nixon is not worthy to hold the office of President"—is "immune" to a claim of defamation.

guage of opinion or humor, the risk of a lawsuit is still present if the work goes beyond a subjective value judgment and asserts (or assumes) a false statement of fact.

The Privilege of "Fair Reporting" and "Neutral Reportage." A basic rule of defamation is that one who *repeats* (or "republishes") another person's defamatory statement is herself liable for defamation. But the republication of a libel may be privileged under the so-called privileges of "fair reporting" and "neutral reportage," which are related but distinct defenses to a defamation action.

Under certain circumstances, and in certain states, an author may report on the official proceedings of a public body—for example, a legislative debate or a press conference by a public official—even if the author's account embodies otherwise defamatory statements by third parties, but only so long as the author's account of the proceedings is fair and accurate.

Similarly, an author may be entitled to repeat the otherwise defamatory statements of a third person without exposing herself to liability so long as the author is giving a "neutral" or "balanced" account of a public controversy. But the privilege of "neutral reportage" is a "conditional" privilege, and the author must be able to show that the speaker whose words are being reported was a credible and responsible public figure and that the subject matter was a matter of legitimate public concern.

Under both privileges, it is important for the author to avoid the appearance of "adopting" the defamatory statement as her own. And it is always a good practice to give the subject of the statement an opportunity to respond to the allegations against him, especially if the author is purporting to give a balanced or neutral report of a public controversy.

Retractions. Under the laws of most states, someone who feels that he has been damaged by a published statement is entitled to demand a retraction—and the publisher who refuses to publish a retraction may be exposed to a greater measure of damages or other impediments to the defense of the case. But retraction alone is usually not enough to *defeat* a defamation case, and the plaintiff is generally allowed to pursue his case for certain kinds of damages even after the retraction is published. And the mere fact that the retraction has been published, of course, amounts to an acknowledgment by the publisher that the offending statement was false or inaccurate in some manner. So the decision to publish a retraction—and the exact wording and placement of the retraction—is a form of damage control, rather than an absolute defense, and must be carefully evaluated by the publisher's legal counsel.

Checklist of Defamation Issues

The following questions must be asked of the author's work in general—and, especially, any statement in the work that expresses a potentially damaging fact about a person or company. "The statement" refers to any statement that has been identified as the basis of a potential claim of defamation, and "the subject" refers to the person (or company) about whom the statement is made.

▷ **Does the statement tend to injure the reputation of a living individual (or a company)?** The threshhold question in vetting a manuscript for defamation issues is whether the statement will, in fact, prompt the reader to think badly of the subject. But defamatory meaning need not appear on the face of the statement. If the implications or references within the statement are susceptible of a defamatory interpretation, then the statement poses a risk of liability.

▷ **Is the subject of the statement a living person (or an existing company or organization) that can be identified by the reader?** Since a dead person (or a defunct company or organization) cannot sue for defamation, the fact that the subject is dead ordinarily eliminates the risk of a defamation suit.

▷ **Can the author demonstrate the factual basis of an statement?** The key to defending any defamation claim is proving the truthfulness of the statement. So it is essential to carefully review the sources that the author relied upon in making the statement to determine if they are accurate, credible and legally admissible.

▷ **Has the author made any promises of confidentiality or other special handling of research materials?** The fact that the author relied on a confidential source raises a special concern if the author cannot cite the source in the defense of a defamation suit. The source should be approached prior to publication to determine if he or she will go "on the record," or else the author ought to identify other sources to support the statement.

▷ **Has the author or publisher received any threats of litigation from someone described, depicted or quoted in the author's work?** If the publisher has, in fact, received a threat or demand from the subject prior to publication, the statement must be vetted with special care because the risk of a lawsuit is greatly heightened.

▷ **Is the individual who is described in the statement a public figure or a private figure?** As a practical matter, a greater degree of caution is necessary if the subject of the problematic statement is a *private* figure, since he or she will face a much less rigorous burden of proof if a defamation claim is actually filed.

▷ **Is the subject of the statement a matter of public controversy or public concern?** Certain privileges and defenses may be available if the author is merely reporting on a person or a matter of legitimate public concern. By contrast, a statement that is unrelated to a public figure or a public concern must be regarded as a high risk.

▷ **Has the author given the subject an opportunity to respond?** It's usually a good practice to contact the subject of the statement and give the subject an opportunity to tell her side of the story, especially if the author purports to be reporting in a neutral fashion on a matter of public controversy. The opportunity to respond also shows an effort by the author and publisher to act in a reasonable and responsible manner. But bear in mind that contacting the subject may result in a "no comment," an outright denial, or even a threat of litigation, all of which raise additional problems for the author or publisher!

▷ **Does the statement constitute an opinion, a work of humor or satire, or a fair comment on a matter of public concern?** Special defenses may be available if the statement falls into one of the protected categories of publication in which a subjective value judgment—rather than a verifiable statement of fact—is expressed by the author. But such defenses arise only after the lawsuit is filed, and the risk that a lawsuit will be filed ought to be considered prior to publication.

▷ **Has the statement already appeared in other media? If so, has a correction or a retraction been published?** The fact that a statement has already been published does *not* immunize the author or publisher from a defamation claim. The rule is that republication of a libel is also libelous. But, as a practical matter, a statement based on a widely reported incident is less likely to draw a lawsuit (if it has not already resulted in litigation against the publisher of an earlier version).

Invasion of Privacy

Confronted with the newborn monster of mass-circulation newspapers, a rather curmudgeonly 19th century jurist came up with the notion of the right "to be let alone," and that's the genesis of a legal claim known as "invasion of privacy." Classically, the right of privacy penalizes the publication (and, in one case, the gathering) of otherwise truthful statements in four distinct categories, and a careful vetting for invasion of privacy issues will consider each one.

Public Disclosure of Private Facts. The most straightforward form of invasion of privacy is the publication of "private" and "embarrassing" facts that are not related to a matter of public concern. For example, if a newspaper runs a profile of a grandmother whose pie won a blue ribbon at the county fair—and then discloses the fact that she was a prostitute in the distant past—the reformed hooker may well be entitled to sue for "private facts" invasion of privacy.

"False Light" Invasion of Privacy. Even if a statement is literally true and not "private" or "embarrassing," it may still amount to an invasion of privacy if the statement suggests something false or misleading about the individual. For example, if a book on organized crime includes a photograph of a prominent accountant sitting next to a notorious mobster—but the photograph has been cropped in a manner that the prevents the reader from seeing that the accountant and the mafia don happened to be sitting next to each other at a baseball game and did not know each other at all—then the accountant may have a claim for "false light" invasion of privacy.

Intrusion. The very act of physically intruding upon an individual's privacy, whether by physically entering someone's property or observing him in a private setting or acquiring a physical object that belongs to him, may amount to an invasion of privacy even without publication of what the intruder observed. For example, stalking a celebrity with a camera or digging through his garbage may give rise to a claim for "intrusion" even if the photographs or the garbage-digger's findings are never actually published.

Misappropriation of Name or Likeness. The claim for the wrongful use of a person's name or image for merchandising or commercial endorsement first developed as a variant of invasion of privacy, but it's a claim that really has nothing to do with privacy at all. Nowadays, it is almost always known by a more accurate phrase: The "right of publicity." For example, if the author once received a private letter from a Pulitzer-winning novelist—and the publisher uses an excerpt from the letter as a "blurb" on the dust jacket of the author's book— the famous novelist may have a claim for "misappropriation" of the right of publicity. ➤ *Right of Publicity—Below*

Distinguishing Between Defamation and Invasion of Privacy. Invasion of privacy sometimes closely resembles defamation, but some distinctions can be made between these two causes of action.
➤ *Defamation—Above*

First, truth is an absolute defense in most defamation lawsuits, but the truthfulness of an offensive statement is generally *not* a defense in an invasion of privacy action.

Second, both individuals and companies are entitled to sue for defamation, but invasion of privacy is a claim that, as a general rule, may be brought by a living person only.

Third, the requirement of publication varies between defamation and invasion of privacy. Disclosure of a defamatory statement to a single person is generally enough to sustain a claim for libel or slander. Invasion of privacy based on "private facts" and "false light" requires a showing that the facts were more widely disseminated. And an "intrusion" claim does not require a showing of disclosure at all.
➤ *Intrusion—Above*

The Expectation of Privacy. A key inquiry in any privacy case—and thus an important factor in vetting a manuscript for privacy issues—is the definition of what constitutes a "reasonable expectation of privacy." Thus, for example, an elected public official or a celebrity who has sought public attention enjoys a narrower expectation of privacy and is less likely to succeed in an invasion of privacy claim than a private person who has not sought to put himself in the limelight. But even a private citizen may forfeit some measure of privacy if he is unlucky enough to find himself the victim of a crime, an illness, or a natural catastrophe, especially when the events or circumstances are found to be "newsworthy" or "of legitimate public concern."

Checklist of Privacy Issues

Here are some of the factors that suggest a potential risk of invasion of privacy.

▷ **Is the subject of the disclosure a living person?** If not, as a general rule, no claim of invasion of privacy can be asserted. (However, a "right of publicity" claim may be asserted by the heirs and successors of a deceased person—*Below*.)

Life Story Rights. "Life story rights" is a term of very recent coinage that refers to the acquisition of the right to depict a living person in a motion picture, a movie-of-the-week, a mini-series—or, for that matter, a book. Essentially, the acquisition of life story rights is functionally and legally equivalent to securing a promise from the person that she will not sue for libel, invasion of privacy, misappropriation of the right of publicity or any other legal claim when and if the producer actually makes the movie.

The acquisition of life story rights from someone who is depicted in a book or movie may not always be necessary in order to tell a true story of a living person. Indeed, even motion picture and television producers will forego life story agreements when the facts are available in court transcripts, newspaper stories, and other public sources. As long as the author's work is not otherwise vulnerable to a lawsuit on the basis of the claims described here, then it's reasonable to argue that anyone is free to tell the story.

Life story rights are more commonly secured for motion pictures and television than for books, and it's still the rare publisher that requires the author to seek permission from the subject or source of a book before publishing it. Still, the best solution to the problem of a potential lawsuit for defamation, invasion of privacy, and misappropriation of the right of publicity is often a life story rights agreement.

▷ **Is the subject of the disclosure identifiable to the readers?** An individual's privacy cannot be invaded if the subject of the disclosure has been obscured or fictionalized in a way that prevents the reader from recognizing him as a living person. But it's not enough to do so with a wink and a nod as in a *roman á clef*. If the reader *can* identify the subject of the disclosure through a physical description or other circumstances, then a potential claim may arise even if the subject is not identified by name.

▷ **Is the fact being disclosed commonly known or available in public records?** The publication of information that is generally available in court files, military records, birth and marriage certificates, and other public documents is usually not enough to sustain an invasion of privacy action.

▷ **Is the fact being disclosed "highly offensive" to a reasonable person?** An innocuous disclosure, no matter how "private," is generally not enough to justify a claim for invasion of privacy. The disclosure must be "outrageous" to the average reader. As a general matter, disclosures relating to sexual issues, criminality, physical and mental ailments, and eccentric conduct ought to be carefully considered in the vetting process.

▷ **Is the fact being disclosed of "legitimate concern to the public"?** The First Amendment and the general notion of "the public's right to know" may justify the publication of intimate and even offensive facts. And "newsworthiness" appears to cover a multitude of sins. Indeed, one legal source observes that newsworthiness extends to virtually any "[matter] of genuine, even if more or less deplorable, popular appeal," including birth, death, crime, disease, suicide, and natural catastrophe. But at least some distinction must be made between what is news-worthy and what is merely gossip in order to measure the risk of a privacy claim.

▷ **Is the disclosure a matter of public conduct?** It's less risky to disclose an embarrassing fact if the disclosure is based on some-thing that happened in a public place or was observed by a large number of people.

▷ **Is the subject of the disclosure a public figure or a private individual?** A public figure enjoys a much more limited "expectation of privacy" than a private individual, and thus it is always riskier to make an intimate disclosure about a private individual. But sometimes it's hard to tell when someone is a private or a public figure. For example, an otherwise obscure individual who finds himself the victim of a noto-rious crime through no fault of his own may be regarded by the courts as a public figure, but a once-notorious criminal may regain the right "to melt into the shadows of obscurity," as one court put it, merely because of the passage of time.

Right of Publicity

The right of publicity generally empowers an individual to prohibit the use of his "persona"—not only his name and likeness but also his signature, voice and other distinguishing characteristics—for "commercial" purposes, and especially in connection with the advertisement or endorsement of a product.

Permissible Uses of the Name, Image or Likeness of Another. The right of publicity is not necessarily violated when, for example, an individual is described or depicted in a book for purposes of reporting, scholarship, commentary or even mere entertainment. Rather, the right of publicity focuses on the use of an individual's persona for a *commercial* purpose—and the mere fact that a book is published for profit is not enough to make it a commercial use.

As a general proposition, the use of the name or likeness of an individual in a work that touches upon a matter of public interest or public concern is unlikely to be a violation of the right of publicity. Thus, for example, it is permissible (and commonplace) to write an "unauthorized" biography of a public figure without violating his right of publicity—but it probably is a violation to falsely claim, whether openly or by implication, that the the public figure has endorsed the book.

Any use of the name or likeness of an individual that implies an endorsement poses a high risk, and so does the use of the individual's name or likeness in the form of merchandise such as a poster. By contrast, the use of an individual's name and likeness as the subject matter of a book, whether it's a biography or a novel, is less likely to constitute a violation of the right of publicity.

However, it is sometimes hard to to distinguish in advance between lawful and unlawful uses of name and likeness in a publishing context. For example, one court held that a fictionalized biography of Agatha Christie, which was published as a novel, was *not* a misappropriation of her right of publicity, but another court upheld a jury verdict in favor of Lucky Luciano's former attorney, whose name was incidentally mentioned in a novel based on the life of Lucky Luciano.

Dead Celebrities and the Right of Publicity. Unlike the right of privacy, which may be exercised only by a living individual, the right of publicity is a property right that may be sold or licensed, and it passes to the heirs of a dead person. As a general proposition, however, the right of publicity in the name, image or likeness of a dead person is recognized only when the individual's name or likeness enjoyed some measure of commercial value during his lifetime or, in some states, if the celebrity actually exploited the commercial value of his name or likeness during his lifetime. So, as a practical matter, only the heirs or assignees of dead *celebrities* are likely to prevail in a claim for the misappropriation of the right of publicity of a dead person.

> OVERPOSSESSIVE. The Lawnmower Man was a motion picture based on a short story by Stephen King, but aside from the title itself, the movie had very little in common with the story. Still, the producers advertised their picture as "Stephen King's The Lawnmower Man" in an unabashed effort to sell tickets to the best selling author's vast readership. King sued on the grounds that the use of the possessive in the title amounted to a false claim that he had actually participated in the making of the movie. Even though the producers had properly acquired the right to make a motion picture based on King's work, the author argued, they had not acquired the right to use his name in a manner that implied an endorsement of the movie—and the court agreed.

Checklist of "Right of Publicity" Issues

▷ **Does the use of the individual's name or likeness imply sponsorship or endorsement?** The very highest risk of liability is presented when the author or publisher appears to claim that the individual has somehow sponsored or endorsed the book, directly or indirectly, whether in the book itself or in the advertising and promotional material.

▷ **Is the individual's name or likeness used in a manner that relates to a matter of public interest?** The very least risk is found in works of politics, history, biography, or some other subject of legitimate public interest where the individual is described in a manner that relates to the editorial contents of the book. A novel or some other work of entertainment may pose somewhat greater risk, but the use of the name or likeness of an individual for purposes of amusing or informing the reader is not necessarily a violation of the right of publicity *if it does not suggest an endorsement.*

▷ **Is the individual a celebrity?** A greater risk is always present when the individual whose name and image are used in the work is, in fact, a celebrity, whether living or dead. Certain living celebrities—Elizabeth Taylor, for example—are known to be especially vigilant in preserving their right of publicity, and so are the estates or licensees of certain dead celebrities, including Marilyn Monroe and Elvis Presley.

▷ **Is the name and likeness of an individual used in merchandise, or in the advertising and publicity materials for a book?** The highest risk of a claim for violation of the right of publicity exists when the name or likeness of an individual appears in an item of merchandise— a poster, for example, or a calendar—or in some promotional setting such as the dust jacket or advertisements for a book.

"Negligent Publication" and Disclaimers

Any book that offers instruction, advice, or other information that the reader may use (or misuse) to his detriment faces a potential claim that the reader was injured or damaged by errors or defects in the book itself. Under the theory of "negligent publication," a textbook publisher was once held liable for the injuries suffered by students who performed one of the experiments in a chemistry textbook—and the experiment blew up. And a publisher was held liable for deaths that resulted when a plane crashed after the pilot followed the erroneous instructions in the book of aeronautical charts.

An author or publisher may be held liable for errors and defects in the books that they write and publish—or for the failure to warn of possible dangers in using the book—only when the risk of injury to the reader is "foreseeable." But the test of foreseeability is applied on a case-by-case-basis, and the courts reach some rather odd and inconsistent results even as they purport to follow the same rule.

For example, *Soldier of Fortune* magazine was held liable for negligence in the death of a murder victim whose paid killer was recruited through a "gun-for-hire" advertisement in the magazine classifieds. But *Hustler* magazine was held *not* to be liable for the death of a young man who tried out a form of "autoerotic asphyxiation" that was tantalizingly described in a magazine article.

More often than not, lawsuits for "negligent publication" have been unsuccessful. For example, publishers have been held *not* to be liable for the injury of a reader who used a constipation remedy prescribed in a nursing textbook, or the death of a woman who followed the advice in a diet book, or the losses of an investor who relied on inaccurate data in a financial publication.

Bear in mind, by the way, that a distinction may be made between the *author* and the *publisher* in measuring the risk of liability for negligent publication. Publishers are frequently excused from liability for errors in materials that were provided to them by "third parties," including the authors of the books published under their imprints. But the author may very well be held to a different and higher standard of care when it comes to injuries resulting from erroneous advice or information that the author herself provided to the reader.

Warnings and Disclaimers. The customary precaution taken by publishers who fear such claims is a warning and disclaimer—that is, a formal warning to the reader of the risks that he may encounter in making use of the book, and/or an announcement by the publisher that it will not accept liability for any injuries caused by the reader's use of the book. Warnings and disclaimers are two separate creatures, however, and each one poses risks of its own.

A warning is a form of advice and instruction from the publisher to the reader: "Be careful when you use the information and advice in this book." But the warning itself can be as defective as the information and advice that it warns against! To be effective, the warning must be carefully and accurately phrased to alert the reader to the actual risks of using the book; if possible, it must give specific information on how to avoid injury or damage; and it must be displayed in a fashion that catches the reader's attention and conveys the publisher's message clearly. Thus, for example, a warning that consists of legal boilerplate in 8-point type buried at the back of the book may be defective in itself!

LIVER AND MUSHROOMS. A pair of mushroom hunters, equipped with a copy of G.P. Putnam's The Encyclopedia of Mushrooms, were rushed to the hospital for emergency liver transplants after they consumed poisonous mushrooms. But a court ruled that the publisher was not liable for any errors in the book because the publisher had neither prepared the text nor guaranteed the contents of the book. (Significantly, The Encyclopedia of Mushrooms had been written by a pair of British authors and printed by a British publisher, and Putnam's had merely purchased copies of the finished work for distribution in the United States.) A publisher does not have the duty to investigate or guarantee the accuracy of the books that it publishes, nor does the publisher have a duty to publish a warning to the reader. "Were we tempted to create this duty," the court observed in Winter v. G. P. Putnam's Sons, "the gentle tug of the First Amendment ...would remind us of the social costs." In other words, the publisher was entitled to rely on the author for the accuracy of the book—but the authors, who were not in court, might have faced a different risk since it was their work that was alleged to be defective.

A disclaimer is an effort by the publisher to disavow any guarantee of the safety, accuracy, or reliability of its book. Essentially, the publisher is trying to say: "We do not accept any responsibility if you are injured or damaged because you rely on information or advice in this book." A disclaimer is rarely effective in avoiding liability that is otherwise imposed on the author or the publisher by law—if, for example, a court finds that the publisher should have warned of the risks in using a book, the mere fact that a disclaimer appears in the book will not be enough to save the publisher from liability. But a disclaimer is more likely to be effective in demonstrating that the publisher did not make any specific guarantees, whether directly or indirectly, regarding the safety or reliability of the book.

Warnings and disclaimers ought to be carefully drafted to reflect the particular risks associated with using the book. An example of a warning and disclaimer that is widely used in publishing circles appears in the Form Library. ➤ *Form 7: Warning and Disclaimer*

(By the way, there's another specimen in the Introduction of this book—it's the warning that *I* drafted to warn the *you* against the possible risks of using the book you are now reading!)

But here's a warning and disclaimer *about* the very notion of warnings and disclaimers: No single boilerplate warning and disclaimer will be sufficient for all publishers and all purposes. The book itself must be carefully reviewed and evaluated, and some measure of expertise must be brought to bear in drafting an effective warning and disclaimer.

Checklist of Negligent Publication Issues

▷ **Does the author's work purport to offer legal, financial, medical or other advice and information that may result in physical, mental or economic injury to the reader?** If so, the risk of a claim for negligent publication must be taken into consideration in checking the accuracy and completeness of the contents of the book. A book on medical self-help, for example, may be a high-risk publishing enterprise that requires more careful research and vetting than a children's book of nursery rhymes. But even a cookbook, for instance, or a "how-to" book may include information and advice that is dangerously inaccurate—or dangerous if misused by the reader.

▷ **Is the author herself an expert in the field?** The publisher needs to be concerned about the qualifications of the author to assemble and present advice and information to the reader. If appropriate, the manuscript ought to be vetted by a specialist in the field.

▷ **Will a warning or disclaimer be effective to reduce the risk of injury or damage to the reader?** A boilerplate warning or disclaimer is not enough. If used, they must be clear and complete, and they must be displayed in a prominent position in the book in order to assure that the reader will, in fact, find them before using the book.

Trademark and Trade Dress Infringement

The law protects the user of a particular trademark against competition from a "confusingly similar" mark, and the very notion of what constitutes a trademark is quite expansive. For example, a press name ("Penguin Books") can be a trademark, and so can a visual image or logo (the distinctive drawing of a penguin on the spine of a Penguin Book). Even the *appearance* of a book—the typography, graphics, color, and other graphic elements of a book cover—can be protected as a special form of trademark called "trade dress." ➤ *Briefs: Trademark and Unfair Competition*

Not every use of someone else's trademark is an infringement. The essential test in trademark infringement is whether the consumer will be misled into believing that the allegedly infringing product is sponsored by or affiliated with the owner of the trademark. And so the particular circumstances in which a trademark is used will determine if a claim for infringement is likely.

Use of Trademark in the Content of a Book. The mere fact that an author incidentally mentions a trademark in the text or depicts a trademark in the illustrations of a book is not enough to constitute trademark infringement as long as no suggestion is made that the author's book is published or sponsored by the trademark owner.

Mention of a trademark to convey information, rather than to identify the source of the book or to claim an endorsement, is usually permissible. Thus, for example, Ian Fleming was perfectly free to invoke the trademarks of Beretta and Aston-Martin in his James Bond novels. And it's probably not trademark infringement to include a photograph of O. J. Simpson under a Hertz sign in a biography of the benighted football hero to illustrate the fact that he once acted as the celebrity spokesman for the rental company.

A closer question is always presented, however, if the trademark appears in the title of a book. Suppose, for example, that the author has written a price guide for collectors of Coca Cola memorabilia. If the book's title uses the Coca Cola trademark in a manner that falsely suggests sponsorship or endorsement of the book by the Coca Cola Company, then the publisher faces a risk of trademark infringement; but the incidental use of the trademark to identify the subject matter of the book is less likely to amount to infringement. Thus *The Official Coca Cola Collector's Handbook* is far risker than *Klockenlocker's Handbook of Coca Cola Collectibles.*

Use of Trademark and Trade Dress by the Publisher. An altogether different (and much greater) risk is presented when the author or the publisher adopt a press name, a series title, or a trade dress that resembles the trademarks actually used in the marketplace by another author or publisher. For example, if the publisher of a travel guide called its series *LET'S GET GOING!*, then the publisher might expect to hear from the attorneys for Harvard's best selling travel series, *LET'S GO!*

Disclaimers. Under some circumstances, a disclaimer may be appropriate to advise the reader that no sponsorship or endorsement is claimed by the author or publisher. For example: "*Klockenlocker's Handbook of Coca Cola Collectibles is not sponsored or endorsed in any manner by the Coca Cola Company.*" But disclaimers are rarely sufficient to defuse a trademark claim if the overall impression of the book *does* suggest an affiliation, especially if the disclaimer is buried in small type somewhere inside the book. A disclaimer, if it is to be effective at all, must be prominent enough to catch the reader's attention *before* the reader concludes that the book is somehow connected with the owner of the mark.

Parody and Satire. Rather like fair use in the field of copyright, a parody of a well-known trademark or trade dress may be defended against a claim of infringement if the parody is broad enough to alert the reader to the fact that no actual affiliation is claimed by the author or publisher of the parody. Thus, if the parody or satire is either too subtle or too literal, the risk of a trademark infringement claim may still be present. A prominent disclaimer may assist in identifying the work as a parody, but only if the disclaimer is effective in distinguishing the author's work from the work that is being parodied.

➤ *Copyright Infringement and Fair Use—Above*

Checklist of Trademark Issues

▷ **Is the trademark of another person or company actually mentioned or depicted in the work?** If so, the precise nature and circumstances of the use must be carefully assessed. Is the mark used to convey information or to identify the source of the work? If the use of the mark suggests an affiliation with the trademark owner, the publisher ought to obtain formal permission from the trademark owner, or else change (or eliminate) the use of the mark.

▷ Is the title, trademark or trade dress adopted by the publisher for its own edition of the author's work confusingly similar to the marks of another publisher? All elements of the book project—including the title, dust jacket, advertising and promotional materials, and the content of the book itself—need to be reviewed to determine if the consumer is likely to believe that the publisher's editions actually originated with another publisher whose marks are similar in appearance.

> THE CITY MARK AND THE COUNTRY MARK. When New York magazine mimicked The Old Farmer's Almanac on the cover of its 1990 Christmas gift issue, the publishers of the Farmer's Almanac sued for trademark infringement on the grounds that the trade dress of their publication—the yellow background, the red and white border, and the "agrarian seasonal vignettes" that frame the cover—had been infringed. But the court found it unlikely that readers would be misled into believing the Christmas issue of "frivolous, trendy, inconstant, stylish" New York was somehow sponsored by the Farmer's Almanac, which is known for its "rusticity, thrift, homespun good sense, homely time-honored adages, practicality, [and] permanence." The New York cover was an "obvious take-off," the court ruled in Yankee Publishing Inc. v. News America Publishing, Inc., and the right of "artistic free expression" outweighed the trademark rights of the Farmer's Almanac.

▷ Is a disclaimer appropriate to reduce the risk of trademark infringement? If used, is the disclaimer clear and prominent enough to warn the reader that no claim of sponsorship is being made? A disclaimer may *not* insulate the author or publisher from liability at all, especially if the placement or phrasing of the disclaimer is not effective in alerting the reader to the actual source of the work.

Other Issues in Vetting

▷ **Rights and Permissions.** Any book that includes elements created by someone other than the author or the publisher must be evaluated to determine if permission is necessary to make use of copyrighted material owned by a third party. For example, it may be necessary— and it's *always* a sensible precaution—to secure formal written permission from the artist or designer who creates the cover art and other graphic elements of the book; the contributors of any prefaces or forewords that may be included in the book; the artist, illustrator or photographer who contributes visual images to the book, including charts, graphs, maps, photographs and incidental artwork; and the authors or publishers of any copyrighted work that is quoted in the book (unless, of course, the quoted material falls within the scope of fair use). ➤ *Chapter 2: Co-Authorship and Copyright & Copyright Infringement and Fair Use—Above*

▷ **Subsidiary Rights.** A special problem arises if the publisher is asked to grant permission to a third-party to make use of copyrighted work in another medium such as audio, electronic, or motion picture and television. Suppose, for example, that an electronic publisher seeks permission from a book publisher to use a portion of a copyrighted book as part of a multi-media software program in a CD-ROM format. Before granting permission to the electronic publisher, the book publisher must confirm that it owns and controls electronic rights in the book itself—and not only the author's text, but also any photographs, illustrations, prefaces or forewards, or other copyrighted material that may appear in the printed volume. Otherwise, the book publisher may inadvertently give permission to use materials that it doesn't own—and the electronic publisher, despite its best intentions, may end up infringing the copyright in someone else's work.

▷ **Son of Sam Laws.** Some states have enacted statutes that allow victims of crime to make a claim on money or other things of value that a criminal may obtain as a "fruit" of his crime, including advances, royalties and option payments for selling his story to a publisher. The "Son of Sam" laws vary from state and state, and—thanks to a recent Supreme Court decision that ruled some aspects of the New York law to be unconstitutional—the statutes in some states may not be fully enforceable unless they have been recently amended to comply with the Supreme Court ruling. But authors and publishers must be cautious about making <u>any</u> payment to a person accused or convicted of a crime—whether the payment is made to him as an author, a source, or a seller of "life story rights"—to ensure that they have complied with any "Son of Sam" law that may apply to the transaction.
➤ *Life Story Rights—Above*

▷ **Obscenity.** A work that contains explicit sexual content, whether verbal or visual, may expose its author or publisher to the risk of prosecution under state or federal obscenity statutes, which usually include a *criminal* penalty such as a monetary fine or a prison term.

Only the most egregious sexual content is likely to raise a risk of an obscenity prosecution—but the approved constitutional definition of what constitutes obscenity offers very little assistance in measuring the risk of a successful prosecution in any given case: "Obscene matter" means matter taken as a whole, which to the averge person, applying contemporary statewide standards, appeals to the prurient interest, and is matter which, taken as a whole, depicts or describes in a patently offensive way sexual conduct; and which, taken as a whole, lacks serious literary, artistic, political, or scientific value."

A more accurate and honest definition of obscenity was once given by Justice Potter Stewart: We can't define it, but we know it when we see it.

Even if a work is *not* legally obscene, federal law requires the publisher of certain materials depicting "sexually explicit conduct" to maintain records regarding the age of individuals who appear in the materials, and to include in every copy a notice of where such records are kept.

The risk of running afoul of the obscenity laws or other laws regarding sexually explicit material is especially high when the work includes *visual* depictions of sexual conduct, and the risk is highest when the sexual content involves individuals who appear to be minors. But obscenity is such a complex and specialized area of the law that the author or publisher who is publishing explicit sexual material ought to seek the advice of an attorney specializing in the defense of obscenity cases.

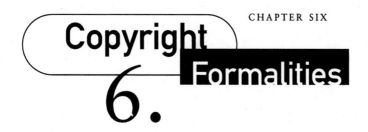

Copyright Formalities

6.

If the Copyright Act is the Bible of copyright law in the United States, then *Nimmer on Copyright* is the Talmud—a commentary so authoritative and so comprehensive that it is routinely cited and relied upon by the Supreme Court. When I bought my first copy of what copyright lawyers call "the Treatise" back in 1976, *Nimmer* consisted of two loose-leaf binders. Today, *Nimmer* takes up six fat volumes—and it's still growing as new cases are decided, new laws are enacted and new treaties are signed.

So the law of copyright is too vast, too various, and too fast-changing to be neatly summed up in a single volume. Indeed, within my own two decades of law practice, the copyright law has been fundamentally recast and revised not once but twice. And so *any* copyright question, even one that appears to be simple and straightforward, may require some fairly subtle analysis and wide-ranging research before it can be decisively answered—if it can be answered at all!

Still, it's possible to summarize some of the basic principles of copyright law as it applies to the publishing industry. The discussion set forth below is current as of the publication date of this edition of *Kirsch's Handbook*, and generally applies to works created or published in the United States after March 1, 1989.

Formalities of Copyright

Starting in 1789, when copyright was enshrined in the Constitution "to promote the Progress of Science and useful Arts," and continuing

Which Copyright Law Applies? The law of copyright in the United States is especially complex because the Copyright Act has been fundamentally revised twice in the last two decades—and even the current law is constantly modified in large and small ways as new cases are decided and new statutes are enacted. Thus, it's always necessary to determine which of the following bodies of law apply to a particular work.

The Copyright Act of 1909 applies to works first created or published prior to January 1, 1978. The 1909 Act placed great emphasis on copyright formalities such as notice, registration, and renewal—and defects in notice or renewal could inject an otherwise protectible work into the public domain. A vast number of pre-1978 works are still under copyright, of course, and thus the 1909 Act will not be a dead letter until well into the 21st century.

The Copyright Act of 1976 went into effect on January 1, 1978. Although the new law was far more forgiving than the 1909 Act, many of the copyright formalities—and the sometimes catastrophic consequences of ignoring them—were preserved in the 1976 Act. The Copyright Act of 1976 in its original form was the prevailing law only between 1978 and 1989, a brief period that Nimmer dubs the "decennial" era of copyright law. Thus, any work created or published between January 1, 1978, and February 28, 1989, is governed by the original provisions of the Copyright Act of 1976.

The Berne Convention Implementation Act of 1988 marked the long-delayed accession of the United States to the international copyright treaty known as the Berne Convention for the Protection of Literary and Artistic Works. In order to join the Berne Convention, the United States was required to substantially amend the 1976 Act to ➔

until 1989, the copyright law of the United States was based on strict compliance with certain "formalities" that determined whether or not an author was entitled to the benefits of the "natural monopoly" bestowed upon artists and inventors by the Framers of the Constitution.

For example, until very recently, the failure to include a proper copyright notice in a published work of authorship caused the work to be injected into the public domain, and so did the failure to renew the copyright at the proper time.

In 1989, however, the United States joined the Berne Convention, an international copyright treaty that flatly prohibits its members from requiring adherence to *any* formalities as a condition of copyright protection. As a result, the copyright law of the United States has been fundamentally revised, and the existence of copyright itself is no longer dependent on notice, registration, or any other formality.

➤ *Which Copyright Law Applies?—Below*

The current copyright law, however, still extends some important benefits to the copyright owner who goes to the trouble of observing certain formalities, including the use of a copyright notice and the registration of copyright. The key formalities of copyright—and the advantages that the copyright owner enjoys by complying with them—are discussed below.

Notice of Copyright

Publication of a notice of copyright in a book or other work is no longer *required* under United States copyright law, and the fact that a work is published without notice—or with defective notice—will no longer cause the work to pass into the public domain. But the publication of a copyright notice still bestows some very important benefits on the copyright owner, and thus *a proper notice ought to be included in every copyrighted work* unless there is a compelling reason to omit it!

→ alter or eliminate various formalities. Works created or published on or after March 1, 1989, are governed by the 1976 Act as amended by the Berne Convention Implementation Act and modified by other recent cases and statutes.

Reminder: The principles of copyright law generally discussed Kirsch's Handbook are based on the current law of copyright as of the date of publication. These principles may not apply to a work created or published prior to March 1, 1989. And, as the law of copyright continues to change and develop, the principles stated here may no longer apply to works created or published after March 1, 1989. So the reader is cautioned to seek the advice of an attorney who is familiar with the most current state of the law before applying any of these principles to a specific legal problem.

The key benefit of including a copyright notice in a published work arises when and if the copyright owner seeks to enforce his rights against an infringer. A defendant who had access to a published work that bears a proper copyright notice cannot raise the defense of "innocent infringement," and thus faces much stiffer penalties for acts of infringement. And, as a practical matter, a copyright notice makes it easier for someone seeking to lawfully acquire rights in a published work to find his way to the copyright owner. ➤ *Remedies for Copyright Infringement—Below*

Notice of Copyright Under the U.C.C. and Other Treaties. The Berne Convention prohibits its member-nations from imposing formalities such as copyright notice as a precondition to copyright protection. For that reason, copyright notice is optional in the United States and all other Berne Convention member-nations.

However, a few countries that belong only to the Universal Copyright Convention (U.C.C.), and *not* to the Berne Convention, still require a particular form of notice to ensure full copyright protection under their own law. The most important element of a U.C.C. notice is the familiar symbol © (and *not* merely the words "Copyright" or "Copr.") immediately followed by the name of the copyright owner and the date of publication.

Yet another international copyright treaty, the Buenos Aires Convention, provides that an additional element must appear in a proper copyright notice: *"All Rights Reserved."* Thus, as a matter of caution—and nearly universal practice among publishers—*all* of these various elements are usually combined in the copyright notice, as illustrated, for example, by the notice that appears in Bruce Chatwin's *The Songlines*:

Copyright © Bruce Chatwin 1987. All Rights Reserved.

How to Formulate a Copyright Notice. The specific contents of a proper copyright notice will vary according to the identity of the author, the kind of materials that are embodied in the work, and the year of first publication. At a minimum, and as a general rule, a copyright notice will usually include each of the following elements:

▷ The word "Copyright," "Copr." and/or the symbol©

▷ The name of the copyright owner

▷ The year of first publication

▷ The phrase: "All Rights Reserved"

There are a number of ways that a copyright notice may be properly stated. For example, here is the copyright notice that appears in the Farrar, Straus and Cudahy edition of *The Slave* by Isaac Bashevis Singer:

Copyright © 1962 by Isaac Bashevis Singer.

But the following variants are equally correct:

Copr. © 1962 by Isaac Bashevis Singer
© 1962 by Isaac Bashevis Singer

And, ideally, each of the foregoing formulations would be followed by:

All Rights Reserved.

Variations in Copyright Notices. Be forewarned: Sometimes the drafting of a proper copyright notice requires a careful evaluation of the contents and copyright status of a published work in order to come up with an accurate and legally correct notice. Bear in mind that the permutations of copyright ownership are almost endless, and it may require expert analysis to formulate a proper notice. Here are a few typical variants.

▷ A special symbol ℗ is used to give notice of copyright in the contents of a sound recording. Thus, for example, the copyright notice on an audiocassette version of *Zen Mind, Beginner's Mind*, a spoken-word performance of Shunryu Suzuki's book by Peter Coyote, is given as follows:

Recording ℗ Copyright 1988 by Audio Literature, Inc.
© Copyright 1970 by Shunryu Suzuki (Weatherhill)

▷ The author is not always the owner of copyright in his own work, and thus it is not always legally correct to give the author's name in the copyright notice. Technically, even if the author has assigned some (but not all) of the "bundle of rights" in his copyrighted work to the publisher, the author is still regarded as the "owner" of copyright and the *author's* name should be stated in the notice. If, on the other hand, the author has granted *all* rights in his work to the publisher, then the name of the *publisher* ought to appear in the notice. As a matter of tradition, however, publishers often agree to state the copyright notice in the name of the author even if all rights have been assigned to the publisher. In any event, since a defect in the copyright notice does not result in any forfeiture of copyright, the choice of names in a copyright notice is no longer a crucial decision, although it may affect the defense of "innocent infringer" if a defendant can prove that he was actually misled by a defect in the notice.

▷ If a copyrighted work was created as a work-for-hire then the publisher is the "author" for purposes of copyright ownership, and *only* the publisher's name should appear in the notice. ➤ *Chapter 2: Co-Authorship and Copyright*

▷ If the work is a revised edition of an earlier copyrighted work, then the notice may include two or more dates— the year of first publication of the work, the years of each subsequent revision, and the year of first publication for the latest revised edition. Thus, for example, the copyright notice in my copy of *Nimmer on Copyright* includes no fewer than *thirty* dates, starting with the year of first publication (1963) and ending with the year of publication of the most recent revised edition.

▷ If the work consists of separately copyrightable work by an author and an illustrator, a photographer, a translator, or some other collaborator, then it may be appropriate to give a separate notice in the name of each contributor. Here is an example from the copyright notice page of the Viking Press edition of *In Russia*, which consists of words by Arthur Miller and photographs by Inge Morath:

Text Copyright © 1969 by Arthur Miller. All Rights Reserved. Illustrations Copyright 1969...by Inge Morath. All Rights Reserved.

▷ If the work is derived from or based on another copyrighted work, then it may be appropriate to give a separate notice for each work. For instance, the copyright notice that appears in the English language version of Nikos Kazantzakis's *Report to Greco* also gives notice of copyright in the original Greek version from which it was translated.

ENGLISH TRANSLATION COPYRIGHT © 1965 BY SIMON AND SCHUSTER, INC. ORIGINAL GREEK LANGUAGE EDITION ENTITLED (. . . . .) COPYRIGHT 1961 BY HELEN N. KAZANTZAKIS. ALL RIGHTS RESERVED.

THE ILLS FROM MISSING DATES. Even if a work has been repeatedly revised over the years, it is usually sufficient to give only the most recent year of publication and omit the previous years in the copyright notice. Still, under certain circumstances, the use of a misleading date in a copyright notice may be regarded as an unfair trade practice or false advertising if the notice tricks the reader into believing that he is buying a new book. Thus, for example, a publisher may run afoul of the law if he makes only slight changes in an old book, gives the book a new title, and publishes the book with a copyright notice that states the current year of publication only.

A better practice is to state plainly, preferably on the cover but at least on the copyright notice page, that the book has been previously published in some form. Here's how New Directions, publisher of Henry Miller's Big Sur and the Oranges of Hieronymous Bosch, solved the problem: COPYRIGHT © 1957 by New Directions Publishing Corporation. The chapter called "Paradise Lost" was published as a separate book and called A Devil in Paradise, Copyright © 1956 by Henry Miller.

Similarly, an abridged edition should be clearly identified as such to avoid any confusion among consumers. For example, Audio Literature, the audio publisher of Peter Coyote's reading of Zen Mind, Beginner's Mind by Shunryu Suzuki, is careful to announce on the cover itself: ABRIDGED. 12 (of 38) sections omitted.

Location of Notice. As long as the notice appears "in such manner and location as to give reasonable notice of the claim of copyright," the precise location of the notice is not crucial. Approved positions for the placement of a copyright notice range from the front cover to the back cover, the frontleaf, the first page of text, the last page of text, and so on. As a general practice, copyright notices are printed on the page immediately following the title page.

If the book as published also includes copyrighted work by someone other than the author—the artist who created the cover illustration, for example, or the author of a preface—then it's useful to include a separate notice of copyright on the dust jacket itself or on the first page of the preface. For example, the Farrar, Straus and Giroux edition of Thomas Merton's *Mystics and Zen Masters* is copyrighted in the name of the Abbey of Gethsemani, but the back cover bears an additional notice: *Cover design © 1986 by Jacqueline Shuman.* Still, under the current law, the consequences of an improper notice— or no notice at all—are no longer catastrophic and will not affect the existence and ownership of copyright.

Copyright Registration

Copyright is a form of "intellectual property" that springs into existence at the moment a work of authorship is created—or, to use the language of the law, when it is "fixed in a tangible medium." Thus, when an author types "THE END" on the final page of her Great American Novel, she is the sole owner of copyright in the work, and she need do nothing more to perfect her rights.

The United States Copyright Office, however, maintains a registry of copyrights. And if the author or publisher goes to the trouble of *registering* the copyright of her work in the Copyright Office, the author and publisher will enjoy some important—and sometimes crucial—advantages in enforcing their rights and preventing infringement of her work. The benefits of registration are so significant—and the formalities of registration are so simple—that every copyright owner ought to register her work in the Copyright Office.

Application for Copyright Registration. The owner of any exclusive rights in a copyrighted work in the United States is entitled to apply for registration of copyright in the work at any time after the work is created, whether before or after publication. The registration process consists of preparing and assembling a completed registration form, an application fee, and—when required—copies of the work itself,

How Long Does a Copyright Last? The answer depends on when the work was created or published because each version of United States copyright law calculates the duration of copyright in a different way.

Works Published Prior to January 1, 1978. Under the old copyright law, a copyrighted work was protected for two consecutive terms of 28 years each, but the copyright was extended into the second term of protection only if it was duly and timely renewed prior the expiration of the first term by filing a renewal application in the Copyright Office. Thus, the total period of copyright protection was 56 years from the year of publication or, for an unpublished work, the year of registration.

Under the Copyright Act of 1976, which went into effect in 1978, the second or "renewal" term was extended to 47 years, with the result that the total period of copyright protection was 75 years. But the renewal term was still conditioned upon the filing of a proper and timely renewal in the Copyright Office.

Then, upon the enactment of the Copyright Renewal Act of 1992, the requirement for the filing of a renewal application was eliminated. Thus, any work which was first published between January 1, 1964, and December 31, 1977, will be automatically renewed without the necessity of filing a renewal application, and copyright protection will continue for an additional 47 years. (Note: Even though renewal is no longer required, there are still some good reasons for most copyright claimants to file a renewal application. An attorney with copyright expertise can advise on whether such a renewal is advisable.)

Works Published after January 1, 1978. The Copyright Act of 1976, which went into effect in 1978, eliminated the 56-year →

and submitting all of these materials to the United States Copyright Office.

The registration form most often used in the publishing industry is Form TX, which generally covers "nondramatic" literary works in printed form, including books of all kinds, magazine articles, catalogues, directories, and so on. The author or publisher will find some useful instructions about the registration process on the Form TX itself, and on other Copyright Office registration forms. (All forms are available without charge from the Copyright Office by calling the 24-hour "Hotline" at (202) 707-3000.)

A separate application, Form SE, may be used for registration of whole copies of a magazine, newspaper or other serial publications. Several variants of the Form SE—including the "short form," and "group registration" forms for daily or weekly periodicals—are available for certain kinds of publications. The group registrations, of course, are especially important to publishers of magazines and newspapers since separate registration of each issue would be prohibitively expensive and burdensome.

Form VA is used for registration of pictorial, graphic and sculptural works, including photographs, illustrations, technical drawings, and similar visual artwork. Under some circumstances—for example, when the writer and the illustrator of a book claim separate copyright in their own work—the text will be registered on Form TX, and the artwork will be separately registered on Form VA.

According to the current fee schedule of the Copyright Office, a fee of $20.00 must accompany each application for copyright registration.

Deposit requirements vary according to the nature of the work being registered. As a general rule, the deposit of two copies of the "best edition" of the work must also accompany each application for registration of a *published* work under most (but not all) circumstances. (The "best" edition is the one with the highest quality paper and binding and the most complete features; for example, if a book is published simultaneously in hardcover and softcover, the hardcover is the best edition.) An unpublished work may be registered with the deposit of a single copy, and special rules may apply to various other kinds of published works. An applicant may also request to be excused from the deposit requirement in special circumstances.

→ period of copyright protection <u>and</u> the requirement of renewal of registration. Instead, the current law provides for a single continuous term of copyright protection. The following rules generally apply to works created after January 1, 1978:

▷ <u>Works Authored by a "Natural" Person</u>: Copyright is measured by the life of the author plus fifty years, that is, copyright will expire 50 years after the death of the author. In the case of jointly authored works, the death of the <u>last</u> surviving author is the benchmark date. (A "natural" person is a human being, as opposed to a corporation or some other entity.)

▷ <u>Works-for-Hire, Works Published Under a Pseudonym, and Anonymous Works</u>. A copyright term of 75 years from the year of first publication, or 100 years from the date of creation, whichever is <u>shorter</u>, applies to "works-for-hire," that is, works that were "specially prepared" by employees in the course and scope of employment or by independent contractors working under a written work-for-hire agreement. The same term also applies to works that may have been created by a natural person writing under a pseudonym, and to works which were published with no natural person as the identified author. Note, however, that an anonymous or pseudonymous work can be converted to the "life plus fifty" term of copyright protection by following certain procedures to identify the author in the records of the Copyright Office.

<u>And Then the Public Domain</u>. Upon the expiration of copyright protection, the work passes into the public domain and may be freely used by anyone without the permission of the copyright owners.

Here's a brief glossary of the terms that are used on the forms and in various agreements relating to copyright:

Author: "Author" is a "term of art" in copyright law that refers to the person who, as a matter of law, created the copyrighted work. In most instances, the author is the human being who sat down at the word processor or the drawing board to create a novel or an illustration. If more than one human being participated in creating the work, then each is a joint author. But if the work is a "work-for-hire" by the publisher's employee—or by an independent contractor who signed a work-for-hire agreement— then the author is the employer or the commissioning party. And the author of a collective work such as a magazine or a newspaper, which is usually created by both employees and independent contractors, is often the corporate entity that owns the publishing enterprise. ➤ *Chapter 2: Co-Authorship and Copyright*

Copyright Claimant. The "copyright claimant" is the person (or, in some instances, the company or organization) that owns the copyright in the work in the United States. Often, but not always, the author and the copyright claimant are one and the same person. If, however, the author has transferred all of the rights in her work to another person or a company, then the recipient of the grant of rights is properly identified on the copyright application as ➜

The Certificate of Copyright Registration. A copyright application is examined and evaluated by the Copyright Office, and some applications are rejected if they are improperly completed or if the work is not entitled to registration. A refusal to register a work of authorship may be appealed in the federal courts, but the fact is that most applications are routinely approved, and a Certificate of Copyright Registration is issued. The certificate bears a serial number and an effective date that will be used to identify the copyrighted work in future dealings with the Copyright Office, and in business transactions regarding the various rights in the work.
➤ *Recordation—Below*

The Benefits of Registration. Although the Copyright Act no longer requires registration as a condition of copyright ownership, the fact remains that registration bestows some very important advantages on the copyright owner. Most of these advantages arise if and when the copyright owner seeks to stop— and punish—an infringer by filing a copyright infringement suit. If the copyright owner waits until after an infringer has been detected to file a registration, then it may be too late to make use of some remedies that are provided for infringement. And so the First

Commandment of copyright law is: Thou shalt register your copyrights promptly!

▷ As a general rule, a copyrighted work *must* be registered before the copyright owner is entitled to file a lawsuit for copyright infringement. (**Important Note:** This requirement does *not* apply to so-called "Berne works"—that is, works created and/or published in a Berne member-nation other than the United States—but it *does* apply to works by United States authors and all works first published in the United States, even if they were authored by a citizen of a Berne member-nation.)

→ the copyright claimant.

A distinction must be made, however, between a copyright claimant, who generally owns all rights in the work, and a "copyright owner" or "copyright proprietor," who owns some but not all of the bundle of rights that make up a copyright. For example, if an author grants book rights to her publisher—but reserves motion picture rights, audio rights, merchandising rights, and various other rights—then the author is still the "copyright claimant" but the publisher is a copyright owner. Since the bundle of rights may be divided up and sold off in a series of separate transactions, it is entirely possible for a work to have many "copyright owners." A copyright owner is entitled to file a copyright application even if someone else is actually the author and/or the copyright claimant—but the author and copyright claimant must be correctly identified in the application itself.

▷ A Certificate of Copyright Registration, if issued before publication or within five years after the first publication of a work, serves as strong evidence that the work is, in fact, entitled to protection under the copyright law. What's more, the mere existence of the certificate is evidence that may be used to prove the facts stated in the application— the identity of the author, the owner of copyright, the nature of the copyrighted work, the year of first publication, and so on. Although a defendant in an infringement lawsuit may present evidence to contest these facts, the "burden of proof" shifts to the defendant. (Even a registration more than five years after publication has some evidentiary weight, although it's up to the judge to decide how much.)

▷ A copyright owner is entitled to seek "statutory damages" and attorneys' fees *only* if the work has been registered—and these statutory remedies are generally available only for acts of infringement that take place *after* the date of registration of the work, whether published or unpublished. (The requirement of registration in order to obtain statutory damages and attorneys' fees, by the way, applies to all authors and copyright owners, both U.S. and foreign.) The statutory remedies are so advantageous that the lack of a timely registration may make it unrealistic for a copyright owner to aggressively pursue an infringer at all! ➤ *Remedies for Copyright Infringement—Below*

Remedies for Copyright Infringement

Copyright owners are entitled to draw upon a daunting arsenal of remedies in prosecuting civil actions for copyright infringement. But the most effective remedies are available only if the the work has been registered in Copyright Office before the act of infringement or within three months after publication.

Plaintiff's Damages and Infringer's Profits. Whether or not the work was registered prior to the infringement, a plaintiff in a copyright infringement suit is entitled to recover his *actual damages* caused by the infringement, that is, the money that he lost as a direct result of the availability of infringing copies of his work. A plaintiff is also entitled to recover the *profits*, if any, that the infringer made by selling the infringing copies. But the plaintiff must be able to prove the amount of his actual damages and the infringer's profits by admissible evidence in court—and, all too often, the plaintiff is simply unable to prove that he lost any money or that the infringer made any money!

Statutory Damages. The Copyright Act, however, bestows a very important right upon the owners of registered works of copyright—the right to seek damages without proof of actual loss by the plaintiff or actual profits by the infringer. Such damages are specified in the statutes that embody the Copyright Act and are awarded "in lieu

---

The Mandatory Deposit. Under most (but not all) circumstances, an application for registration of copyright in a published work must be accompanied by a "deposit" of one or two copies of the "best edition" of the work. But even if the copyright owner decides **not** to register the copyright in her work, the fact remains that a deposit may still be required under the law. As a general rule, according to the Copyright Act, two copies of the "best edition" of every work published in the United States must be deposited in the Library of Congress within three months after publication—and anyone who refuses to make a deposit after demand from the Register of Copyrights faces a fine of up to $2,500! The point of the mandatory deposit has nothing at all to do with copyright—it's a mechanism to ensure that the Library of Congress is able to acquire books and other publications at the expense of the publisher! As a practical matter, however, most deposits are made by authors or publishers who are, in fact, registering the copyright in their works, and thus the deposit is made to serve both functions at once.

SUITABLE FOR FRAMING. Sometimes it hardly pays to sue for copyright infringement unless statutory damages and attorneys' fees are available. That's what celebrated editor and author Gordon Lish learned when he sued Harper's Magazine for copyright infringement after the magazine published a private letter that Lish circulates to students in his writing classes. Lish won his lawsuit, but since he had not bothered to register his unpublished letter in the Copyright Office prior to the infringement by Harper's, he was not entitled to statutory damages or attorneys' fees. The trial court tried to figure out what his "actual" damages might be, and came up with an award of $2,000, even though the judge admitted that the letter had "no true market value." Later, an appeals court affirmed the judgment in favor of Lish but struck down the $2,000 damage award. As a result, Lish won a judgment that may look impressive on the wall of his study, but it's not good for much else. The lesson? Always register your works promptly upon publication in order to secure the all-important right to seek statutory damages and attorneys' fees in case of an infringement!

of" actual damages. (That's why statutory damages under the Copyright Act are sometimes called "in lieu damages.") The Copyright Act prescribes a range of statutory damages, but it is left to the discretion of the court to decide the exact amount.

Important Note: Statutory damages are available only for acts of infringement that took place *after* the date of registration. However, if a work is registered within three months of first publication, then statutory damages will be available for *all* acts of infringement, whether the infringement took place before or after registration. And both U.S. and foreign authors and copyright owners are required to register their works before they are entitled to claim statutory damages or attorneys' fees.

Statutory damages for "innocent" infringement are currently $200 per act of infringement. An innocent infringer is one who can prove that he acted in good faith and without knowledge that he was infringing a valid copyright. But a defendant cannot claim to be innocent if he had access to copies of the work bearing a proper copyright notice. ➤ *Notice of Copyright—Above*

Statutory damages for "willful infringement" are currently set at a maximum of $100,000 per act of infringement. An infringer who has actual knowledge that he is infringing another's copyright—or even an infringer who acts in "reckless disregard" of the rights of the copyright owner—may face the high range of statutory damages.

Most copyright infringement falls into a middle range of statutory damages. If an infringement is characterized as neither innocent nor willful, the range of statutory damages is $500 to $20,000 per act of infringement. Generally, it's up to the discretion of the court to decide where a particular act of infringment falls in the vast range between innocence and willfulness, but the decision is often influenced by the degree of knowledge and intent of the defendant.

An "act of infringement," for purposes of calculating statutory damages, does not refer to a *copy* of an infringing work. Rather, all infringing copies of a particular copyrighted work amount to *one* act of infringement. For example, if a rogue publisher printed 10,000 "bootlegged" copies of a best-selling novel and sold out the entire edition, he would be liable for *one* act of infringement. If he went on to distribute 10,000 "bootlegged" videocassettes of the movie version of the novel, he would be liable for a second act of infringement.

Attorneys' Fees. The successful party in a copyright infringement action, whether plaintiff or defendant, is entitled to recover "costs of suit" and attorneys' fees in an amount that the court finds to be reasonable. Attorneys' fees are available *only* if the copyrighted work at issue was registered prior to the act of infringement or within three months after publication—and this requirement applies to both U.S. *and* foreign authors and copyright owners.

Other remedies. The Copyright Act also empowers a court to order a preliminary or permanent injunction against further acts of infringement, to order the seizure, impoundment and destruction of infringing copies, and to award interest on the damages suffered by the plaintiff. Registration of a copyright prior to the act of infringement is *not* required in order to obtain these remedies.

The Copyright Act also provides for severe *criminal* penalties, including monetary fines and imprisonment, for copyright infringers who are prosecuted by the United States Attorney and convicted in the federal courts. Rarely, however, does the federal government treat copyright infringement as a criminal matter—and, of course, criminal penalties are not available in a civil lawsuit by the copyright owner against the copyright infringer.

Copyright Recordation

Copyright is a form of intellectual property that may be sold, licensed, or mortgaged like any other asset. Indeed, copyright may be divided up into an almost unlimited number of rights—book rights, movie rights, electronic rights, and so on—and the author is entitled to sell or license each one of these rights to whomever she chooses. ➤ *Chapter 7: Electronic and Other Subsidiary Rights*

In order to be valid and enforceable, however, any assignment of an exclusive right in a copyrighted work must be embodied in a writing that bears the signature of the copyright owner or her agent. A nonexclusive license need not be in writing, since a license conveys the right to *use* the copyrighted work but not actual ownership of copyright, but it's still a good practice to confirm even a non-exclusive license in a writing signed by the copyright owner.

> Get It in Writing. Although a nonexclusive license need not be embodied in a signed writing, it is always a good practice to secure "rights and permissions" in a formal agreement signed by the licensor—and then to record the license in the Copyright Office. By following these formalities, the author and publisher who are relying on the permission of another copyright owner will be able to continue to use the copyrighted material in future editions of their book even if the publisher who gave permission later transfers the rights to the material to another publisher. ➤ *Recordation—Above & Form 4: Permissions Agreement*

In order to clarify the ownership of rights in any particular copyrighted work—and to protect copyright owners against conflicting assignments—the Copyright Office maintains a document registry where copyright agreements may be recorded as a public record. Just as a homeowner will routinely record a grant deed in the county recorder's office, the owner of an exclusive right in a copyrighted work is entitled to record the legal document by which such rights were conveyed. Once recorded, the law decrees that the world is "on notice" of its contents, and thus no one can claim to have acted in ignorance of a document that has been properly recorded.

Recordation is strictly optional, but it affords some important benefits to the copyright owner. As a general rule, if the author makes a conflicting grant of rights in a copyrighted work—for example, he purports to sell the audio rights to his work to both his book publisher and an audio publisher—then the agreement that is recorded first in the Copyright Office will prevail even if it was signed *after* the conflicting agreement. (Some exceptions apply, especially if an agreement has been recorded promptly after signing; it is necessary to carefully analyze any conflicting agreements to determine which is entitled to priority.) And, as a practical matter, a recorded document is more readily admissible into evidence in a lawsuit for copyright infringement than is an unrecorded document.

The Recordation Process. Any document bearing the original signature of the signer may be recorded without further authentication. A photocopy of a document may be recorded only if it is accompanied by a notarized or sworn statement by one of the signers (or the signer's authorized representative) to the effect that the photocopy is a true copy of the original. For convenience, the Copyright Office provides a standard Document Cover Sheet which may be used to mail the document to be recorded to the Copyright Office at the following address:

Documents Unit, LM-462
Cataloging Division
Copyright Office
Library of Congress
Washington, D.C. 20559-6000

The document to be recorded must be accompanied by the applicable recording fee, which is currently $20.00 for a document of six pages or less regarding a single copyrighted work. Other fees apply to longer documents or documents relating to multiple titles.

"Short Form" Documents. Authors and publishers are understandably reluctant to turn a book contract into a public record by recording the whole contract in the Copyright Office since it discloses the financial details of the transaction for the world to see. Instead, at the same time the book contract is signed, it's a common practice for the author and publisher to also sign a "short form" or summary version of the book contract that omits the financial details and describes the grant of rights only. Then the short form—and not the entire contract—may be recorded in the Copyright Office.

➤ *Form 5: Instrument of Recordation*

Electronic and Other Subsidiary Rights

7.

CHAPTER SEVEN

When I was a fledgling freelance journalist with my first novel under contract, I earned a coveted invitation to join a group of writers and editors who met regularly at a restaurant on the Sunset Strip in West Hollywood for what I imagined to be a West Coast version of the Algonquin Round Table. I expected witty repartee, war stories, dirty little secrets, and maybe even some lofty talk about the art and craft of writing—but what I heard was a lot of green-eyed gossip about the number of zeroes in the movie deals that everyone *else* seemed to be making on their latest books.

It was a moment of revelation for a young writer, and the home truth of the publishing industry has not changed. Only a tiny fraction of the books published will actually "earn out" their modest advances and start to pay royalties to the author. An advance is often the only money that an author will ever see for all the blood, sweat and tears that have been poured into a writing project. And so authors are still sustained in their efforts by a shining dream—a movie-of-the-week based on their novel, or maybe a spoken-word edition featuring the author's own voice, or some ill-defined but surely lucrative multimedia software product on CD-ROM.

All of these rights—electronic, audio, motion picture and television—are generally known as "secondary" or "subsidiary" rights, at least in the context of a book deal, and they represent a potential source of additional money for authors and publishers alike. Since so few books are actually made into a spoken-word product or a

CD-interactive program or a motion picture, the ownership and control of subsidiary rights is rather like buying a lottery ticket—the odds that it will ever pay off are long indeed. But it's a lottery that every author and publisher wants to play.

Primary, Secondary and Subsidiary Rights. Exactly what is the difference between a "primary" and a "secondary" right? What is the difference between "secondary" and "subsidiary" rights? And what exactly are "allied" and "ancillary" rights? Although these terms appear frequently in copyright agreements, there are no precise legal definitions for them. As a general proposition, the "primary" right in any particular contract is the right that the purchaser himself intends to exploit—the primary right in a book contract, for example, is the right to publish the author's work in book form. Everything else is "secondary" or "subsidiary"—the two terms are functionally interchangeable for most purposes. And certain rights may be "allied" or "ancillary" to certain other rights—arguably, the right to authorize the publication of an excerpt of a novel for promotional purpoes is "ancillary" to the right to publish the novel in the first place. Such shorthand phrases, however, are the seeds of misunderstanding—and worse. A better practice is to spell out what rights are granted and what rights are reserved with as much clarity and precision as possible. (For the sake of consistency, all such rights will be generally referred to as "subsidiary rights" in Kirsch's Handbook.)

The "sexiest" subsidiary rights in the publishing industry nowadays are electronic rights and audio rights, although motion picture and television rights are still the glittering prizes with the richest payoffs. But the bundle of subsidiary rights in a book includes a great many other rights, everything from Braille editions and Bengali translations to calendars and comic books, each of which may be separately bought and sold. So the negotiation of a basic book deal and the drafting of a book contract ought to include a clear and careful allocation of these rights between the author and the publisher.

➤ *Chapter 4: The Book Publishing Contract*

Ownership of Subsidiary Rights in a Book

In most book deals, the author starts out with ownership and control of *all* rights in her work. When she enters into a contract with a book publisher, she assigns certain rights to the publisher, and she may reserve certain rights for herself. The book contract, then, will determine who owns and controls subsidiary rights in the author's work—and the book contract will determine how the author and publisher share the revenues from exploitation of such rights. Thus, the exploitation of subsidiary rights in a book may take any of the following forms:

▷ If the author has *reserved* some or all subsidiary rights in her work—audio rights, for instance, or electronic rights—then she is free to sell or license these rights to an audio publisher or an electronic publisher, and the book publisher will not participate in the compensation paid to the author for the subsidiary rights.

▷ If, however, the author has *granted* some or all subsidiary rights to the book publisher, then it is the book publisher who will generally make use of the rights or else license the rights to another user. If the book publisher owns audio rights, too, and creates an audio edition of the author's work, then the book contract will determine how the author is to be compensated for *both* the print edition and the audio edition.

▷ If the author has granted subsidiary rights to the book publisher—and, for example, the book publisher licenses the electronic rights to a publisher specializing in electronic media—then the electronic publisher will pay the book publisher for use of the electronic rights, and the book publisher will share the revenues with the author according to the provisions of the book contract. According to most book contracts, the author and the book publisher share all revenues from subsidiary rights according to a fixed split, sometimes fifty-fifty, sometimes more or less.

Thus, when a subsidiary rights deal is negotiated, it may be the author or the book publisher that actually conducts the negotiations and signs the contracts with an audio publisher, an electronic publisher, a motion picture producer, or so on. Bear in mind, however, that the book contract is the document that will decide who owns and controls the sub-

> The Merger-and-Acquisition Jungle. The fact that so many publishing houses are owned by media conglomerates makes for some treacherous negotiations in book deals. For example, how can the author ensure that he is getting a fair deal if the publisher acquires audio rights in his book—and then licenses the rights to an audio publisher that happens to be a subsidiary of the same conglomerate? Generally, the author will be able to secure a promise that any such deal will be "on terms no less favorable to author than an arm's length transaction with a third party"—but such language is mostly meaningless unless there *is* an offer from another publisher to use as a benchmark. A better approach, at least from the author's perspective, is to grant the publisher an option to acquire such subsidiary rights on the same terms as the best offer from a third-party purchaser.

sidiary rights and how the author and publisher will share in the revenues from a subsidiary rights deal.

Print Publication Rights

The right to "print, publish and sell the work in book form" is, of course, the primary right in a book publishing contract. But the right to publish a work in printed form may be subdivided into a number of related but separate rights, and each one may represent a separate product or market. For example, until very recently, most books appeared first in hardcover, and the right to reprint the book in a paperback version—either in a "trade" or "quality" softcover edition (that is, a full-sized book with softcover binding), but more often in a "rack" or "mass market" edition (that is, a cheaper version of the book for sale at newsstands and check-out counters as well as bookstores)— was a valuable subsidiary right that the author and publisher usually shared in equal percentages. ➤ *Chapter 4—The Book Publishing Contract*

Back in the good old days, the most fortunate authors were able to put up paperback rights for auction at a six- or seven-figure price. Nowadays, an increasing number of books are published as "paperback originals," and so paperback reprint rights are less valuable than they once were. Even books that appear in hardback first editions are sometimes accompanied by a simultaneous trade paperback edition. And publishers are likely to ask for what's called a "hard-soft" deal— that is, the publisher acquires the right to publish in hardback *and* paperback.

Hard-soft deals are especially treacherous for authors if the publisher is part of a conglomerate. Rather than selling off the reprint rights to a paperback publisher at the best available price, one division may publish the hardback edition and a different division of the same company will publish the paperback. Thus, the author must approach a hard-soft deal with caution to make sure that the advance and royalty reflect the real economic value of *both* hardback and paperback rights.

Some of the categories and configurations of "print publication rights" that are often granted by an author to a publisher are discussed in Chapter 4, including Hardcover Rights, Softcover Trade Edition Rights, Mass Market Reprint Rights, and General Publication Rights. Here is a checklist of other print-related rights that may be included in a book deal, whether defined as primary or subsidiary rights.

➤ *Chapter 4—The Book Publishing Contract*

AND WHO OWNS THE FINNO-UGRIC COMIC BOOK RIGHTS? Subsidiary rights are sometimes defined by specific (and often highly specialized) markets and products. One children's book publisher, for example, characterizes the right to sell the author's book at school book fairs as a separate subsidiary right. One major book publisher specifically asks the author for the right to adapt the author's work in a "printed cartoon version" such as a comic book or a "graphic novel." The author of a book of aphorisms and advice was asked to license the right to turn his book into a "screen-saver" for personal computers. And another author recently signed a subsidiary rights deal for the right to make her book into an opera.

▷ Foreign Rights: The right to publish the book in its original language in countries other than the United States. Of course, the territory in which the original publisher is entitled to publish the author's work is a fundamental term of the book contract. At a minimum, United States publishers typically seek to acquire the right to publish in the United States, Canada and, often, the Phillipines; some publishers will ask for "world rights," that is, the right to publish anywhere in the world More commonly, however, the right to publish in various foreign countries around the world is the subject of negotiation between author and publisher. ➤ *Chapter 4—The Book Publishing Contract*

▷ Translation Rights: The right to create and publish a translation of the author's work in a foreign language. Translation rights are different from, but related to, foreign rights. For example, the author may grant to one publisher the right to distribute the original English-language edition of the author's work throughout the world, including France, and grant to a different publisher the right to translate his work into French and publish the French-language edition in France and other French-speaking countries. The first publisher enjoys foreign rights in the English edition but no translation rights at all, and the second publisher enjoys *both* foreign and translation rights in a specified language and territory.

▷ Direct-Response Marketing Rights: The right to sell the publisher's editions of the author's work through various forms of "direct-response marketing." Examples of direct-response marketing include print or television advertisements that offer the work for mail-order purchase by the consumer; the sale of books over a home-shopping network; and the sale of books (sometimes packaged with other products) through "infomercials." Publishers have long secured the right to sell copies of

Foreign Language Rights. A translation of a copyrighted work into another language is a "derivative work" that cannot be lawfully published without the permission of the owner of copyright in the original work—but the translation itself is also a copyrighted work that may be owned and protected wholly apart from the original work. That's why it is important to specify who owns and controls the copyright in the translation itself when drafting a foreign rights contract that contemplates the translation of an existing copyrighted work into a foreign language. By contrast, anyone may translate a work that is already in the public domain and publish the translation without anyone's permission—and yet the copyright in the translation itself belongs to the person who performed or commissioned the translation. Of course, two different translations of the same work into the same language will be very similar—but each translator owns his own copyright in those portions of the translation that are original to his work.

➤ *Chapter 8: Remaindering, Reversion and Copyright Termination*

a book by mail-order directly to the consumer, but direct-response marketing is a broader category of distribution nowadays.

▷ **Book Club Edition:** The right to publish and sell the author's work, whether "complete, condensed or abridged", for sale to members of a book club. Some book clubs order quantities of books from the publisher itself, and the publisher arranges for its printer to imprint the books with the name, logo, price and other particulars specified by the book club. Other book clubs simply acquire the right to produce their own version, and use the film or printing plates to manufacture their own copies.

▷ **Premium Sales and Special Editions:** The right to publish the work, whether in a complete or condensed version, as a special edition to be sold in bulk to a specific customer such as a corporation, an academic institution, or some other organization for use as a promotional item. Premium editions often include special imprints on the cover or additional text or other features designed for the premium purchaser. Because premium sales are usually in bulk and non-returnable—and because some premium purchasers may order significant quantities—premium rights can be especially valuable.

▷ **Bulk Sales:** The right to sell books in bulk quantity, usually at a deep discount. A bulk sale is often a one-time, non-returnable sale of a large quantity of books to a single purchaser outside the customary channels of trade in the book publishing industry. A common form of bulk sale is the purchase of books in bulk by a discount chain for sale through their stores.

▷ Anthologies and Collections: The right to select portions of the original work and print the selection—or, more commonly, to license another publisher to print the excerpt—in an anthology, a textbook or other collection.

▷ Periodical or Serial Rights: The right to print an excerpt, a condensation or the entire work in serial form in a periodical. Periodical rights can be subdivided into even more specific categories: magazines, newspapers, digests, newspaper syndicates, and so on. Another familiar distinction is based on

> **Permissions, Selections and Other Antiquities.** "Permissions" and "selections" are hoary old publishing terms that sometimes show up in book contracts to indicate the right of the publisher to grant permission to quote or publish excerpts from the author's work, whether in a book, anthology, or periodical. Some older contracts refer to "abridgement and condensation rights" as a separate category of subsidiary rights. And "transcription rights" is the now-obsolete term that some publishers are forced to rely upon when they claim audio or electronic rights. It's a good practice to freshen up older contract forms from time to time, and to avoid old words and phrases that no longer mean much in the fast-changing publishing industry.

the *timing* of publication in a magazine or newspaper. First serial rights refer to the right to publish a selection from the work *before* the work is first published in book form, and second serial rights refer to publication in a periodical *after* book publication.

▷ School Editions: The right to publish the work, whether in its original form or in an abridged, condensed or other form, for the school book market. Such editions are usually produced with cheaper typography, paper and binding and sold at a reduced price as a textbook or for other classroom use. Sometimes the right is further distinguished among elementary, junior high, senior high and college markets.

▷ Cheap Editions: The right to publish and sell the author's work in a lower-priced hardcover edition. "Cheap editions" are a rarity in contemporary publishing; however, a few publishers continue the fine old tradition of presenting books in durable hardcover bindings but at a lower cost than a conventional hardback book. The Modern Library is the most enduring and praiseworthy example of a cheap edition.

▷ Unbound Sheets: The right to sell the author's work in the form of printed but unbound sheets that are delivered to another publisher who cuts, binds, and distributes the work under its own imprint. The practice of simply printing the author's work and then selling it off to another publisher for distribution is fast-disappearing among trade publishers, although some book clubs actually produce their editions in a similar manner. Still, some older contract forms refer to the sale of unbound sheets as a separate right.

▷ **Microfilm and Microfiche Rights:** The right to reproduce the author's work in the form of microfilm or fiche. Microfilm technology is *not* equivalent to data storage or retrieval on a computer— essentially, it's microphotography of a book, page by page, for reproduction on a microfilm reader—and thus it's a less valuable right because of the availability of new and better computer-based technologies. ➤ *Electronic Rights—Below*

▷ **Photocopying Rights:** The right to grant permission for photocopying of some or all of the work for "in-house" use, usually by the employees or staff of a business, university, or other institution. Special photocopying privileges are extended to libraries under the Copyright Act, and certain kinds of library photocopying do not require the permission of the copyright owner. Although authors and publishers will rarely entertain requests for permission to photocopy on an individual basis, the Copyright Clearance Center allows the copyright owner an opportunity to issue a blanket license for photocopying in exchange for a specified royalty.

▷ **Braille, Large Print and Other Editions for the Handicapped:** The right to adapt the work to make it accessible to handicapped readers, including Braille, large print and spoken-word recordings. The Copyright Office forms routinely solicit the permission of the copyright owner to make royalty-free Braille editions, and publishers often ask authors to specifically approve such editions in the book contract. Obviously, a Braille edition is not likely to injure the sales of the work in print, and most authors are willing to give permission for a Braille version of their work. But some authors are cautious about granting permission for royalty-free spoken-word recordings for the blind, since a commercial audio version is an increasingly important product in the book industry. Similarly, large print editions, which are intended for vision-impaired readers, are a commercial product on which royalties are usually paid. Clearly, if the publisher intends to exploit any of these rights for profit, then a royalty or a share of revenues ought to be paid to the author. However, the author may be willing to forego a royalty if the rights are granted to "recognized non-profit organizations for the handicapped," and to waive compensation only if the publisher, too, is receiving no payment for such rights.

▷ **Publicity: The right to adapt, condense and publish or broadcast portions of the work, usually on a royalty-free basis, to publicize and promote the sale of the work in print.** Most publishers feel free to make use of the author's work for publicity purposes even without a clause in the contract that specifically provides for publicity rights. But a cautious publisher may prefer to secure such rights in the book contract itself to avoid any misunderstanding later on.

Electronic Rights

The single hottest topic of conversation and concern in contemporary publishing circles is the exploitation of so-called electronic and multi-media rights, and yet the right to adapt an author's work in an electronic medium is so new and so unfamiliar that most authors and publishers are only beginning to understand how electronic rights are actually turned into a marketable product.

Electronic rights are still regarded as "secondary" to print publica-tion rights in a book contract—but the fact is that both printed books and some important electronic products, notably books in the form of computer-readable CD-ROM disks, are often marketed through the same channels of distribution and end up on the shelves of the same bookstores. Even when electronic publishing takes a somewhat more exotic form—a subscription database such as Nexus, for example, or a subscription computer network such as CompuServe or Prodigy—the electronic product may compete directly with the printed book.

So electronic rights in a book are probably more accurately characterized as primary rights. Indeed, book publishers tend to regard electronic rights as inextricably linked to print rights—and a publisher may insist on acquiring both print *and* electronic rights as part of a basic book deal. Authors, on the other hand, are justifiably concerned that book publishers are taking too much and paying too little when it comes to electronic rights. Indeed, as technological changes in the publishing industry make electronic rights ever more valuable, electronic publishing may replace printed books as the primary right in a book contract.

"Electronic rights," Kurt Vonnegut, Jr. once told *The Authors Guild Bulletin*, "are the paramount authors' right to be protected."

The threshold questions in negotiating and drafting the electronic rights clause in a book contract may appear to be simple.

▷ How are electronic rights actually defined?

▷ Who owns and controls electronic rights in the author's work, the author or the publisher?

> A NEW ERA IN ELECTRONIC RIGHTS NOW BEGINS. A revolution in subsidiary rights was sparked when Cyan, Inc., a software publisher, auctioned off the right to turn its best selling computer game, Myst, into a series of books. Thirteen publishers joined in the bidding for three novels to be written by the designers of the CD-ROM game, Rand and Robyn Miller, and Hyperion, a division of Disney Book Publishing, Inc., won the print rights with a seven-figure bid. A new era has begun—book rights are now one of the subsidiary rights in an electronic game!

▷ If the publisher acquires electronic rights from the author, how will the author participate in the revenues generated by the exploitation of such rights?

▷ What degree of control, if any, will the author or the publisher enjoy in determining how the electronic rights are actually exploited?

But, as discussed below, even these basic questions are more challenging than they seem precisely because electronic rights are so new and so vaguely understood by authors and publishers.

What Are Electronic and Multimedia Rights? The very definition of electronic rights is hazy at best, and the publishing industry has not yet arrived at a common understanding of what actually constitutes a product that requires ownership of such rights. Older contracts, which may ignore the subject altogether or else refer to such abstruse or obsolete technologies as "ephemeral screen flashing" or "punch cards," are simply inadequate to the task of defining and allocating electronic rights. And various words and phrases of more recent coinage—"multimedia," "new media," or "interactive media"—are not much more helpful. For purposes of discussion, the right to use a copyrighted work in all such media and technologies will be described as electronic rights.

The problem is further complicated by the fact that certain forms of book publishing are intended to make use of computer-based technology to deliver a printed product to the consumer. For example, "publishing on demand" is a new form of marketing that will allow a consumer to order a book of his choice from the publisher's catalogue—the text will be transmitted in digital form from a computer database to a remote printer in a retail bookstore, and the book buyer will be handed a printed copy of the author's work. Is publishing on demand an electronic right or a print publication right—or both?

So the task of the author and publisher in negotiating and drafting an electronic rights clause is to define with precision what rights are being offered for sale or license—and only then will it be possible to divide up the ownership of such rights.

> **No Rights Without a Writing.** Articles and artwork created by freelance writers, artists and photographers are usually acquired with little or no paperwork—and yet some publishers are all too casual about reusing such materials in their own publications or, even more critically, selling electronic rights in their back issues to multimedia publishers or database operators. Although the law is still unsettled, the best reading of current Copyright Act is that publishers do not automatically acquire subsidiary rights when they pay a fee to a freelance contributor. And no rights can be acquired from a freelancer and owned exclusively by the publisher unless the author has signed a copyright assignment or a work-for-hire agreement. So the vigilant freelancer—and the prudent publisher—will take care to specify in a signed writing what rights are being acquired in freelance submissions.
>
> ➤ *Chapter 2: Co-Authorship and Copyright*

Varieties of Electronic Rights. A basic and sometimes crucial question is whether and how the author's work will be adapted or manipulated in an electronic medium. Each of the following uses of the author's work may be regarded as a separate electronic right:

▷ The right to reproduce the entirety of the author's work in its original form on some medium of electronic data storage which is then sold to the consumer for personal use, e.g., an encyclopedia or dictionary in the form of CD-ROM. (CD-ROM, which stands for "Compact Disc—Read Only Memory," is one popular form of portable data storage in a computer system; other forms include the familiar floppy disk or the more durable diskette, and yet more exotic products may well come into the marketplace.)

▷ The right to reproduce the entirety of the author's work in its original form through an electronic storage, retrieval and output system, where the product which is sold to the consumer is actually a printed book, i.e., a book published on demand.

▷ The right to reproduce the entirety of the author's work in its original form on an electronic database, which is then made accessible to the consumer for personal use over a subscription computer network or database service that is accessed by telephone, e.g., a computer service such as Nexus, where the contents of the *New York Times,* the *Los Angeles Times* and hundreds of other periodicals may be accessed and "downloaded" by subscribers through their personal computers.

> **TEXTBOOKS ON LINE AND ON DEMAND.** Among the earliest innovations in electronic publishing-on-demand—and, some say, an augury of the future of book publishing—is McGraw-Hill's Primis system. Primis offers college professors an opportunity to create and publish their own textbooks by selecting various materials from the McGraw-Hill database. The materials are then paginated, printed, indexed, and delivered to the college bookstore for sale to students.

▷ The right to reproduce and adapt selected portions of the author's work for use in conjunction with words, images and sounds from other sources as part of a multimedia or interactive product, whether on a CD-ROM disc, a subscription database, a game cartridge, or similar products and services, e.g., a computer video game based on Michael Crichton's novel *Jurassic Park.*

Book contracts and even electronic publishing contracts do not always distinguish among these various electronic goods and services, but such distinctions will become ever more important as electronic rights are more widely exploited in the publishing marketplace. A cautious author or publisher may wish to divide up electronic rights into various categories, including the ones described above.

A Model Electronic Rights Clause. Here's an all-inclusive electronic rights clause that seeks to expansively define electronic rights— and the clause can be adapted to allocate the rights to either the publisher or the author. The clause may be used in a book contract to allocate electronic rights to either the author or the book publisher, or in a contract between an author or book publisher and an electronic publisher. ➤ *Chapter 4: The Book Publishing Contract*

Electronic Rights

Author [hereby grants and assigns to Publisher] [or:] [hereby reserves] any and all electronic rights in and to the Work, in perpetuity and throughout the world, including the exclusive right to use, adapt or otherwise exploit the Work, or any portion thereof, in electronic data entry, storage, processing, transmission, retrieval, display and output systems of any and all kinds, whether now known or hereafter invented. Without limiting the generality of the foregoing, "Electronic Rights" include but are not limited to mechanical, electronic or other technologies such as microprocessors and computers of all kinds; information storage and processing systems in the form of CD-ROM and other compact disk media, digital media, interactive media, and/or multimedia; and/or the transmission, display, output and reproduction of any such media and technologies, whether by screen display, print-out, direct-to-disk transfer, photoreproduction, photocopy or otherwise, and whether stored on hard drives, disks, diskettes, remote or on-line data bases, magnetic tape, or other computer media or technologies or like processes attaining similar results.

If the author wishes to assign some, but not all, forms of electronic rights to the publisher, the following clause may be used in addition to the model clause set forth above. By striking out the phrases that do not apply to the specific deal that the author and publisher have struck, it's possible to use the following clause to assign some rights to the publisher and reserve other rights to the author.

Notwithstanding the foregoing, Author and Publisher acknowledge that the following Electronic Rights are [assigned by Author to Publisher] [or] [reserved by Author]: (1) The right to reproduce the entirety of the Work in any form of portable data storage now known or hereafter devised, including, by way of illustration only, disks and diskettes, for sale to consumers; (2) The right to enter the entirety of the Work in an electronic database or network for sale to consumers by means of electronic transmission to a facility where copies are printed out and/or transferred to any data storage media now known or hereafter devised, including, by way of illustration only, "publication on demand;" (3) The right to reproduce the entirety of the Work in a remote electronic database or network for use by consumers who are licensed to access the database and download the Work for their own personal use only; and/or [4] The right to reproduce and adapt the Work in its entirety, or any portions thereof, for use as part of an interactive or multimedia product in any medium or mode of transmission, display and output now known or hereafter invented.

Compensation for Electronic Rights. The mechanisms for compensating an author or a book publisher for exploitation of electronic rights remains an unsettled question in the publishing industry precisely because the technologies, the products, and the marketplace for exploitation of electronic rights are so new.

The Author's Guild and the American Society of Journalists and Authors have recommended that authors receive a "conventional" advance and royalty when the book publisher exploits electronic rights in an author's work through one of its own divisions, and 85% to 90% of revenues paid to the book publisher when electronic rights are licensed to a third party.

Some book and magazine publishers, on the other hand, tend to regard electronic rights as an incidental benefit of acquiring print publication rights in the author's work, and do not routinely offer to pay *anything* for such rights. Or, more commonly, the exploitation of electronic rights is lumped into a catch-all subsidiary rights clause that allocates to the author a fixed percentage—sometimes fifty percent, sometimes more or less—of revenues received by the publisher for the exploitation of *all* subsidiary rights.

How and when the author and book publisher are compensated for exploitation of electronic rights is determined by how these rights were allocated in the book contract.

▷ If the *author* has retained electronic rights in her work, then it is the author who will negotiate and enter into a contract directly with one or more electronic publishers—and the electronic publisher will pay the author an advance, a royalty, a flat fee, or some other form of compensation.

▷ If the *book publisher* has acquired electronic rights from the author as part of a book deal, then the publisher may choose to create and distribute an electronic version of the author's work through one of its own imprints and divisions—and then pay the author an advance and royalty or some other form of compensation for the electronic product according to the terms of the book contract.

▷ If the *book publisher* has acquired electronic rights in the author's work but chooses to license the rights to an *electronic publisher*, then the compensation will be paid by the electronic publisher to the book publisher, and then by the book publisher to the author. For example, the book publisher will license rights to the electronic publisher, who pays a royalty, a flat fee or some other form of compensation to the book publisher; then the book publisher will share the payments with the author according to the subsidiary rights provisions of the underlying book contract, which usually consists of a split of gross revenues from the electronic publisher.

The form of compensation will depend largely on the form of the electronic product itself. An electronic rights deal between an author or book publisher, on the one hand, and an electronic publisher who distributes the author's work in the form of a CD-ROM disk, on the other hand, is likely to resemble a conventional book contract—the electronic publisher will probably be willing to pay an advance against royalties, and the royalties will be calculated on the selling price or the net revenues of the CD-ROM edition. But conventional royalties may not be applicable to other kinds of electronic products and services.

For example, the operator of an on-line database or a subscription computer network will make an author's work accessible to consumers who may pay the operator a membership or subscription fee on a monthly or yearly basis, a charge based on the cost of linking up with the database or network by telephone, a fee for each file that is accessed by the consumer, a fee for files that are downloaded by the consumer, a charge based on the amount of time spent "on-line," or some combination of these charges.

Or, as another example, the publisher of multimedia or interactive computer software may wish to extract only portions of the author's work—text, images, or both—for use in conjunction with other words and images. When the consumer purchases the software in the form of CD-ROM disks, the author's contribution to the final product may be small and even unrecognizable. Thus, even though the CD-ROM product itself is sold rather like a book, the author's contribution to the electronic product may be relatively small in quantity and difficult to value.

Under these circumstances, the electronic publisher may offer to pay the author or book publisher a one-time fee, a monthly or yearly licensing fee, a royalty based on a specified percentage of access fees and time charges collected for the entire database, a royalty based on a percentage of fees and charges collected for use of the author's work in particular, or according to some other formula.

Cast ashore in a brave new world of electronic media, the publishing industry does not yet know enough about the economic value of electronic rights—or the impact of electronic products on the sale of conventional books—to calculate a fair and viable method of compensation. Until electronic rights have proven their value in the marketplace, the allocation of rights and revenues will be mostly a matter of gut instinct and hard negotiation.

Right to Control the Electronic Product. Once electronic rights are sold or licensed to an electronic publisher, the very nature of an electronic product may make it difficult for the author or publisher to retain any meaningful right to restrict how the author's work is adapted and used in the end product. Indeed, the use of bits and pieces of the author's work in a multimedia or interactive media product may result in the creation of something rich and strange but no longer recognizable.

An author or publisher who seeks to control how the author's original work is used in an electronic product may wish to ask for contractual provisions that provide for one or more of the following terms:

▷ The electronic publisher is obliged to use the author's work in its entirety and without modification or alteration.

▷ The electronic publisher is obliged to credit the author and publisher of the underlying work, and to include an appropriate copyright notice in the name of the author or publisher in the electronic product.

▷ The electronic publisher is obliged to impose certain limits on the end user of the electronic product to preserve and protect the author's or publisher's copyright interests in the underlying work. For instance, the purchase of computer software often takes the form of a *license*, not a sale, and the consumer is required to comply with certain licensing terms in making use of the software—notably, the consumer is not allowed to make or distribute copies of the software.

▷ The author or publisher retains the right to review and approve how the author's work is adapted and used in the end product.

The nature of the electronic product will determine whether the electronic publisher is willing to grant these assurances. If the author's work is simply to be reproduced in its entirety in the form of a CD-ROM disk, for example, such protections ought to be acceptable to the electronic publisher. But if the electronic publisher is creating a multimedia product that incorporates only bits and pieces of the author's work, it's much less likely that the electronic publisher will agree to such demands.

Audio Rights

The right to make a spoken-word recording of some or all of the text of the author's work in the form of an audiocassette or other sound recording is, rather like electronic rights, a secondary right that has taken on new importance in book publishing as the market for audio products grows and expands. Indeed, the conventional wisdom in publishing is that the audio version of a book is a product that must reach the bookstores at the same time the book itself is published. So book publishers may begin to regard audio as simply another form of book publishing.

> Sale or License? Most book contracts are structured as an outright sale of certain rights by the author to the publisher. Subsidiary rights, on the other hand, and especially electronic rights, are often only licensed for a specified number of years and under certain specified conditions. Licensing allows the author or publisher to recapture the rights after the term of the license has expired—and, even more crucially, licensing allows the author or publisher to impose legal restrictions on how the electronic publisher makes use of the product. And, for the same reason, electronic products and services are usually licensed by the electronic publisher to the consumer. Thus, for example, the "fine print" that accompanies a package of computer software is actually a license that, among other things, prevents the consumer from copying, transmitting or reselling the software.

Audio rights in a book may be subdivided into a number of separate products and markets, each of which are separately owned and exploited. Some audio publishers specialize in *unabridged* readings of the complete text of an author's work in the form of a package of recordings that are often rented rather than sold. Other audio publishers produce only *abridged* readings of a book, consisting of one or two audiocassettes, which are packaged and sold in bookstores with covers that resemble the print edition of the book. Still others may wish to *dramatize* the audio recording of the author's work by turning the text into dialogue and narration and then adding music and sound effects. Indeed, a best-selling novel might well appear in all three versions at the same time—and so each of these audio formats may be treated as a separate subsidiary right. ➤ *Dramatic Rights—Below*

For the protection of both the author and the audio publisher, a well-drafted audio contract ought to specify exactly how much of the author's work may be used and in what manner. The audio publisher may seek the right to edit and abridge the text of the author's work; to add musical interludes and sound effects; to use more than one voice to read the work aloud, especially when the text includes dialogue; to create and insert introductions, conclusions, summaries, and narrative bridges; or to actually dramatize the work by rendering the text in scenes, dialogues, music, and sound effects. If so, the audio contract should spell out the scope of the audio rights and any restrictions that the author has placed on the exercise of the rights.

Book contracts that predate the emergence of spoken-word audio-cassettes as a book-industry product are probably obsolete when it comes to defining and allocating audio rights. Indeed, some of the oldest book contracts still in use may not refer to sound recordings at all. Under such circumstances, audio rights may arguably fall into the rather antique category of "transcription rights," which still appears in some older contracts, or the categories of "dramatic rights," "public readings," or even "allied and ancillary" rights that may accompany the right to make a motion picture or television program. And it may turn out that the book publisher has acquired no audio rights of any kind!

For all of these reasons, it's treacherous to rely on the oblique and sometimes obsolete language of older contract forms. Both the author and the publisher are better served by a straightforward clause that defines audio rights and then allocates such rights according to the deal that the parties have reached.

The Author as Performer. If the author expects to perform her own work in a spoken-word recording, the audio rights clause (or the contract between the author and the audio publisher) must say so in clear terms. And the publisher who is willing to engage the author as an audio performer must secure rights in the author's *performance* as well as copyright in the author's *book*—a standard book contract is *not* sufficient for the purpose of engaging the author as a spoken-word performer.

If, on the other hand, the book or audio publisher is uncertain about the author's performance skills and wants the right to use a professional actor for the audio version, then the audio clause or audio publication contract must expressly reserve the right to audition the author and make the final decision on whether or not the author's voice will be used.

An author who performs on a spoken-word recording of his own work is often paid a higher royalty than the author who merely licenses the audio rights to the work.

Conflict With Other Subsidiary Rights. An important distinction must be made between the right to make a spoken-word recording of the author's work, whether the complete text or an abridged version, and the right to "dramatize" the work by converting the text into dialogue that is spoken by actors with added narration, background music, and sound effects. Technically, the right to dramatize the author's work in audio form may conflict with other important subsidiary rights such as motion picture, television, radio, dramatic and public reading rights.

It's customary in book publishing deals to restrict audio rights to *non*-dramatic uses—that is, the recording of a verbatim reading of the text without dialogue, music or sound effects—and to grant or reserve motion picture, radio, television and dramatic rights in separate clauses. Such distinctions are crucial when the author wants to grant audio rights to a book publisher or an audio publisher, for example, and then grant motion picture, television, radio or dramatic rights to a producer or a studio.

A Model Audio Rights Clause. Here's a model audio rights clause that embraces a broad general definition of audio products but carefully distinguishes between audio rights and dramatic rights.

<u>Audio Rights</u>

Author grants to Publisher, for the full term of copyright in the Work, the sole and exclusive right throughout the world to prepare, produce, publish, distribute and otherwise exploit sound recordings of the text of the Work in the English language, whether in the form of audiocassettes, compact discs, or any other audio recording and reproduction technologies now known or hereafter devised. Such recordings shall be limited to verbatim text of the Work, whether in its entirety or in an abridged or condensed form, and shall not include any dialogue, dramatization, sound effects, settings of text to music, narration, or any other adaptation or dramatization of the Work, except incidental music between segments of the text of the Work and short introductory or transitional narrative passages before, between or after segments of the text of the Work, all of which shall be subject to Author's prior written approval.

Note that the model clause is *not* applicable to audio deals where the author is making a distinction between abridged readings and unabridged readings, or where the author is granting rights to dramatize the text for purposes of an audio product. If the author intends to assign some of these audio rights and reserve others, then the model clause must be carefully adapted to reflect the specific allocation of rights between author and publisher.

Note, too, that the model clause assigns rights in the English language only. Audio rights, like virtually every other primary and secondary right in a book, can be subdivided into different languages and different territories throughout the world.

Compensation for Audio Rights. Audio publishing contracts usually adopt the same mechanism of compensation as a standard book publishing contract—an advance against royalties, and a royalty based on a percentage of revenues.

Although ten percent is a fairly typical royalty rate in an audio deal, the rates may vary according to the commercial appeal of the author or the work, and the actual value of audio royalties is often lower than the value of book royalties using the same percentages since the author is usually paid a percentage of net revenues rather than suggested retail price or gross revenues. Indeed, the definition of "net revenues" is often a hotly negotiated deal point in an audio deal, since the audio publisher generally seeks the right to deduct various costs of production and manufacture from gross revenues *before* calculating the author's royalty.

If the definition of net revenues entitles the audio publisher to recoup its production, manufacturing or other costs before paying royalties to the author, then the accounting clause of the contract ought to specify the cost items that the publisher is required to disclose in statements of account—and the audit clause ought to entitle the author to inspect the underlying books and records that relate to the cost items.

A somewhat higher royalty rate may be paid by the audio publisher when the author's voice is actually used in the audio edition, since the audio publisher is acquiring both audio rights in the book *and* the services of the author as an audio performer.

Some audio products are packaged with a print product and sold as a single unit. If so, the audio publishing contract must carefully define how the royalties are calculated. Some contracts, for example, may set one royalty rate for the audio product and a different one for the print product, and other contracts will set a single royalty rate that is paid on the combined price of the audio and print items.

Motion Picture, Television and Radio Rights

Motion picture and television rights are still regarded as the most desirable subsidiary rights in the publishing industry. The fact is that the advance and royalties paid by a book publisher for sales of a bestseller may be dwarfed by the option payment and purchase price that a motion picture studio or producer is willing to pay.

Motion picture and television rights are the ultimate lottery in the publishing industry. Few books or magazine articles are optioned by the entertainment industry, fewer still are developed into scripts, and only a handful are actually made into movies and then released. But the amount of money that a motion picture producer may be willing to spend to acquire rights in a book is so much greater than the customary advances and royalties in the book industry that a movie deal is still the big score for most authors.

Holdbacks. Even if the author is successful in reserving some or all of the subsidiary rights in his book, the book publisher or the producer who buys movie rights may still ask the author to "hold back" a competing version of the work. For example, an author who reserves paperback rights may be asked by the hardback publisher to promise that no reprint of the book will be published until the hardback edition has been in distribution for a certain number of months or years. And an author who sells movie rights but reserves stage rights may be asked to promise that no stage production will be mounted until after the movie version is first released or broadcast. But holdbacks can be especially damaging to certain subsidiary rights. The conventional wisdom in audio publishing, for instance, is that the audio edition of a popular book must be released at the same time as the print edition in order to succeed in the marketplace—and thus a holdback on audio rights might prevent the author from fully exploiting the sales potential of the audio edition.

Motion picture and television rights in a book, whether they are reserved by the author or granted by the author to the book publisher, may be sought by a variety of potential purchasers: an individual actor, producer or director, an independent production company, a broadcast network such as ABC or CBS, a cable network such as HBO or Showtime, or a studio. The hottest books are circulated within the motion picture industry as manuscripts or galleys, but even a published book may catch the attention of a "reader" employed by a studio, a network or an independent producer in search of raw material for a movie. For purposes of the discussion here, however, we will refer to "theproducer" as the potential buyer of movie rights.

The Scope of Motion Picture and Television Rights. "Motion picture and television rights" is a shorthand phrase that is intended to describe the right to create a motion picture based on some or all of the elements of another work: the title, the characters, the story line, the setting, the theme, and so on.

Once in a great while, of course, the movie version of a book is a faithful retelling of the original story in the form of scenes and dialogue—but, even more commonly, the producer feels free to pick and choose among the various elements in the author's work to create a movie that may not resemble the original story at all. Indeed, a producer may be willing to buy the motion picture and television rights in a book just to use the *title* and not much else!

Once a producer has acquired movie rights, however, he generally wants the right to exploit the author's work as freely—and in as many different

CURIOUS GEORGE GOES TO COURT. The character of Curious George, the lovable but mischievous monkey who appears in a series of classic children's books by Margret and H. A. Rey, was licensed to a production company in 1979 in a contract that provided for the making of a series of animated cartoons "for television viewing."When the cartoons ended up on videocassettes for sale to the public, Margret Rey sued on the grounds that "television viewing" did not include home video products. The court agreed in Rey v. Lafferty that the phrase "television viewing" did not include distribution of videocassettes in the home video market, a form of technology that did not exist when the contract was first signed. As the disappointed cartoon-makers and the happy author discovered, the language of a subsidiary rights contract must be both precise and flexible in order to capture "new uses" that may come along only after the deal is made.

forms—as possible. That's why the language of a contract for motion picture and television rights often defines "motion picture rights" in a manner that encompasses not merely the right to make a movie version of the book, but also to make sequels and prequels, a movie-of-the-week for broadcast television, a spin-off television series, and even a "novelized" version of the *movie* for publication as a *book*, all of which are sometimes concealed behind the bland phrase "allied and ancillary rights."

Until recently, motion picture and television rights were often treated as separate and distinct subsidiary rights, and such rights were sometimes bought and sold separately. And, at least in theory, it's still possible for an author or book publisher to sell motion picture and television rights to a producer, for example, but reserve certain "allied" rights such as the right to create a television series based on the book or the right to make sequels and prequels.

Nowadays, however, the producer of a theatrical motion picture is usually forced to rely on various secondary markets in order to make money on a movie project—not merely the exhibition of the movie in theaters, but also a sale of broadcast rights to network television, perhaps another sale to a cable network, a home video release on videocassette and laser disc, a foreign theatrical release, and so on. That's why a producer will almost invariably seek to acquire *all* movie and video rights in a book from the outset.

Some deals start out as a motion picture project and later go to television, home video and other media; some deals start out as a television or cable project and include an additional payment to the author or book publisher if the mini-series or made-for-TV movie is later released for exhibition in theaters, whether in the United States or abroad. But it's rare indeed for a producer to buy *only* movie rights or *only* television rights. Indeed, the term television rights may no longer be sufficient to convey the array of *video* rights that the typical product seeks to own.

Here's a typical clause from a commonly-used contract form that illustrates how expansively the phrase "motion picture and television rights" is often defined:

> The Man of Steal. Authors and publishers ought to be cautious when granting motion picture and television rights because producers will usually demand not only the right to make a movie version of a novel, for example, but also the right to use the characters and settings in sequels, remakes and television spin-offs. If the author sells the rights to a character that he has created—and not merely the plot of a specific book—then it is the producer, and not the author, who has the right to use the character in future movies without bothering to acquire rights in any of the author's other books.

Author hereby grants to the Producer, forever and throughout the world, all motion picture, television, video and allied rights in and to the Work, and any and all parts thereof, including without limitation the title, story, plot, characters, attire, physical characteristics, settings, and circumstances contained therein, for adaptation and use by Producer as a theatrical motion picture, television motion picture, television series, television special, theatrical remake, theatrical sequel, television remake, television sequel, videocassette, and/or videodisc; for transmission, exhibition, display, distribution, rental, sale and other use by any and all video media, including but not limited to satellite, cable, broadcast, telephone line, "pay-per-view," "in-flight," home video, and video display in hospitals, hotels, military bases, ships, and like settings; and, without limitation, all recording, non-theatrical, merchandising and commercial tie-in rights in the Work and all rights derived therefrom or ancillary thereto.

Since the grant of rights in a movie deal is so expansive, the author or book publisher must carefully review the underlying book contract and any other subsidiary rights deals to make sure that the same rights are not granted to more than one buyer.

Reserved Rights in a Motion Picture or Television Deal. The author or book publisher must be mindful in negotiating a motion picture or television deal to make sure that certain important print, audio, electronic or other rights are not granted to the producer. For example, producers will often seek the right to publish the screenplay itself or a "novelized" version of the movie in book form, a product that may directly compete with the print editions of the author's work. Similarly, a producer may wish to produce a home video or even an audio version of a motion picture based on a book, and such products may conflict with rights granted by the author or publisher to another purchaser.

When acquiring rights in a book, most producers are willing to allow the author or book publisher to reserve certain print-related rights. But the producer may insist on at least *some* print rights. Here's an example of a reservation of rights clause that allocates print rights to both the author and the producer:

Author hereby reserves print publication rights in the Work subject to the following rights which are granted to Producer: (1) The right to use excerpts, synopses, scenarios and other versions of the Work in print publication form (each not exceeding 7,500 words in length) for advertising and publicity purposes; (2) The right to publish, or authorize the publiction of, any screenplays, teleplays, "making of" books, production history, personal commentary, and/or souvenir publications.

LONESOME DOVE CRASHES AND BURNS. When Larry McMurtry signed a contract with Simon & Schuster for his epic Western novel, Lonesome Dove, he granted electronic rights to his book publisher and reserved motion picture and television rights for himself. Later, McMurtry sold the movie, television and "allied" rights to a production company, and the novel was made into a successful mini-series. But when the mini-series producer licensed the soundtrack to Dove Audio for release in the form of an audio-cassette, Simon & Schuster went to court—and won a preliminary injunction. According to Simon & Schuster, the electronic rights clause in its standard book contract—which extended to "photographic, video, audio, digital or any other form or method of copying"—prevented the mini-series producer from turning its television program into an audio product. A trial judge agreed, and the Dove audio version of the soundtrack was banned from the bookstore shelves. The lawsuit was ultimately settled on "amicable terms," and Dove later released an unabridged reading of McMurtry's book.

If the author or book publisher has reserved certain performance rights—stage rights or radio rights, for example—then the producer may ask for a contractual commitment that such rights will be held back for a specified period of time so that the producer may release the movie or television version of the author's work before the author exploits the reserved rights. ➤ *Dramatic Rights—Below*

Compensation for Motion Picture and Television Rights. The actual amounts that a producer is willing to pay to acquire motion picture and television rights in a book is based on a number of factors: the popularity of the author, the sales performance of the book, the number and kind of subsidiary rights to be granted to the producer, the appeal of the screenwriter, director, or actors who are "attached" to the project, and other variables and imponderables. Some movie deals, of course, are worth millions of dollars to the author or publisher, but seven-figure deals are a rarity.

Motion picture and television rights, by the way, are rarely purchased outright. Rather, a producer, a studio, or a network will acquire the option to purchase such rights at a later date for a specified sum; it's a mechanism that permits the producer, for example, to develop a script, arrange for financing, and line up a director and a cast *before* obliging himself to pay the purchase price to the author or book publisher. Under a typical option agreement, the author is paid a certain amount for the option itself, and another, usually much larger amount if and when the option is exercised and the rights are actually purchased. ➤ *Options in Subsidiary Rights Deals—Below*

Regardless of the specific dollar amounts that may be offered, a movie or television deal is likely to include some or all of the following elements:

▷ **Fixed Compensation:** The producer will generally agree to pay a specified dollar amount for the purchase of rights in the author's work, usually in a single payment, but sometimes as a "step deal" in which the producer pays the money in installments as the project is developed. For example, the producer may pay a certain amount on signing of a contract, another amount when the project is "set up" at a studio, a third payment on the commencement (or completion) of "principal photography," and so on.

▷ **Contingent Compensation:** The producer may be willing to pay additional sums of money if certain specified deals are made. For

211

example, the producer may pay a bonus or "kicker" in a specified dollar amount if a theatrical motion picture is budgeted at a certain dollar amount, if a project intended as a mini-series or a made-for-TV movie is released as a theatrical motion picture, if a sale of foreign rights is made, if a sequel or remake is produced, or if the book itself reaches the bestseller lists.

▷ **Royalties:** The producer may agree to pay a specified royalty if the project is made into an episodic television series. Generally, the royalty is paid to the author or book publisher for each episode of the series, and the amount may vary according to the length of the episode—one royalty payment if the episode is 30 minutes long, a higher royalty payment if it's 60 minutes long. And there may be an additional (but smaller) royalty for rebroadcasts, syndication, and other uses of the series. (Unlike royalties in book contracts, the royalty for a television series is usually expressed as a fixed dollar amount per episode or per broadcast and *not* as a percentage of revenue.)

▷ **Deferred Compensation:** Motion picture and television deals often bestow upon the author or book publisher a certain percentage (or "points") of revenues generated by the project—but the value of these so-called "back end" deals is speculative at best. Ideally, the author or book publisher will secure a percentage of *gross revenues* rather than net profits, but such deals are rare indeed. Almost invariably, the author or book publisher will be offered a certain percentage of "net revenues" or, even more commonly, "net profits"—and net profits are defined in a way that permits the producer to deduct a great many costs and expenses *before* any money is due to the participants. Indeed, the "Net Profit Definition" in a movie deal is often a lengthy and complex legal document in itself, and it's the rare profit participant who ever sees any profits. "Net points," as Eddie Murphy once observed during his lawsuit with Art Buchwald, are known in the entertainment industry as "monkey points" because the studio accountants monkey around with the figures until there's nothing left for the profit participants to participate in.

Credit and Other "Perks" in a Movie Deal. Authors who are fortunate enough to make a movie deal will often ask for additional perquisites—the opportunity to write the screenplay, the right to review and approve the screenplay, a small acting role in the movie, or a job (or sometimes merely a credit) as an associate producer. If the producer is willing to make such commitments, these must be set out in detail in the contract between the author or publisher and the producer—but such "perks" are rarely included in a movie deal because they burden the project with additional expense or, even worse, a would-be screenwriter, actor or producer with no experience in the business. At best, the producer may be willing to assure the author a screen credit "according to the rules and procedures of the Writers Guild of America," and possibly a strictly honorary screen credit as associate producer. And a producer may agree to *read* the author's first crack at a screenplay, but it's rare that the producer will promise to pay additional compensation unless he actually decides to buy the screenplay.

Radio Rights. The right to adapt and dramatize an author's work for broadcast over the radio is a separate subsidiary right that is often lumped together with motion picture and television rights in a single deal. Generally, radio rights are distinct from audio rights, especially if the audio rights are restricted to a verbatim, non-dramatic reading of the author's work rather than a dramatization of the work in scenes and dialogue. In any event, the author or book publisher must carefully evaluate *all* deals for subsidiary rights to ensure that the rights sold to various buyers do not overlap or conflict with each other.

Dramatic Rights

Dramatic rights, also sometimes called "stage rights" or "theatrical rights," are defined as the right to adapt and perform a work "on the speaking stage with living actors...in the immediate presence of an audience," according to the Producer-Writers Guild Theatrical Basic Agreement.

"Dramatizing" generally refers to the process of converting text into scenes and dialogue that are performed by actors. Clearly, a book must be dramatized before it can be performed as a movie, a television show, or a radio program, and so there is always a danger that dramatic rights will overlap with motion picture, television, radio, and even audio rights. So care must taken in the drafting of book contracts and other agreements to make sure that the author or publisher has not granted the same rights to more than one buyer:

Here's a model dramatic rights clause that is intended to grant "live stage" rights *only*, and specifically reserves motion picture and television rights to the author.

<u>Dramatic Rights</u>

Author grants to Producer, for the full term of copyright in the Work throughout the world, the sole and exclusive right to use, adapt or otherwise exploit, or authorize others to use, adapt or otherwise exploit the Work or any element thereof (including but not limited to characters, plot, title, scenes, settings, attire and physical characteristics) in the English language in any form of stage presentation to be performed by living actors in the presence of an audience. The rights granted here do not include the right to film, record, photograph or otherwise fix the stage presentation in any tangible medium, and Author expressly reserves all motion picture, television, radio, audio, video and other rights in and to the Work.

Compensation for dramatic rights may take the form of a flat one-time payment by the theatrical producer to the author or book publisher, an advance and a royalty on box office receipts, or a share of profits, if any. Dramatic rights, like motion picture and television rights, are often *optioned* rather than purchased outright. ➤ *Options in Subsidiary Rights Deals—Below*

Public Reading Rights. Some older book contracts still identify "public reading rights" as a separate subsidiary right. Technically, a verbatim reading of the author's work by an actor on a stage is *not* a dramatic right, since the work has not been rendered into scenes and dialogue, nor is it an audio right if the reading is not being recorded for distribution. Although public reading rights are rarely exploited for profit—and few authors or publishers pay much attention to securing the right to read the author's work aloud at a bookstore signing or a writer's conference—a cautious author or publisher may wish to clarify the ownership of such rights in the book contract.

Options in Subsidiary Rights Deals

Some subsidiary rights deals—and virtually *all* motion picture and television deals—start out as an *option* rather than an outright sale or license of the author's work. An option is the right to buy a work of authorship within some specified period on certain specified terms—but the work is not actually purchased unless and until the buyer exercises his option. An option allows a producer, a studio or some other buyer of rights to "develop" the project—that is, commission the screenplay, line up actors and a director, secure financing and distribution deals, and so on—*before* the rights in the author's work are actually bought and paid for.

An option agreement is essentially two contracts in one. The option itself entitles the producer to acquire certain rights in the author's work at a stated price within a specific period of time. If the producer exercises his right to buy the author's work during the option period, then a second agreement comes into effect—a literary purchase agreement by which the producer actually buys and owns rights in the author's work.

Of course, if the buyer does *not* exercise (or extend) his option, then the whole transaction comes to an end—the producer has no further rights in the author's work, and the author is free to sell her work to someone else.

A formal option agreement, therefore, may consist of two rather elaborate contracts, one to define the terms of the option and one to define the terms of the purchase of rights. Both the author or book publisher *and* the producer who acquires rights from them are better protected if a formal option and purchase agreement is negotiated, drafted and signed. But many movie and television deals begin with a shorter contract that summarizes the key terms of the agreement— a so-called "deal memo." If properly drafted, a deal memo is a binding contract with as much legal effect as a full-length contract.

Here are the essential terms of a deal memo for an option of motion picture and television rights in a book or magazine article. (Once again, use the term "producer" to identify the party who is paying for the option—but the optioning party may be a studio, a network, a production company, or some other buyer of rights.)

▷ **Rights to Be Acquired:** Any option agreement must include a specific and comprehensive definition of the rights to be acquired if and when the option is exercised. If, for example, the producer is given the right to acquire some but not all motion picture and television rights in the author's work, then the rights to be granted to the producer and the rights to be reserved by the author must be clearly stated.

▷ **Option Payment:** In most deals, the producer will agree to pay the author or publisher a fixed dollar amount in exchange for the right to buy movie and television rights in the author's work at some later date. The option payment is usually a flat fee paid upon signing of the deal memo or the option agreement.

▷ **Option Term:** The option term is the period of time during which the producer may exercise the option to purchase rights in the author's work. An initial option term may range from six months to several years, and it's common for the producer to ask for the right to extend the option for one or more additional terms by making an additional option payment.

▷ **Purchase Price:** When and if the producer actually exercises his option to purchase rights in the author's work, he will be obliged to pay a stated price, whether a fixed dollar amount, a royalty, a percentage of revenues or profits, or some combination of these forms of compensation.

Since revenue or profit participation depends on a specific definition, it's not unusual for a deal memo to simply state, for example, that the author or book publisher will receive a specified percentage of profits "according to a net profit definition to be negotiated in good faith."

Generally, however, at least *some* specified lump-sum payment ought to be required in order to exercise the option and actually purchase rights in the author's work. And a well-drafted deal memo will make it clear that the option is exercised by actually making payment of the purchase price (and *not* merely giving notice that the option is being exercised).

▷ **Credit and Other Participation:** If the author has bargained for specific screen credit, participation in the project as an associate producer, or any other deal points, these, too, ought to be included in the deal memo.

▷ **"Applicable" and "Non-Applicable" Option Payments:** The producer may ask for the right to "apply" the option payments to the purchase price. For example, if the deal memo specifies that the option payment is $5000 and the purchase price is $50,000—and the option payment is "applicable" to the purchase price—then the producer may exercise his option to purchase rights in the author's work by paying the difference, that is, $45,000. Frequently the deal memo will specify that the *initial* option payment is applicable and any *additional* option payments for an extended term are not applicable.

▷ **Additional Documents:** A deal memo will often make reference to the intention of the parties to negotiate and enter into a "long-form" option and purchase agreement—and, just as often, the author and the producer never get around to drafting or signing the longer and more elaborate documents. That's why it's customary—and sensible—to include a clause that confirms the binding effect of the deal memo itself:

> The parties contemplate that they will enter into a long-form option and purchase agreement containing additional terms and provisions consistent with the terms and conditions set forth here. In the event that no such long-form agreement is executed, however, this deal memo will bind the parties and govern their respective rights and duties.

Note that options in motion picture and television deals are usually slightly different than options in book contracts. An option in a movie deal almost invariably embodies the right of the producer to make an outright purchase of movie rights for a stated price within a specific period of time. An option in a book contract, by contrast, may entitle the book publisher to a period of exclusive negotiation with the author, or the right to match the best deal offered by some other publisher, or the right to acquire rights in the author's next work no matter when it is written.

BOOKS AND TAMPONS. The right merchandising deal can turn a book into a best seller on the strength of a single sale. When Tambrands, the maker of Tampax brand tampons, sought to present itself to the public as an environmentally correct manufacturer, the company arranged to give away a copy of EarthWorks Press's Fifty Simple Things You Can Do to Save the Earth with each package of tampons. Virtually overnight, the publisher managed to sell a total of 1.3 million non-returnable copies of a special edition of the book—a sales record that any author on the New York Times bestseller list ought to envy. Of course, Fifty Simple Things was a already a best seller even before the Tambrands edition appeared on the shelves.

Merchandising Rights

Merchandising or "commercial" rights are an increasingly valuable subsidiary right in the publishing industry as both book publishers and marketeers of all kinds devise ever more ingenious approaches to pitching their products to the public. Nowadays, merchandising rights in books are being exploited to sell everything from calendars to computer games—and books are being sold along with mood rings and baseball cards on various home-shopping cable shows.

Generally, a manufacturer or distributor must secure merchandising rights in order to adapt and use the author's work in the form of merchandise other than a book. Thus, for example, if a game manufacturer seeks to create a board game based on a best-selling book—or if a clothing manufacturer wants to put a character or quotations from a book on a tee shirt—then it is necessary to secure merchandising rights from the author or publisher.

But merchandising rights may also be necessary for a promoter to package and sell a book with another item of merchandise. If a promoter wants to sell a videocassette of an old movie starring Humphrey Bogart and a biogrphy of Bogart in a single shrink-wrapped package, for example, then the promoter *probably* needs to secure merchandising rights from the author or the publisher. And certain special editions of a book, where the bulk purchaser wants to put its own logo and message on the author's work for promotional purposes, may also require a grant of merchandising rights.

The scope of merchandising rights is vast indeed, as the following merchandising rights clause will demonstrate:

Merchandising Rights

Author grants to Publisher, for the full term of copyright in the Work, the sole and exclusive right throughout the world to manufacture, sell and otherwise distribute, or to authorize others to manufacture, sell and otherwise distribute, products, by-products, services, facilities, merchandise and other commodities of every nature or description, whether now in existence or hereafter devised, including but not limited to photographs, illustrations, drawings, posters and other artwork, toys, games, wearing apparel, foods, beverages, cosmetics, toiletries and similar items, which may refer to or embody the Work, or any derivative works based on the Work, including but not limited to characters, plot, title, scenes, settings, attire and physical characteristics, and to adapt, rebind, retitle, repackage and/or sell the Work in conjunction with other items of merchandise.

The author, of course, may balk at the prospect of seeing the characters from her novel used to hawk alcoholic beverages or intimate apparel, and may reasonably demand some right to review and approve the merchandising uses to which her work is put. However, unless the right of approval is included in the merchandising rights clause of a book contract—or in a merchandising contract between an author and a buyer of merchandising rights—then the author must be prepared to see her beloved book put to any use that an innovative entrepreneur can imagine.

Compensation for merchandising rights will depend on the specific nature of the goods that are being sold, but it is usually expressed as a royalty on revenues from the sale of the merchandise itself.

Rights in "Future Technology"

Subsidiary rights clauses in book contracts often include language by which the book publisher or other purchasers of rights seek to acquire rights in media and technologies that are not yet in existence. A typical clause might bestow upon the publisher *"... the right to disseminate, use, adapt or otherwise exploit, or authorize others to disseminate, use, adapt or otherwise exploit, the Work in any medium of communication now in existence or hereafter invented...."*

Such clauses—sometimes known as "future technologies," "new uses," or "new media clauses"—are nothing new. Attorneys have been trying to devise ways to capture the rights in technologies not yet invented ever since talkies replaced silent movies. But the case law on future technologies clauses is uneven and unpredictable—some courts have enforced future technology clauses when they see a new medium as a logical extension of an existing medium, and some have refused to enforce such clauses when the medium is so new that the parties could not have contemplated the new use when they signed the original contract.

The author, of course, will wish to define *any* grant of rights narrowly enough to prevent the inadvertent sale of some profitable new use that may emerge in the marketplace much later. And the publisher will seek to insert a future technologies clause that is prescient enough to anticipate and capture precisely the same new uses. But a sensible alternative, both for publisher and author, is for the author to simply grant the publisher a right of first refusal to acquire the rights to any new technologies that may emerge from cyberspace or some other realm yet undreamed of.

Remaindering,
Reversion and Copyright
8.

Martindale's Bookstore was once a cherished landmark of Beverly Hills in the days before *Beverly Hills 90210*, a bookstore where one might (and I *did*!) encounter Henry Fonda, Cary Grant, Lucille Ball, and Jimmy Stewart as they browsed among the bookshelves. Today, of course, Martindale's is long gone, Rodeo Drive is glutted with tourists from all over the world who are searching for designer souvenirs rather than Penguin Classics, and not a single independent bookstore can be found within the so-called Golden Triangle.

Long ago, a kindly clerk at Martindale's invited me to sign copies of my first novel, a paperback original entitled *Bad Moon Rising*, and he cheerfully offered to put the books on display near the cash register. Only a week or so later, when I wandered in again to see how the books were selling, the same clerk was considerably less kindly and cheerful.

"There'll a be a lot of *ripped covers* on that one!" he snapped.

Thus did I learn a hard lesson about what the publishing industry calls "returns." A bookstore is generally free to return any unsold copies of a book to the publisher for full credit. Hardback books are literally boxed up and *returned* to the publisher, but paperbacks are deemed to be unworthy of the effort or the shipping costs—and so bookstores are asked by the publisher to rip off and return the covers only, just to prove that the books have been destroyed, and consign the coverless books to the dumpster in the back alley.

Returns, if they come too early or in too great numbers, are the death throes of a book. Next comes "remaindering"—a distress sale of the publisher's inventory of the author's work — and then, if the book contract so provides, the reversion of rights to the author. And these are not the only ways that the life of a book comes to an end. As we will discuss here, neither book contracts nor even copyright itself last forever.

Returns

The near-universal custom and practice of the publishing industry bestows upon a wholesaler, distributor or retailer the right to return an unsold book or magazine to the publisher, and the publisher will grant a credit (or, in some cases, a refund) to the customer. Although some books are returned because they were defectively printed and bound or damaged in transit, most returns are simply books that the bookseller did not sell.

Sometimes a book is sold to a retailer on a "non-returnable" basis—when only a single copy or a small number of copies is ordered, for example, or when a deep discount is given by the publisher—but *most* books that are sold through the trade are returnable. Thus, the author and the publisher do not really know how many books have been sold until the returns are netted out of the gross sales.

The mechanism of returns is rarely specifically defined or authorized in a contract between an author and a publisher, although the right of return *is* addressed in agreements between publishers and their distributors and wholesalers, and—most importantly—in the terms of sale that a publisher announces to the book industry in its own catalogues and circulars or in advertisements that appear in book industry publications such as *Publishers Weekly*.

Still, returns play a crucial role in the royalty and accounting provisions of most contracts between an author and a publisher, even if returns are mentioned only obliquely. The book contract almost always authorizes the publisher to calculate and pay the author's royalties on the number of books actually sold *after* returns have been "netted out"—"net copies sold less returns" is the phrase that often appears in the contract. And publishers usually enjoy a contractual right to hold back some royalties as a "reserve against returns," that is, some portion of the royalties otherwise payable to the author are held back by the publisher as a precaution against books that are sold but later returned by the retailers. ➤ *Chapter 4: The Book Publishing Contract*

Returns are commonplace in the publishing industry. Copies of even the most successful books may be returned to the publisher now and then, and returns are often placed back into the publisher's inventory and resold later on. But returns are also an early and unmistakable sign of a book that is not selling well. If the returns are sizable enough, then the publisher is likely to consider taking the book out of print and "remaindering" the inventory. ➤ *Remaindering and Out of Print—Below*

Remaindering

"Remaindering" is another custom and practice of the publishing industry, a term that refers to the publisher's decision to take a slow-selling book out of active distribution, sell off the existing inventory at the best price available, and—sometimes but not always—declare the book "out of print" and allow the rights to revert to the author.
➤ *Out of Print and Reversion of Rights—Below*

Remainders are often sold in bulk to a distributor (or to a "remainder house") or a catalogue publisher that specializes in the sale of remaindered books through retail bookstores or by direct mail to consumers. Some remaindered books are purchased by their own authors, and a great many first novels are stacked up in cardboard boxes in garages and basements all over America. And some books suffer the ignominious fate of old horses and junked cars—the remaindered books are sent to a paper recycling company to be shredded!

Remaindering, like returns, is so commonplace that some book contracts do not mention it at all. But most contracts specifically define the rights and duties of the author and the publisher when a book is remaindered. The model book contract in Chapter 4 specifies some fairly typical procedures for remaindering, but here is a basic checklist:

▷ **The right to remainder:** Since the publisher generally undertakes the duty to "print, publish and sell" the author's work in a book contract, it's sensible to specify in the contract that the publisher is entitled to take the author's work out of print and remainder the existing inventory.

▷ **Restrictions on remaindering:** Most book contracts empower the publisher to remainder the author's book at the publisher's sole discretion or upon the publisher's determination that there is no longer a commercial demand for the book. Less commonly, the book contract may require the publisher to continue printing and selling the author's work unless sales fall below some specific number of copies in a specified period of time.

TRASHY BOOKS. Some remainders are shipped straight to the paper-shredder. But at least one publisher was surprised to discover copies of a remaindered book for sale on the bargain table of a bookstore when the books should have been turned into confetti by a paper recycling company. As it turned out, the recycling company had sold off the remaindered books instead of turning them into pulp—an entrepreneurial venture that amounted to blatant copyright infringement, as the recycler learned when the publisher filed (and won) a lawsuit.

And publishers are alert to enterprising but unscrupulous booksellers who "rip and return" the covers of paperback books for credit—and then sell the coverless books anyway. Here's a typical warning that Ballantine prints in copies of A Gathering of Angels by Morris B. Margolies to caution ethical bookbuyers against less-than-angelic bookselling practices: "Sale of this book without a front cover may be unauthorized. If this book is coverless, it may have been reported to the publisher as 'unsold or destroyed' and neither the author nor the publisher may have received payment for it."

▷ **Notice of Remaindering:** Rarely is the publisher specifically obliged by contract to notify the author of its decision to remainder a book, but it *is* fairly common for the author to enjoy the right to purchase the remaindered copies before the publisher may sell them. As a practical matter, then, the publisher may be required to notify the author of an intention to remainder the books in order to determine if the author wishes to purchase the stock on hand.

▷ **Opportunity to Purchase Books and Production Materials:** An author is often granted the right to purchase remaindered copies "at the best available price," or "at the actual cost of manufacture," or at some other specified price or pricing mechanism. Some contracts also give the author the opportunity to purchase film, plates, unbound sheets and covers, and other production materials at cost or at some specified price.

▷ **Royalties on Remainders:** Typically, the book contract will provide that *no* royalties need be paid on the sale of remainders, or else that a greatly reduced royalty will apply to "amounts actually received by Publisher in excess of the costs of manufacture." Thus, even if the author's remaindered book are still being sold through a remainder house, it's unlikely that any royalties will be paid to the author.

▷ **Consequences of Remaindering:** The fact that a book has been remaindered is often (but not always) an indication that the publisher no longer wishes to publish and sell the book. Thus, remaindering is sometimes accompanied by a declaration that the book is "out of print"—and most book contracts provide that the rights to a book that has been declared or taken out of print will revert to the author. Or, if the publisher does not actually declare the book to be out of print, the author may wish to do so in order to trigger a reversion of rights. However, if a publisher wishes to remainder only one edition of author's work, and continue to publish the work in some other form, remaindering may *not* result in taking the author's work out of print and may *not* trigger a reversion of rights. ➤ *Out of Print & Reversion of Rights—Below*

Out of Print

A book is "out of print," according to book industry practice, when it is no longer generally available to consumers through ordinary channels of trade in the book industry. And, according to most book contracts, the fact that a book is out of print often triggers a reversion of rights to the author, who is then free to sell the rights to another publisher or exploit the rights herself. That's why the out-of-print clause is sometimes a point of hot negotiation between author and publisher. ➤ *Reversion of Rights—Below*

When Is a Book Out of Print? Although common sense dictates that a book is out of print when a book buyer can no longer buy a copy, the precise definition of out of print—and the precise legal consequences of taking a book out of print—may vary significantly from contract to contract. Most standard out-of-print clauses are highly favorable to the publisher, but an assertive author may be successful in negotiating an out-of-print clause that is more protective of the author's rights.

The publisher prefers a definition of out of print that is broad enough or general enough to allow the publisher to retain rights for as long as possible. Thus, a publisher-oriented out-of-print clause might provide that a book is deemed to remain in print as long as copies of the author's work are available for sale in any form anywhere in the world, even if, for example, the work is only published in a foreign language edition or an audio edition under a license from the publisher.

The author, on the other hand, will argue for a definition that declares the work to be out of print if the publisher itself ceases to actively publish and distribute the work in a commercial hardcover or paperback edition in United States, a medium and a market that represent the most valuable print rights in an author's work.

Thus, an author-oriented clause might specify that a work is out of print if the book is no longer listed in the current catalogue of the publisher (or its licensee), if the book is no longer in stock in the warehouse of the publisher or the publisher's wholesalers and distributors, or if the book is no longer readily available and offered for sale in the United States in ordinary retail channels of trade in an English-language edition.

Sometimes the definition of out of print will make reference to an objective standard—the book is deemed to be in print as long as it is listed in the current edition of *Books in Print*, a standard industry reference work, for instance, or the publisher's current trade catalogue. And such benchmarks are useful enough if the author and publisher can agree on one. More often, however, the out-of-print clause is ambiguous enough to permit the author *and* the publisher to take and defend a stand if a dispute arises.

How to Declare a Book Out of Print. The mechanism for declaring a book out of print may be specified in the book contract, but many contracts are simply silent on the subject.

Rarely does a book contract require that the *publisher* notify the *author* when it intends to take a book out of print. Indeed, a publisher who chooses to declare a book out of print usually announces the fact not to the author but to the book trade, often in an advertisement in trade publications or announcements to the publisher's wholesale and retail accounts.

The point of an out-of-print announcement by the publisher is usually to set a cut-off date after which the publisher will no

THE ETERNAL BACKLIST. A publisher once boasted to me that his publishing house <u>never</u> declares a book out of print. "You never know when somebody is going to be elected President," he said, "and if I've got a book that the guy wrote when he was a nobody, I still want to have it on the day he's sworn in!" So the publisher claims that he maintains a small stock of <u>every</u> book that the house has ever published, and he maintains two catalogues—one is the catalogue that's actually used by sales representatives in the field, and the other is a kind of eternal and all-encompassing backlist that is available only upon request. Since the books on the list are technically available for purchase, or so the publisher asserts, the author cannot demand a reversion of rights. Of course, any author whose book is only available on the publisher's "B" list (or, more to the point, the author's attorney) is likely to take a very skeptical view of the publisher's practices, whether or not the author lives in the White House.

225

longer accept unsold books as returns. Here's a typical example from an issue of *Publishers Weekly*:

> <u>OUT OF PRINT</u>
> The University of Chicago Press announces that the 13th edition of the Chicago Manual of Style, ISBN 0-226-10390-0, is out-of-print effective June 30, 1994. Last date of returns is September 1, 1994. The revised 14th edition of the Chicago Manual of Style, ISBN 0-226-10389-7, is available.

More commonly, a book contract may bestow upon the author the right to declare a book out of print if she discovers (or suspects) that the publisher is no longer actively publishing the work. Typically, the author's declaration takes the form of a demand that the publisher either put her book back into print or to allow the rights in the work to revert.

Some book contracts restrict the right of the author to declare a book out of print for a certain period of time after the signing of the book contract or the initial publication of the author's work.

A typical mechanism by which the author notifies the publisher that her book is out of print is set forth in the model contract in Chapter 4, which is fairly typical of similar clauses in standard book contracts. The author's notice triggers a series of deadlines by which the publisher must either publish a new edition of the author's book or allow the rights to revert to the author. ➤ *Chapter 4: The Book Publishing Contract*

The Consequences of Declaring a Book Out of Print. Under some circumstances, the declaration that a certain edition has been taken out of print has *no* consequences at all for the author and the publisher, especially if the publisher is still actively publishing the work in another edition or if the book contract does not provide for a reversion of rights. More commonly, however, the determination that a book is out of print will trigger the all-important reversionary clause of the book contract, which may well result in the transfer of rights in the author's work from the publisher to the author. ➤ *Reversion of Rights—Below*

Reversion of Rights

A book contract, an audio or electronic rights agreement, a movie option, and most other deals regarding copyright, trademark or other "intellectual property" are based on a conveyance of rights from one person to another person. Sometimes the conveyance is "in perpetuity," sometimes "for the full term of copyright," sometimes for a specified number of years—but there are almost always some circumstances under which the rights will "revert" to the person who conveyed the rights in the first place.

The legal effect of a reversion of rights, of course, is that ownership and control of the rights are now in the hands of the person who initially conveyed them. For instance, once the rights in a work have reverted from the publisher to the author, then the author is perfectly free to sell the rights to another publisher, or otherwise exploit the rights herself. And, by contrast, the publisher no longer owns the rights that have reverted to the author—and thus the publisher may no longer publish the author's work or participate in the subsidiary rights.

In the conventional book deal, it is the *author* who grants rights to the *publisher*, and thus it is the author to whom the rights revert under certain circumstances. But the same principle applies to *any* grant of right—if a *book publisher* licenses a *French publisher* to publish a French-language edition of the author's work, for example, then the French-language translation rights will revert from the French publisher to the book publisher (and *not* directly to the author) if the foreign rights contract includes a reversion-of-rights clause.

As discussed above, a book contract often provides that rights will revert from the publisher to the author when a book goes out of print. But there are numerous other mechanisms that trigger a reversion of rights, whether in a book contract or in some other agreement for the conveyance of intellectual

A MacGUFFIN WORTHY OF THE MASTER. Stuart Abend was a kind of copyright prospector who bought up old copyrights wherever he could find them in the hopes that he'd strike gold—and he did. Abend paid $650 for the rights to "It Had to Be Murder" by Cornell Woolrich, a mystery story that first appeared in Dime Detective Magazine in 1942. The movie rights to Woolrich's story were purchased by a production company owned by Alfred Hitchcock and Jimmy Stewart, which turned the "pulp" into the enduring classic, Rear Window. Thanks to the vagaries of the Copyright Act of 1909, however, the movie rights in Woolrich's now-forgotten short story reverted to Woolrich's estate after the first term of copyright, and when Abend bought the rights to the short story, he promptly sued the owners of Rear Window for copyright infringement. After years of litigation, the Supreme Court finally ruled in Stewart v. Abend that Rear Window could no longer be shown without Abend's permission because the motion picture rights in the underlying short story now belonged to him! The case sent studio lawyers running to the contract files to see if the studios still owned the rights to thousands of classic movies that were based on books and short stories.

property rights. The precise circumstances of such reversions will depend on the particular contract, but here are some examples of typical contractual provisions that may trigger a reversion of rights.

▷ **Out of Print:** As discussed above, the most common triggering event for a reversion of rights is a determination that the author's work is out of print. However, the book contract will often impose specific (and sometimes complex) procedures that must be followed by the author. Rights that have been licensed to a third party will generally remain in effect even if the publisher's rights revert to the author. And, typically, the publisher is entitled to retain all rights if the author's work is put back into print within a specified period of time after the author demands a reversion of rights.

▷ **Expiration of the Contract:** If a contract grants the right to exploit a copyrighted work for a specified period of years, then the expiration of the contract term will generally trigger an automatic reversion of rights.

▷ **Failure to Meet Contract Requirements:** Some contracts are drafted to provide that the rights will revert to the author (or other grantor of rights) if the purchaser of rights fails to achieve certain specified results. For example, a contract for the foreign edition of a book may provide that the contract will renew automatically from year to year as long as a specified number of copies are sold or a certain amount of royalties is paid—and, if not, the rights revert to the author.

▷ **Breach of Contract:** The failure of the author or the publisher to comply with certain basic terms of a contract will often trigger a termination of the contract and a reversion of rights. For example, a book contract commonly provides that the publisher may terminate the contract if the author fails to deliver a satisfactory manuscript by the specified deadline—and then, upon repayment of the advance, the rights will revert to the author. Similarly, a book contract often entitles the author to a reversion of rights if the publisher fails to publish the book within a specified period of time after delivery of the manuscript.

Procedures and Formalities in Reversionary Clauses. A book contract may prescribe certain procedures and formalities that determine when and how the rights will revert to the author, or it may provide that a reversion takes place automatically upon certain contingencies, or it may be entirely silent on the subject.

The author generally prefers a reversion-of-rights clause that functions automatically if, for example, the publisher fails to publish the work within a specified period of time or allows the work to go out of print. If the contract provides for an automatic reversion, then the author is entitled to treat the rights as her own even if the publisher neglects or refuses to acknowledge that the rights have reverted to the author.

The publisher, on the other hand, generally insists on a clause that requires the publisher to affirmatively acknowledge a reversion of rights before the author may claim ownership of the rights in her work. A formal mechanism for confirming a reversion of rights is a reassurance to the publisher that the author will not simply declare herself to be the owner of rights previously granted to the publisher.

A fair compromise is a reversion-of-rights clause that allows either party to declare its belief that rights have reverted—and then puts the burden on the other party to respond in a specified manner or within a certain number of days if it disagrees. Under such a clause, for example, the author may give a formal notice to the publisher that she believes her work to be out of print, and if the publisher fails to respond in writing within a given number of days with a statement that the book is (or will be) in print, then the contract will deem that the rights have reverted to the author.

Effect of a Reversion of Rights. Generally, a reversion-of-rights clause will provide that *all* rights granted by the author to the publisher will revert to the author in the event of certain specified conditions. Once the rights have, in fact, reverted to the author, then it is the author—and *not* the publisher—who is now entitled to use, sell or otherwise exploit the rights.

A common exception to the general rule, however, arises whenever the publisher has entered into a transaction with a third party for the publication of the author's work or the exploitation of subsidiary rights in the work. Most reversion-of-rights clauses provide that such third-party contracts will remain in effect even after the rights to the author's work have reverted from the publisher to the author.

Suppose, for instance, the original American publisher of the author's work has licensed an audio edition of the author's work while the book contract was still in effect. Even if the book publisher allows its own editions to go out of print, and the rights generally revert to the author, the *audio publisher* will generally be entitled to continue to publish and distribute the audio edition of the author's work. And, under most circumstances, the book publisher will be entitled to collect royalties from the audio publisher and share them with the author in the manner prescribed by the underlying book contract.

Recordation

Sometimes a contract will decree that a reversion of rights is automatic, that is, the rights in a work are deemed to go back to the person who granted them in the first place without any notice or other formalities. And sometimes a contract will provide for a formal mechanism— a notice in writing, a release, or some other document—to confirm that the rights have reverted from one person to another. In either case, however, the Copyright Office maintains a public registry in which a reversion of rights may be put in the public record.

The Copyright Office accepts and records documents of all kinds that bear on the ownership of a copyrighted work. For example, when an author grants rights to a publisher in a book contract— or, to cite another example, when a book publisher grants rights to an audio publisher in an audio contract— the publisher who is acquiring these rights is entitled to record the contract in the Copyright Office as a way of giving public notice of its ownership of rights.

➤ *Chapter 6: Copyright Formalities*

The very same process of recordation is available when rights to a copyrighted work have reverted to the author or publisher who granted the rights in the first instance. And the very same purpose is served when a document embodying the reversion of rights is recorded in the Copyright Office—the party to whom the rights have reverted is giving formal notice of the identity of the copyright owner.

Recordation of the *reversion* of rights is especially important when the *grant* of rights was recorded in the first instance. If, for example, the publisher records the book contract by which it acquired rights, but the author fails to record a reversion of rights, then the public record will show that the publisher still owns and controls the copyright in the author's work. The absence of a recorded document that confirms the reversion of rights to the author may make it more difficult for the author to sell the rights to another publisher or to enforce her rights against an infringer.

As a practical matter, a great variety of documents—some of them quite informal—may be recorded in the Copyright Office to show that rights have reverted from one party to another party. A formal "Notice of Reversion of Rights" may be prepared, signed and recorded. But, then, a simple letter from the publisher to the author, confirming the fact that the rights in the author's book have reverted to the author, is sometimes the very best evidence of a reversion of rights— and such a letter, too, can be recorded in the Copyright Office.

➤ *Form 8: Notice of Reversion*

Ideally, the reversion will be embodied in a document that originates with or is signed by the person who previously owned the rights that are now reverting. For example, if the author is claiming a reversion of rights in her work from the book publisher, it's always best to have a confirming document signed by the publisher. But even if the publisher fails to confirm the fact that rights have reverted, it is still possible to prepare and record a document by which the author simply announces her claim of ownership of rights. While a unilateral declaration by the author is not always enough to prove that a reversion of rights has taken place, the recordation of such a document *is* effective as a public notice that she claims to own the rights to her work. ➤ *Chapter 6: Copyright Formalities*

Termination of Transfers

One of the best-kept secrets of copyright law in the United States is the right of an author to simply cancel a book contract—or any other contract that transfers rights under copyright—and reclaim the rights in her work. "Termination of transfer," as the mechanism is known in the language of copyright law, is a right that belongs to every author and cannot be waived or otherwise limited by contract. Thus, no matter what a book contract says about the ownership or duration of rights in the author's work, the author may take back the rights in her work as provided by the doctrine of termination of transfer.

The rationale for bestowing upon authors the right to terminate a transfer of copyright will warm the heart of any struggling novelist or starving artist. The copyright law recognizes that an author will be tempted to sell her work on disadvantageous terms when she is poor and unknown—and, the law decrees, the author whose work turns out to be valuable ought to be able to take back the rights and sell them at a higher price later on.

The right to terminate a transfer must be exercised in strict compliance with some highly technical rules and procedures. Here is a simplified summary of the basic requirements for termination of transfers under the current copyright law:

▷ The right to terminate a transfer, when available, must be exercised during a five-year "window of opportunity" which is specifically defined by the applicable copyright law. The precise timing and duration of the right will depend on the nature of the original grant of rights.

Pre-1978 Book Contracts. As a general proposition, a book contract signed *before* January 1, 1978, may be terminated during a five-year period that begins at the end of 56 years after the date of copyright of the author's work.

Post-1978 Book Contracts. As a general proposition, a book contract signed *in* or *after* 1978 may be terminated during a five-year period that begins with the *earlier* of the following dates: (a) The end of 35 years after the date of publication under the book contract, or (b) the end of 40 years after the date of signing the book contract.

Important Note: A careful review of the facts and circumstances of any grant of rights in a copyrighted work must be undertaken to determine exactly *when* the right of termination of transfer comes into existence and *how long* it may be exercised. The rules vary, for example, if the transfer of rights did *not* include the right to publish the author's work.

▷ If the right to terminate a transfer is *not* exercised within the "window of opportunity" defined by law, the right is lost forever and the original grant of rights remains in effect on its own terms.

▷ The right to terminate a transfer may be exercised by the author (or a majority of joint authors) who signed the original grant of rights. If the author (or one of the joint authors) is dead, the right may be exercised by the dead author's surviving spouse, children or other lineal descendants.

▷ To exercise a termination of transfer, the author must serve a formal notice on the person who owns the rights that are to be terminated. The content, timing, service, and recordation of the notice are all closely prescribed by the copyright law, and a close scrutiny of the applicable statutes and regulations must be undertaken to make sure that the notice is legally sufficient.

▷ The termination of transfer must take place within the applicable five-year window, but *notice* of termination must be served on the current copyright owner no earlier than ten years before the date of termination and no later than *two* years before the date of termination.

▷ The right to terminate a transfer does *not* apply to works made for hire. Thus, an author whose work is characterized as a work-for-hire may *not* terminate the rights of the employer or commissioning party who obtained the rights in the first place. Indeed, one of the principal benefits of work-for-hire, at least for the owner of rights, is that the owner of rights need not worry about a later termination of transfer.

▷ The right to terminate a transfer does *not* apply to "derivative works" that were created on the basis of the author's work. Suppose, for example, that an author sold her novel to a book publisher and then sold motion picture rights to a movie producer. The author is entitled to terminate the transfer of rights to her book publisher, who may not thereafter publish the book, but she may *not* prevent the motion picture producer from distributing the movie version of the book. However, if the author terminates the transfer of the movie rights, the movie producer may *not* make any sequels or remakes of the movie version.

▷ The right does *not* apply to grants that appear in a will. In other words, if an author bequeaths the copyright in her best-selling novel to her favorite charity, the surviving spouse or children may *not* terminate the bequest.

TOO CLEVER BY HALF. One crafty publisher (or, more accurately, one publisher's crafty lawyers) came up with a clever approach to cutting off the right of an author to terminate the transfer of rights in a book contract. The publisher's standard book contract characterizes every book that it publishes as a "derivative work" created by the editorial staff on the basis of the author's manuscript. Thus, under the special rule that applies the derivative works, the publisher is entitled to continue to publish its own editions of the author's work even after a termination of transfer! But the publisher may be too clever—the clause is so baffling that an author may be prompted to seek legal advice from a lawyer who will be more likely to spot the gambit and demand that the offending language be stricken from the contract!

Ownership of Copyright After the Death of Author

Copyright in a work of authorship is a form of property that may be owned, licensed, sold, mortgaged, or bequeathed by will. So, if the author has executed a valid will that bequeaths her copyrights to a specified person or institution, then the beneficiaries will own the copyrights upon her death.

If, however, the author dies without a will, then the applicable laws of the state where the dead author was domiciled will determine who inherits her property, including her copyrights. Generally, the so-called "law of intestate succession" will give the property (including copyrights) to her spouse and children or their descendants—but the question becomes a matter of probate law, not copyright law, and requires the expertise of a probate attorney who is familiar with the laws of the author's domicile.

There is one narrow exception to the general rule that applies to the copyrights of an author who has died without a will, but only if the author's work is governed by the pre-1978 law of copyright, and the author died while her work was still in its first term of copyright protection. Under these circumstances, if the renewal rights have not vested in a publisher or some other party to whom the author granted rights in her work, then the Copyright Act specifies exactly who will be entitled to own and exercise the right to renew the copyright— specifically, the surviving spouse and children, the author's executor, or the author's "next of kin."

One who inherits the copyrights of a dead author "steps into the shoes" of the author and owns only such rights as the author herself enjoyed at the time of her death. So, for example, if the author's work is subject to a contract with a book publisher that remains in effect at the time of death, then the beneficiary is generally entitled to collect royalties, to declare a reversion of rights, and to terminate the transfer to the extent that the author would have been entitled to do so.

Expiration of Copyright and the Public Domain

Even if a book contract grants rights to the publisher "for the full term of copyright," the fact is that protection under the law of copyright eventually comes to an end and the author's work passes into the public domain. Exactly how long a specific work of authorship is protected under copyright, however, depends on when it was first created or published and which body of copyright law applies.

Works Published Prior to January 1, 1978. Under the old copyright law, a copyrighted work was protected for two consecutive terms of 28 years each, but the copyright was extended into the second term of protection only if it was duly and timely *renewed* prior the expiration of the first term by filing a renewal application in the Copyright Office. Thus, the total period of copyright protection was 56 years from the year of publication or, for an unpublished work, the year of registration.

Under the Copyright Act of 1976, which went into effect in 1978, the second or renewal term was extended to 47 years, with the result that the total period of copyright protection was 75 years. But the renewal term was still conditioned upon the filing of a proper and timely renewal in the Copyright Office.

Then, upon the enactment of the Copyright Renewal Act of 1992, the requirement for the filing of a formal renewal application was eliminated. Thus, any work which was first published between January 1, 1964, and December 31, 1977, will be *automatically* renewed without the necessity of filing a renewal application, and copyright protection will continue for an additional 47 years. Thus, for *most* (but not all) works published before January 1, 1978, the term of copyright protection is 75 years.

Note: Even though renewal is no longer *required*, there are still some good reasons for most copyright claimants to file a renewal application, especially the heirs or successors of a deceased author. An attorney with copyright expertise can advise on whether the filing of such a renewal is advisable. ➤ *Chapter 6: Copyright Formalities*

Works Published after January 1, 1978. The Copyright Act of 1976, which went into effect in 1978, eliminated the 56-year period of copyright protection *and* the requirement of renewal of registration. Instead, the current law provides for a single continuous term of copyright protection. The following rules generally apply to works created after January 1, 1978:

▷ **Works authored by a "natural" person:** Copyright is measured by the life of the author plus fifty years, that is, copyright will expire 50 years after the death of the author. In the case of jointly authored works, the death of the *last* surviving author is the benchmark date. (A "natural" person is a human being, as opposed to a corporation or some other entity.)

▷ **Works-for-Hire, Works Published Under a Pseudonym, and Anonymous Works:** A copyright term of 75 years from the year of first publication, or 100 years from the date of creation, whichever is *shorter,* applies to "works made for hire," that is, works that were "specially prepared" by employees in the course and scope of employment or by independent contractors working under a written work-for-hire agreement. The same term also applies to works that may have been created by a "natural" person writing under a pseudonym, and works which were published with no "natural person" as the identified author. Note, however, that an anonymous or pseudonymous work can be converted to the "life plus fifty" term of copyright protection by following certain procedures to identify the author in the records of the Copyright Office.

Thus, for most works created or published after January 1, 1978, the term of copyright protection is currently "life of the author plus fifty years" or 75 years, depending on the status of authorship.

▷ **Works Created Before 1978 But Never Published or Registered:** If a work was created prior to January 1, 1978, but the work was never published or registered, the basic term of copyright protection is currently "life of the author plus fifty years." However, the law provides that copyright in such works will remain in effect at least until December 31, 2002. And, if such works are published before December 31, 2002, then the term of copyright protection will extend to December 31, 2027.

And Then the Public Domain: Upon the expiration of copyright protection, the work passes into the public domain and may be freely used without the permission of the *former* copyright owners. Public domain, as the term is used in copyright law, simply indicates that no legal protection under copyright is applicable to a particular work (or, under some circumstances, cetain portions of a particular work) in a particular country.

Thus, for example, *anyone* may publish a new edition of *Moby Dick*, or translate the book into Esperanto, or produce a musical comedy based on the zany exploits of Ishmael and Queequeg, or share the choicer passages with other subscribers to a computer bulletin board, all without fear of a lawsuit from

> **Copyrights Without Borders.** The particulars of copyright law vary from country to country, which means that a work that has passed into the public domain in the United States may still be protected under the copyright laws of another sovereign nation. For that reason, it's necessary to analyze the copyright status of a work in each country where the work is to be published or otherwise exploited to be sure that the work is not subject to copyright <u>somewhere</u> in the world.

LES MIZ. A work cannot be dragged back into copyright once it has passed into the public domain. However, if an author creates a new work on the basis of a work in the public domain, then the author may be entitled to separate copyright protection for the new and original elements that he has added to the old work. A good example is Les Miserables—the musical version of Victor Hugo's classic novel is entitled to copyright protection, but the underlying work remains in the public domain, and anyone may try his own hand at turning the heavy tome into light opera. The elements that are drawn directly from the novel may be used freely by any lyricist—but, of course, the original words and music in the hit musical are protected under copyright.

the heirs of Herman Melville, whoever and wherever they might be!

Finis

From the first bang of inspiration to the last whimper of copyright, we have surveyed the law of publishing in all of its sweep and some of its detail. As you can now see, publishing law is like some vast coral reef, a remarkable construction of fabulous complexity and dreamlike eccentricity that continues to add to itself as new technologies come along. Indeed, the very fact that publishing law is so ancient, so elaborate, and yet so vital is proof of how deep and persistent in the human heart and soul is the urge to write and publish

"We're all creative in the end, only most of us squelched it, do you see?" Henry Miller once told me during a memorable interview conducted from his bed. "We all have the urge to sing, to dance, to paint, to write. We have as an excuse that we have to earn a living. Well, we didn't have to earn a living—we could starve! Do you know what I mean?"

The ideal of publishing law is to allow the author and the publisher to have it both ways—to create *and* to eat. So write well, publish long, and prosper!

Briefs

Briefs are short sumaries of various aspects of publishing law that have not been treated in detail in the main chapters of *Kirsch's Handbook.*

1. TRADEMARK AND UNFAIR COMPETITION

Copyright does *not* protect titles, but a body of law known as "trademark and unfair competition" affords legal protection to titles, characters, bylines, press names and logos, and other words, symbols and graphic elements.

Trademark and copyright are distinct forms of "intellectual property". Essentially, copyright protects "works of authorship fixed in a tangible form," and trademark protects words and symbols that are used to identify one who provides goods and services in the marketplace.

Trademark law is embodied in case law—that is, cases decided by various appellate courts—and in state and federal statues, including the principal federal law of trademark and unfair competition, the Lanham Act. Although registration of trademarks is available at both the state and federal levels, and in various countries around the world, the fact is that trademark rights are acquired and maintained by actual *use* of a valid mark in the marketplace. The longer and more pervasive the use of a mark, the stronger and more readily protected the mark becomes—and a trademark, unlike a copyright, potentially lasts forever.

What Is a Trademark? A trademark is a word, image, or symbol — or a combination of such elements—that is used to identify an individual, a company or an organization as a source of particular goods and services. (Technically, a mark that is used to identify the source of *services*, rather than *goods*, is known as a service mark.) Thus, for example, the phrase BANTAM BOOKS is a trademark, and so is the rooster in the Bantam logo.

Trade Dress. The physical or visual appearance of a product may be protected as a trademark if it is distinctive in appearance and used consistently as a source-identifier. Trade dress may consist of a variety of elements: shape, color, typography, graphic design, and other graphic elements as used in a specific configuration. The dust jacket design of a book or the cover of a magazine may amount to trade dress that is entitled to protection under trademark law.

Titles. As noted, the title of a book or other copyrighted work is *not* protected under the law of copyright, but some limited protection of titles is available under trademark law.

▷ The title of a *single* work is *not* readily protected under trademark law; under most circumstances, the Patent and Trademark Office (PTO) will not accept an application for registration of a single title as a trademark. However, the courts may be willing to afford trademark protection to a single title if it has acquired what is known in trademark law as "secondary meaning"—that is, the title is widely known and recognized by the public as the work of a specific author or publisher.

▷ The title of a *series* of books, by contrast, is more readily protected and more likely to be accepted for registration as a trademark by the PTO. The same is true of any word or symbol that is used to describe not merely a single work but a series or category of publications—the title of a magazine, a newspaper or even a column may be registered and protected as trademarks.

Pseudonyms. A pseudonym used by a publisher or an author may be entitled to legal protection, although the name of a living author is generally *not* entitled to trademark registration. For example, romance publishers generally require their authors to use a pseudonym—and the publisher acquires the right to use the pseudonym to identify the work of various writers. So the pseudonym functions as a trademark rather than the name of a living author.

Characters. If a character in a book or other work achieves "secondary meaning," then the character itself may amount to a trademark that may be registered and protected under trademark law. Mickey Mouse, for instance, first appeared as a character in a short black-and-white cartoon, but today the figure of Mickey Mouse—and even various stylized elements of the figure, such as the shape of Mickey's head and ears—are routinely used by Disney to identify its goods and services.

Acquisition of Trademark Rights. Trademark rights are acquired and maintained by *actual use* of a valid mark in commerce. Generally, trademark rights belong to the *first* (or "senior") user in a specific geographical territory or for a particular line of goods or services, and ownership of trademark continues in effect as long as the owner continues to actively use the mark. No registration of any kind is required to own and protect a trademark, although registration bestows some important benefits on a trademark owner. ➤ *Registration & Loss of Trademark Rights—Below*

Remedies for Trademark Infringement. Trademark infringement generally consists of the use of a "confusingly similar" mark that creates a likelihood of confusion in the marketplace between the goods and services of the trademark owner and those of the alleged infringer.

Federal, state and common law establish various remedies for the owner of a trademark that has been infringed, including monetary damages, recovery of attorneys' fees, an injunction to prevent future infringements, and even the seizure and destruction of infringing goods. Not every remedy will be available in every case of trademark infringement, but the courts are often quite creative in making the punishment fit the crime. The federal courts, for example, are empowered to "treble" (or triple) the monetary damages in appropriate cases, and one publisher that featured an infringing mark in an advertisement in *Publishers Weekly* was ordered to run a corrective advertisement in *PW* to correct the misimpression of the earlier ad!

Strength of Trademarks. Trademarks may be characterized as "weak" or "strong" according to certain legal standards. And trademark status may change according to circumstances: weak marks may grow stronger, and strong marks can weaken!

▷   Generally, a mark that is simply a generic term for a class of goods and services is not recognized as a trademark and will not be accepted for registration. THE BOOK PUBLISHING PRESS, for example, will probably *never* be entitled to registration or protection as a trademark for a book publisher!

▷ A mark that is "merely descriptive" of the goods and services offered by the trademark user is considered to be weak and is generally not worthy of registration. WORLD BOOK, MOTOR TREND, and FARMER'S ALMANAC were all characterized by the PTO as "merely descriptive" of the contents of each publication.

▷ A mark that is merely descriptive may acquire strength as a trademark and eventually be entitled to registration if and when the mark has acquired "secondary meaning" through long and pervasive use—that is, the mark has come to be known and recognized by the public as the symbol of a particular source of goods and services.

▷ A mark that is highly arbitrary and distinctive is generally considered to be the "strongest" mark.

Registration. A mark that is used in interstate or international commerce may be registered in the Patent and Trademark Office. Registration is also available in many foreign countries and in most of the fifty states, although state-by-state registration is not a practical approach to protecting a trademark that is used on a national basis.

Trademark registration is a method of *confirming* ownership of a trademark, but it is *not* necessary to acquire trademark rights in the first place. Many marks of great value and long use have never been registered at all. However, the registration of a trademark bestows some important advantages on the owner, including the legal presumptions that the trademark is owned exclusively by the registrant and that any infringing use of the mark is willful and knowing (but only *if* the trademark owner has used the proper trademark notice).

➤ *Trademark Notice—Below*

Trademark registration in the PTO is a demanding process, and trademark registrations are not approved in the routine manner that generally applies to copyright registrations. Upon the filing of a trademark application in the PTO, an examining attorney is assigned and a formal review and evaluation is conducted. Registration may be refused if the mark is not used in interstate or international commerce, if the mark is considered to be generic or merely descriptive, if an application for a "confusingly similar" mark is already pending, or if a similar mark has already been registered.

Trademark applications in the PTO fall into three categories. A mark which is not yet being used may still be registered on an "intent-to-use" basis, which functions as a reservation of trademark rights and does not ripen into a formal registration unless and until the mark is actually used in commerce. Under certain circumstances, a mark which is not entitled to full protection as a trademark—for example, because it is "merely descriptive"—may be registered on the so-called Supplemental Register, where the mark will enjoy some limited federal protection. A mark which is entitled to the fullest range of protection will be registered on the Principal Register.

A mark must be registered in one or more particular categories of goods and services. Books and magazines, for example, are registered in International Class 16. A trademark owner may apply for registration in every category in which the mark is (or will be) used, but a separate application is required for each such category.

The filing fee for a trademark application is currently $245 per application, and the applicant must submit a completed application form, a "drawing" of the mark that meets technical specifications of the PTO, and—for "actual use" registrations—"specimens" or samples of the mark as actually used.

Once an application has been approved by the examining attorney, the mark is "published for opposition" in the Official Gazette, a publication of the U.S. government. Anyone who objects to the registration of the published mark is entitled to file an opposition, and additional proceedings in the PTO will be required to determine if an opposition is meritorious. Generally, an "opposer" is someone who uses (or intends to use) a mark that he considers to be "confusingly similar" to the published mark. Only about three percent of all applications are opposed, and even an opposition may be settled without litigation if the parties enter into a trademark license or a "concurrent use" agreement.

If no opposition is filed, or if the opposition is withdrawn because the parties have reached a settlement, or if the applicant prevails in the opposition proceedings, then the mark will be registered in the PTO, whether on the Principal Register or the Supplemental Register, or—if the application is made on an "intent-to-use" basis—a "Notice of Allowance" is issued.

A registration, once granted, remains in effect for an initial term of ten years and can be renewed indefinitely as long as the mark is still being used. After the first five years of the initial term, however, two different declarations must be filed in order to maintain the registration in effect and obtain the maximum protection under federal law.

A Notice of Allowance for a mark registered on an "intent-to-use" basis is effective for an initial period of six months and may be extended for up to three years. Eventually, however, the applicant must actually begin to use the mark, and then a "statement of use" must be filed in order to protect the mark.

Trademark Notice. Two basic kinds of trademark notice may be used to claim trademark rights in a particular mark.

If a mark is *not* registered in the Patent and Trademark Office, then the symbol TM (or, for service marks, the symbol SM) may be used immediately adjacent to the mark itself to give public notice that the user of the mark claims exclusive rights under trademark law. However, the mere use of these symbols does not actually confer legal rights on the user; rather, trademark rights are acquired by actual use in commerce, and the symbols TM or SM merely indicate that the trademark owner is asserting such rights.

If a mark *is* registered on the Principal Register or the Supplemental Register of the Patent and Trademark Office, then (and *only* then) the user may (and should) use the statutory trademark notice in one of the approved forms: the symbol ® next to the mark, or the words "Registered in the U.S. Patent and Trademark Office" or the legend "Reg.U.S. Pat. & TM Off." If one of these forms of notice has *not* been used in connection with the mark, and the trademark owner has *not* given actual notice to an alleged infringer, then the Lanham Act precludes an award of certain kinds of monetary damages.

Important Note: The symbol ® may be used *only* if a mark is actually registered in the Patent and Trademark Office, and under no other circumstances. The symbols TM and SM *may* be used for an unregistered mark or a mark that has been registered only at the state level.

Termination of Trademark Rights. As a basic proposition, trademark rights in a mark last as long as the mark is used exclusively by its owner. However, trademark rights can terminate in several ways.

▷ **Abandonment:** A trademark that is no longer used by its owner is deemed "abandoned," and the trademark rights are forfeited. Exactly what constitutes abandonment is a subtle legal inquiry, and an interruption in use of a mark does not necessarily result in abandonment if the owner can show that he intends to use the mark again.

▷ **Loss of Meaning as a Source Identifier:** A mark that comes to be known as a generic term rather than a source-identifier loses its trademark significance and is no longer entitled to protection as a trademark. A good example in the publishing industry is "Webster's," which no longer refers to any particular publisher of dictionaries and is now a generic or descriptive term for dictionaries in general. Trademark owners sometimes make an effort to "police" the market-place and discourage the use of their marks as generic terms. Common usage of a trademark as a generic term may "dilute" or even obliterate the trademark rights in a particular mark.

▷ **Sale or License of a Trademark:** A trademark, like any other form of intellectual property, can be sold by the original owner and user to a purchaser who will then own the trademark rights. However, strict rules apply to any *licensing* of trademark rights, and a poorly drafted trademark licensing agreement may result in loss of trademark rights by the original owner.

▷ **Effect of Expiration of Trademark Registration:** If a trademark owner fails to renew its state or federal registration, then the registration itself may expire and the trademark owner will forfeit the benefits that go along with a current and valid registration. However, the underlying rights in the mark itself are *not* automatically forfeited even if the registration expires so long as the other circumstances described above do not apply.

2. MORAL RIGHTS

"Droits moral" ("moral rights") is a principle of European intellectual property law that affords a special kind of legal protection to authors and artists even after they have sold the copyrights in their work. Essentially, an author enjoys the "moral" right to be credited as the author of her work, to prevent her name from being used in connection with work that she did not create, and to prevent a subsequent owner of the author's work from altering the work in a manner that impugns its artistic integrity.

United States law does *not* recognize moral rights in the publishing context, although the fine arts enjoy a certain degree of protection under recently-enacted state and federal laws. Still, it is possible for an author in the United States to invoke certain principles of common law and copyright law in order to protect the authorship and artistic integrity of her work.

The most important sources of law for the protection of moral rights in the United States are the Lanham Act, which governs the federal law of trademark, and the common-law doctrine of unfair competition, both of which have been successfully used in lawsuits by authors seeking to prevent a publisher from misidentifying the author of a work or altering the author's work. Thus, for example, Ken Follett relied in large part on the law of unfair competition to prevent New American Library from crediting him as the principal author of a book which he had edited and revised (but not written) long before he became a best-selling novelist.

Other legal theories—including contract law, libel and defamation, and copyright law—have also been used by disgruntled authors and artists as a basis to protect their moral rights. As a practical matter, however, any author who seeks to protect her moral rights in a work of authorship in the United States is best served by addressing the issue in the contract by which rights in the work are conveyed to a publisher or a producer.

3. INSURANCE

A special kind of insurance is available for authors and publishers to cover many of the legal risks that may result from the publication of a book, a magazine, or other audio, audio-visual or electronic products. Such coverage is known variously as "Media Risks," "Media Perils," "Publisher's Errors and Omissions" or "Author's Errors and Omissions." Like any insurance policy, a media risks policy will cover some claims and exclude others—but a media risks policy is generally intended to cover certain kinds of media-related claims that are ordinarily excluded from general liability and casualty policies.

Important Note: To determine the terms of coverage in any particular insurance policy, it's necessary to carefully read the policy, including all definitions, declaration pages, riders and exclusions. The general comments set forth here may *not* apply in every media risks policy.

Who Is the Insured, Author or Publisher? Generally, it is the *publisher* that secures media risks insurance, and thus the publisher is the principal beneficiary (or "named insured") of the policy. Although an author is certainly entitled to buy a media risks policy of her own, very few authors actually do so, mostly because the premiums for such coverage are so high. The premium for a basic media risks policy is seldom less than $5,000 per year, and may be much higher.

However, it is increasingly common for authors to ask—and for publishers to agree—to add the author to the publisher's media risks insurance as an "additional insured," which means that *both* the author and the publisher are entitled to coverage under the policy. If the publisher agrees to include the author on its insurance policy, the cautious author will ask to see a "Declarations" page that shows the author's name as an "Additional Insured" to be sure that coverage extends to the author, too. Even if the author *is* added to the publisher's insurance policy, the coverage of the author may be limited in scope; the author must carefully review the policy itself to determine exactly what claims and what damages will be covered.

The term "insured" is used here to describe the person whom the insurance policy is intended to cover, whether it's the publisher, the author, or both.

Scope of Media Risks Coverage. Media risks insurance generally covers claims for copyright and trademark infringement, defamation and invasion of privacy, trade libel and product disparagement, and idea misappropriation arising out of the preparation, publication, distribution and advertising of books, magazines, audio and audiovisual works (such as audiocassettes, videocassettes and motion pictures), computer software, and electronic products. Certain related claims, such as unfair competition or intentional infliction of emotional distress, may also be covered. Even claims for trespass, eavesdropping, and false arrest may be covered under a media risks policy if the wrongful conduct occurred "in the gathering, acquisition or obtaining" of material for publication.

Excluded Claims. Many media risks policies may *exclude* specific categories of liability, including claims based on bodily injury or property damage, breach of contract, "dishonest, fraudulent or criminal" conduct, antitrust violations or unfair business practices, false advertising, or patent infringement. For example, an action against a insured for "negligent publication"—that is, a claim that a book contains false or inaccurate information that leads to death, physical injury or property damage—would be excluded from coverage under many media risk policies. The exclusions in any particular policy must be carefully evaluated, and some publishers may choose to obtain additional insurance policies (including, for example, a general liability policy) to cover claims that are excluded from a media risks policy. ➤ *Chapter 5: Preparing the Manuscript*

Benefits of Insurance. The single most important benefit of a media risks policy—or any other insurance policy—is that the insurance company hires and pays a lawyer or law firm to defend against a covered claim. Because it costs so much money to litigate even a small or spurious claim, the mere fact that the insurance company is paying some or all of the legal fees represents a savings of tens or even hundreds of thousands of dollars for the insured.

The second important benefit, of course, is that an insurance company is obligated to pay a judgment entered against the insured on a covered claim, and the insurance company will generally try to settle a claim at its own expense prior to trial. But the insurance company is only obligated to pay a settlement or satisfy a judgment in excess of any applicable "deductible"—and only up to the stated dollar amount (or "policy limit") of the insurance policy. So the insured may still be required to pay a substantial amount of money on a covered claim even though a media risks policy is in effect. ➤ *Deductibles—Below*

"Deductibles" and Self-Insured Retention. A media risks policy, like an automobile insurance policy, often requires the insured to pay a certain specified portion of the costs of defending, settling and/or satisfying a judgment resulting from a claim. Technically, the insured's contribution is generally known as a "deductible" if the insurance company lays out the money and then collects it from the insured, or "self-insured retention" if the insured is required to pay its share *before* the insurance company is obliged to pay out any money. Even if an author is named as an "additional insured" on the insured's media risk policy, the author may still be asked to pay some or all of the deductible as part of her obligations under the indemnity clause.
➤ *Insurance and the Indemnity Clause—Below*

Period of Coverage. Most media risk policies are "claims made" policies, which means that the insurance applies to claims that are filed within the stated period of coverage and which arise from conduct that took place within the same period.

Some policies are "occurrence" policies, which means that the insurance applies to claims which arise from conduct that took place within the stated period of coverage, regardless of when the claim is actually made.

As a practical matter, of course, a book may remain in print—and on the bookshelves of bookstores and libraries—almost indefinitely as new printings and new editions are published and distributed. For that reason, a publisher seeking to insure itself against future claims will probably wish to keep media risks policy in effect on a continuous basis by renewing the policy each year.

The Decision to Settle a Claim. Generally, a media risks policy will require the approval of both the insurance company and the insured to settle a claim. Media defendants, however, are sometimes reluctant to settle any claim that is regarded as spurious, both as a matter of principle and as a deterrent against future lawsuits. And the author or publisher whose legal fees are being paid by the insurance company may be more inclined to stand on principle than an author or publisher who is paying his own lawyers! So a media risks policy is likely to include a mechanism that allows the insurance company to withdraw from the defense of a claim if the insurer is willing to settle on the claimant's terms but the insured is not.

(The relationship between insurance companies and their insureds is weighty and complex, especially when a conflict arises over settlement of a claim. An insured who finds himself in such a conflict ought to seek expert legal advice to determine what rights and responsibilities apply to the insurance company and the insured.)

Insurance and the Indemnity Clause. The obligations of an author toward her publisher under the indemnity clause of a book publishing contract may be affected by the publisher's media risks insurance, but rarely are the author's obligations entirely eliminated merely because the publisher has such insurance. Even if the author is named on the publisher's policy as an additional insured, the indemnity clause may still impose some substantial burdens on the author.

➤ *Chapter 4: The Book Publishing Contract*

▷ If the publisher carries media risk insurance, but the author is *not* named as an additional insured on the publisher's policy, then the *insurance company* may be entitled to make a claim against the author for reimbursement of any amounts that the insurance company spent to defend and indemnify the publisher. A legal mechanism called "subrogation" allows an insurance company to "step into the shoes" of its insured and pursue any claims the insured may have against a third party. Since the publisher may be entitled to indemnification by the author under the indemnity clause of the book contract, the insurance company is probably entitled to sue the author on the same grounds that were available to the publisher under the indemnity clause.

▷ Even if the author *is* named as an additional insured, the author is probably still responsible to the publisher for the deductible that the publisher is required to pay under the insurance policy *and* for any amounts spent on defense, settlement or judgment in excess of policy limits. Thus, the fact that an author is covered by publisher's insurance does not necessarily eliminate or even cap the potential liability of the author under an indemnity clause. And because the deductibles under media risk policies tend to be so high, the author's exposure may be considerable.

4. A PUBLISHING LAW LIBRARY

The books and periodicals listed here are the ones that I keep in *my* office library and use on a routine basis in my practice. A great many other reference works are available in the field of copyright, trademark, entertainment law, and intellectual property law, and the list is not a comprehensive bibliography. But these are the works that I use and find to be reliable.

Legal Reference Works

Many of the following books are written *by* lawyers *for* lawyers, and non-lawyers may find some of them difficult to understand and use. And, to make reliable use of the lawbooks described below, the user must have access to a current and updated edition. Lawbooks generally consist of looseleaf volumes that are continuously expanded and updated by their publishers as new statutes and regulations are enacted and new cases are decided. For that reason, *any legal reference work that has not been updated on a regular and continuous basis is usually regarded as unreliable and unusable by a practicing lawyer.*

Important Note: *Kirsch's Handbook* is not routinely updated. The reader is cautioned to consult an attorney to determine the current state of the law before relying upon any of the general statements of law in this book.

> Copyright Registration Practice by James E. Hawes (Clark Board Callaghan).
> A comprehensive one-volume guide to the fundamentals and mechanics
> of Copyright Office filings, including copyright registrations, recordation
> of copyright documents, renewal of copyright, and other formalities.
>
> Trademark Registration Practice by James E. Hawes (Clark Boardman
> Callaghan). A comprehensive one-volume guide to filing, prosecuting and
> maintaining federal trademark registrations in the Patent and Trademark Office.

The Publishing Law Handbook by E. Gabriel Perle and John Taylor Williams (Prentice Hall Law & Business). A two-volume survey of various aspects of publishing law featuring useful overviews and checklists.

Nimmer on Copyright by Melville B. Nimmer and David Nimmer (Matthew Bender). A six-volume treatise on copyright law by the late Melville B. Nimmer and his son and successor, David Nimmer. Nimmer is an ever-expanding legal reference work that remains the most comprehensive and authoritative study of copyright law, including both theoretical and practical issues treated in great depth, and the full text of most applicable statutes, regulations and treaties.

McCarthy on Trademarks and Unfair Competition by J. Thomas McCarthy (Clark Boardman Callaghan). A comprehensive four-volume treatise on trademark law and the related law of unfair competition, including both the historical and analytical underpinnings of the law and practical advice on the mechanics of acquiring, registering, and defending trademark rights.

International Copyright Law and Practice by Paul Geller, General Editor (Matthew Bender). A two-volume, nation-by-nation survey of copyright law in many countries around the world, including a useful analysis of the scope of copyright protection under national law and how it applies in other countries under various international treaties. The original editors were Paul Geller, a distinguished copyright expert in his own right, and the late Melville B. Nimmer; Geller continues to edit the treatise.

Lindey on Entertainment, Publishing, and the Arts: Agreements and the Law (Clark Boardman Callaghan). A four-volume collection of annotated contracts and other legal forms for business transactions in the entertainment industry in particular and the media in general, including not only book publishing but also advertising, stage, music, motion pictures and television, electronic media, and computer software.

Periodicals

BNA'S Patent, Trademark and Copyright Journal. (Bureau of National Affairs, 1231 25th Street, N.W., Washington, D.C. 20037). A weekly reporting service for attorneys that summarizes cases, statutes, regulations, and pending legislation relating to the law of patents, trademarks and copyrights.

Entertainment Law Reporter, Lionel S. Sobel, Editor, (Entertainment Law Reporter Publishing Company, 2118 Wilshire Blvd., Suite 311, Santa Monica, CA 90403). A monthly journal for attorneys and entertainment industry professionals featuring essays and updates on new and significant cases in the area of motion pictures, television, radio, music, theater, publishing and sports.

Authors Guild Bulletin (The Authors Guild, 330 West 42nd Street, 29th Floor, New York, N.Y. 10036). The quarterly membership publication of The Authors Guild, a professional association of published authors, which includes information on markets and techniques and also some very sophisticated coverage of publishing law issues from the author's perspective.

PMA Newsletter (Publishers Marketing Association, 2401 Pacific Coast Highway, Suite 102, Hermosa Beach, CA 90254). The monthly membership publication of Publishers Marketing Association, a trade association of independent book, audio and video publishers, which emphasizes the nuts-and-bolts of book publishing and marketing techniques, but also includes occasional coverage of legal topics.

Other Reference Works

Literary Market Place: The Directory of the American Book Publishing Industry (R.R. Bowker): The definitive resource for tracking down the current names, titles, addresses, telephone and facsimile numbers of book publishers, and various sources of goods and services in the publishing industry, ranging from agents to wholesalers.

Huenefeld Guide to Book Publishing by John Huenefeld (Mills & Sanderson, Publishers). A businesslike overview of how to start and run a book publishing company by one of the preeminent consultants in the publishing industry.

The Self-Publishing Manual by Dan Poynter (Para Publishing). A nuts-and-bolt primer on self-publishing that has helped countless authors and entrepreneurs turn themselves into book publishers.

6. INFORMATION RESOURCES AND OTHER SERVICES

Here are some basic sources for copyright and trademark registration forms, information searches, and other general information and advice about book publishing. A great many other sources of copyright and trademark research are now available, including on-line services that allow individual users to conduct research on their own.

Copyright Forms and Information
Copyright Office
Library of Congress
Washington, D.C. 20559
(202) 707-3000 (General Information and "Hotline"
for ordering copyright forms.)

Trademark Forms and Information
Patent and Trademark Office
Department of Commerce
Washington, D.C. 20231
(703) 557-INFO (General Information and "Hotline"
for ordering trademark forms.)

Copyright and Trademark Searches
Thomson & Thomson (Trademark)
500 Victory Road
North Quincy, MA 02171-1545
(800) 692-8833

Thomson & Thomson Copyright Research Group
1750 "K" Street N.W., Suite 200
Washington, D.C. 20006-2305
(800) 356-8630

ISBN Information and Procedures. (ISBN refers to "International Standard Book Number," which is an industry-wide system for identifying books and their insureds by a standardized serial number. The use of ISBN is *not* required by law, but it's essential in commercial book distribution.)

International Standard Book Numbering Agency
C/o Reed Reference Publishing
121 Chanlon Road
New Providence, NJ 07974
(908) 464-6800

CIP Information and Procedures. (Cataloguing in Publication, or "CIP," is a service provided by the Library of Congress and consists of standardized cataloguing information that publishers generally print on the copyright notice page of their books to assist libraries in maintaining their own catalogues. CIP is *not* required by law, but most libraries will not buy books that do not include CIP information.)

Cataloguing in Publication
Library of Congress
Washington, D.C. 20540
(202) 707-6372

Writers Guild of America Registration Service. The WGA maintains script registries where story materials for screenplays and teleplays as well as novels, short stories, poems and other dramatic works may be registered.

Writers Guild of America, West Registration Service
9009 Beverly Boulevard
West Hollywood, CA 90048
(310) 205-2540, (310) 550-1000

Writers Guild of America, East Registration Service
555 West 57th Street, Suite 1230
New York, NY 10019
(212) 757-4360, (212) 767-7800

Copyright Clearance Center. The Copyright Clearance Center is a service that represents copyright owners in granting blanket photocopying licenses and collecting fees for the photocopying of copyrighted works.

Copyright Clearance Center (CCC)
27 Congress Street
Salem, MA 01970
(508) 750-8400

Forms Library

The library of legal forms provided here are based on typical contracts, notices, and other documents commonly used in publishing transactions.

Important Caution: Bear in mind that no single form can anticipate and answer all of the legal issues that may arise in a particular deal. Before making use of any of these forms, it's important to evaluate the deal points and other special circumstances of *your* transaction under the laws of *your* state. Ideally, you will consult with an attorney before making any use of blank forms.

A Checklist of Contract Procedures

▷ All contracts should be carefully drafted to identify the name, address, and legal capacity of the parties, e.g., whether each party is an individual, a partnership or joint venture, a corporation, or some other legal entity. The contract should make it clear that one who signs on behalf of a corporation or other legal entity is acting as an officer not merely as an individual.

▷ Whenever a word, phrase or number in a typed or printed contract is deleted, inserted or modified, *all* parties should initial the change in the margins, and then sign the document where indicated, usually on the last page.

▷   Carefully examine each clause of a contract or other legal document to make sure that it accurately states the deal that you intend to make. *You must satisfy yourself that the "boilerplate"—that is, standard legal provisions from a contract form—actually applies to your transaction.*

▷   Although copyright law and certain aspects of trademark law are based on federal statutes that apply throughout the United States, contracts are generally governed by state law. Make sure that all contract provisions satisfy the laws of *your* state.

▷   Ideally, review *any* legal document with a qualified attorney before signing it!

Book Publishing Contract

A complete book publishing contract appears with clause-by-clause annotations in Chapter 4. When the annotations are removed, the basic clauses include all of the provisions that typically appear in a book contract. However, any book contract—including the one in Chapter 4—must be carefully evaluated to make sure that the allocation of rights and duties actually reflect the deal that author and publisher intend to make. ➤ *Chapter 4: The Book Publishing Contract*

Form 1: Collaboration Agreement

A collaboration agreement may be used when two or more individuals participate in the preparation of a single work of authorship, whether as joint authors, principal author and ghostwriter, author and illustrator, or some other form of collaboration. The form set forth here assumes that all participants in the project will be joint authors and joint owners of copyright in equal shares, and that all of them will participate equally in the preparation of the work; some collaborators may agree to different allocation of responsibility, authorship credit, and copyright ownership.

Bear in mind, too, that the work of a ghostwriter, an artist, or most other collaborators and contributors can be characterized as "work-for-hire" under the proper circumstances; if so, the contributor of work-for-hire is neither an author nor a copyright owner.

➤ *Chapter 2: Co-Authorship and Copyright & Form 2: Work-for-Hire Agreement*

COLLABORATION AGREEMENT
Dated as of _____ , 1994

THIS COLLABORATION AGREEMENT ("Agreement") is entered into as of the date first written above by and between [Insert name of first collaborator] and [Insert name of second collaborator, etc.] regarding a project presently titled [Insert working title and short description of project] ("the Work").

Terms and Conditions

1. Joint Authorship of the Project. We agree to cooperate with each other as joint authors of the Work, and to share equally in all tasks and responsibilities as may be necessary to complete the Work and secure its publication and other exploitation, including research, writing, and editing of the Work. Hov. ever, in order to clarify our respective responsibilities, we agree to the following division of responsibility:

[Insert any special allocation of responsibilities here.]

2. Author Credit. All references to the authorship of the Work, now and in the future, whether orally or in writing, shall be as follows: [Specify the order of names and any other particulars of authorship credit.] To the extent that we are able to determine the style and manner of author credit in connection with the Work, each of us shall be credited as a joint authors.

3. Approval Required. All editorial, business and other decisions affecting the Work which require the consent of the author shall be made jointly by all of us, and no agreement regarding the Work shall be valid without the signatures of all of us. We will reasonably consult with each other on such matters, and we agree not to unreasonably withhold our consent to any such decisions or agreements.

4. Joint Ownership of Rights. All rights in and to the Work (including but not limited to the copyright therein), and all materials created in connection therewith (including but not limited to notes, tape recordings, transcripts, computer disks, photographs, books, research materials, databases, and the like) shall be owned by us in equal shares, and all notices, contracts and other documents relating to the Work shall so state.

5. Payments. Any and all monies paid by reason of exploitation of the Work, or any rights in the Work, in any language, form or media throughout the world shall be divided equally between us. We agree that any contract or other agreement for exploitation of rights in the Work shall provide that each of us shall be paid our shares directly, or through our joint or respective agent(s), if we so designate in writing, and that duplicate copies of all notices, statements, and other communications shall be sent separately to each of us.

6. Derivative Works. No derivative work based on the Work shall be developed, created or exploited without the equal participation of all of us. However, if any one of us declines to participate in such a derivative work, then the other(s) shall be free to go forward on his/their own, and the non-participating collaborator shall be entitled to receive, out of any net proceeds of such

derivative works, one-half of the amount that would have been payable to the non-participating collaborator if the derivative work had been jointly prepared.

7. <u>Communication with Agents and Editors</u>. We agree that any communication by one of us to or from our editor(s), or from our joint agent(s) so long as we are jointly represented by the same agent(s), must be promptly provided by fax to the other collaborator in a manner that details the nature and substance of the communication.

8. <u>Expenses</u>. We agree that each of us shall bear our own expenses unless we agree otherwise in advance and in writing. Each of us specifically promises that no debt or liability will be incurred on behalf of the others without prior consent in writing. Except as otherwise provided above, none of us will represent or imply to third parties that he or she is authorized to bind or obligate the others without their prior written consent.

9. <u>Completion of the Work</u>. Unless terminated earlier by agreement of the parties or by arbitration, this Agreement shall remain in effect for the duration of the copyright and any other rights in and to the Work, and shall be binding upon each of our heirs and successors. However, in the event of the death or disability of either/any of us at any time during the term of this Agreement or the copyright in the Work, we agree as follows:

9.1 If one of us dies or is disabled prior to the completion of the Work, the other collaborator(s) shall have the sole and unrestricted right to complete the Work, alone or in conjunction with others.

9.2 If one of us dies, whether before or after the completion of the Work, the other collaborator(s) shall have the sole and unrestricted right to exploit the Work in all media, to make all literary, editorial and business decisions with respect to the Work, and to execute all documents necessary to exploit the Work, subject to the rights of the deceased collaborator's successors to participate in the proceeds of such exploitation of rights as described below.

9.3 If one of us is disabled, the disabled collaborator shall continue to participate in all proceeds from the exploitation of the Work.

9.4 If one of us is deceased, then the estate (or other heirs or successors) of the deceased collaborator shall succeed to such collaborator's share of all proceeds from the exploitation of the Work.

9.5 Any expenses incurred in completing the Work by reason of the death or disability of one of us (i.e., any fees paid to a new collaborator) shall be charged equally against our respective shares of all proceeds from the exploitation of the Work.

10. <u>Agency Representation</u>. We agree to jointly retain an agent to represent the Work and other works jointly originated by us. All of the rights and duties under any agency agreement shall be shared equally by us.

11. <u>Termination</u>. We look forward to a successful collaboration on the Work. However, except as provided in Paragraph 9 above, we also agree to follow the following procedures, if necessary, to terminate this Agreement:

> 11.1 If any one of us withdraws from the collaboration before the final manuscript of the Work is fully completed and accepted for publication by a publisher, then the rights of the withdrawing collaborator (including but not limited to the rights to copyright and financial participation, if any) shall be determined by an agreement in writing signed by all of us, or, if we cannot reach such an agreement, by confidential binding arbitration as set forth below.

> 11.2 If we find that we are unable to continue to work together through the completion of the Work despite our best efforts to do so, then we will submit to confidential binding arbitration as set forth below the question of (a) which of us is entitled to complete the Work; and (b) what authorship credit and compensation, if any, shall be paid to the collaborator who does not participate in the completion of the Work.

12. <u>Non-Disclosure and Non-Competition</u>.

> 12.1 Each of us agrees to hold in trust and confidence all material and information disclosed by one of us to the other(s) in connection with the Work, and not to disclose any such material or information to any third person without the prior written consent of the other(s). All such information and materials shall be regarded as proprietary trade secrets jointly owned and controlled by us.

> 12.2 Each of us agrees not to prepare, or participate in the preparation of, any other work which directly competes with or injures the sales of the Work.

13. <u>No Assignment</u>. This Agreement may not be assigned or transferred in whole or part by either/any of us without the prior written consent of the other.

14. <u>No Partnership</u>. We acknowledge and agree that no partnership, joint venture or relationship of principal-agent or employer-employee is created between us. Our relationship is to be governed by the terms of this Agreement and the rights and duties of joint authors of a single work as defined under the copyright law of the United States.

15. <u>Warranties and Representations</u>. We each warrant and represent to the other(s) that each of us is free to enter into and perform this Agreement, and that any material written or provided by each us in connection with the Work is not defamatory and will not infringe upon any copyright or other proprietary right of any other person, or violate any right of privacy or publicity. We each agree to indemnify the other(s) for any loss, liability and/or expense resulting from the actual breach of the foregoing warranties.

16. <u>Arbitration</u>. Any disputes arising under this Agreement shall be submitted to confidential binding arbitration under the rules of the American Arbitration Association, and any award issued through arbitration shall be fully enforceable

as a judgment. To the extent that the arbitration arises under Paragraph 11.2 above, the arbitrator(s) are specifically directed to consider the amount, substantiality and value of each collaborator's contribution to the Work in relation to the contributions and continuing responsibilities of the other collaborator(s) in determining what authorship credit and compensation, if any, shall be payable to the collaborator who does not complete the Work.

17. Jurisdiction. This Agreement is entered into at, and shall be subject to the laws of the State of [Insert state] and any arbitration shall be conducted in [Insert city and state].

18. Entire Agreement. This Agreement constitutes our entire agreement regarding the Work, and supersedes all prior agreements or understandings between us. No waiver or modification of any of the terms of the Agreement shall be binding unless in writing and signed by both of us.

Agreed and confirmed:
[Insert name(s) and signatures of collaborators]

Form 2: Work-for-Hire Agreement

In order to acquire ownership of copyright in a work created by an independent contractor as work-for-hire, a written work-for-hire agreement must be signed before the creation of the work, and the work itself must fall into one of the specific categories specified in the Copyright Act.

The form provided here refers to the person contributing work as "the Contributor," and the person acquiring rights in the Contributor's work as "the Commissioning Party." If appropriate, the party acquiring rights may be identified as "Author," "Publisher," or some other appropriate designation.

As a general rule, no written agreement is necessary for an employer to acquire ownership of work-for-hire created by an employee within the course and scope of employment. Bear in mind, however, that an individual's employment status will be determined by various objective tests under state law, and not merely by the way the relationship is characterized in an agreement. Furthermore, if an individual is, in fact, found to be an employee, then the employer will be responsible for complying with various state and federal laws regarding employment.

For that reason, it is very important to analyze the employment status of an individual rendering services before concluding that the individual is an employee or that his or her work is work-for-hire.

➤ *Chapter 2: Co-Authorship and Copyright*

WORK-FOR-HIRE AGREEMENT
(Independent Contractor)

Dated as of _____ , 19___ .

This WORK-FOR-HIRE AGREEMENT ("Agreement") is entered into as of the date first written above by and between [Insert name and address of person acquiring rights in work contributed by another person] ("Commissioning Party") and [Insert name and address of person from whom rights are being acquired] ("Contributor") regarding the services to be rendered and work to be created by Contributor for The Commissioning Party ("the Contributor's Work") in connection with a work described as [Insert title and short description of the work for which contributor is providing material or services) ("the Commissioning Party's Work").

1. The Contributor's Work shall consist of the following: [Insert description of the work that will be contributed by the Contributor, e.g., writing and rewriting portions of the Commissioning Party's Work, design and execution of cover art, and so on].

2. The Commisioning Party shall pay Contributor as follows for the Contributor's Work upon the delivery of the Contributor's Work in a form reasonably satisfactory to the Commissioning Party: [Describe how the Contributor will be compensated].

3. To the extent that Contributor's Work includes any work of authorship entitled to protection under the laws of copyright, the parties acknowledge and agree that (i) Contributor's Work has been specially ordered and commissioned by the Commissioning Party as a contribution to a collective work, a supplementary work, or such other category of work as may be eligible for treatment as a "work made for hire" under the United States Copyright Act; (ii) Contributor is an independent contractor and not an employee, partner, joint author or joint venturer of the Commissioning Party; (iii) Contributor's Work shall be deemed a "commissioned work" and "work made for hire" to the greatest extent permitted by law; and (iv) the Commissioning Party shall be the sole author of Contributor's Work and any work embodying the Contributor's Work pursuant to the United States Copyright Act, including but not limited to the Commissioning Party's Work, and the sole owner of the original materials embodying Contributor's Work, and/or any works derived therefrom.

4. To the extent that Contributor's Work is not properly characterized as "work made for hire," then Contributor hereby irrevocably grants to the Commissioning Party all right, title and interest in and to Contributor's Work (including but not limited to the copyright therein), and any and all ideas and information embodied therein, in perpetuity and throughout the world.

5. Any ideas, information, formats, methods, procedures, programs, data, or other matter which may be disclosed by the Commissioning Party to Contributor, or which Contributor may learn or observe in the course and scope of the Contributor's Work ("the Confidential Matter"), are private and confidential, and/or proprietary trade secrets of the Commissioning Party.

The Confidential Matter is made available to Contributor in strict and complete trust and confidence. Contributor shall hold the Confidential Matter in trust and confidence, shall not make any copies of the Confidential Matter, shall not disclose the Confidential Matter to third persons, and shall not use the Confidential Matter at any time except with the prior written permission of the Commissioning Party.

6. Contributor has not prepared or published, and shall not hereafter prepare or publish, or participate in the preparation or publication of, any work that embodies or is derived from the Contributor's Work or the Confidential Matter.

7. Contributor shall not accept employment with, or otherwise render services to, whether directly or indirectly, any person or entity that competes with the Commissioning Party for a period of two (2) years following the termination of Contributor's business relationship with the Commissioning Party.

8. Contributor acknowledges that, in addition to the Confidential Matter, the Commissioning Party may entrust to Contributor various items of personal property, including computers, computer programs, databases, and other software, office equipment, and other property ("the Commissioning Party's Property"). Contributor agrees to return all of the Commissioning Party's Property to the Commissioning Party upon the Commissioning Party's request, or upon the termination of the business relationship between Contributor and the Commissioning Party.

9. Additional Documents. The parties agree to sign such other documents as may be necessary to give full force and effect to the rights granted under this Agreement.

10. Arbitration. Any dispute arising from this Agreement shall be submitted to binding and confidential arbitration under rules of the American Arbitration Association in the County of [Insert county], State of [Insert state], and any award issued in such arbitration may be entered and enforced as a judgment any court of competent jurisdiction. The prevailing party in any such arbitration shall be entitled to recover attorneys fees and costs.

11. Termination. Contributor and the Commissioning Party acknowledge and agree that Contributor's independent contractor relationship with Publisher may be terminated at will by either party. Upon such termination, Contributor shall be entitled to a proportionate share of the compensation described above based on the portion of Contributor's Work that has been completed in a form satisfactory to the Commissioning Party and delivered to the Commissioning Party at the date of termination. The terms and conditions set forth above shall survive the termination of such relationship.

Agreed and confirmed:
[Insert names and signatures of all parties]

Form 3: Agency Agreement

An agency agreement ought to specify, among other things, (i) which works of the author, and which rights in those works, are represented by the agent; (ii) what commission rates is to be paid by the author; and (iii) how long the agency agreement remains in effect. Two different approaches are illustrated below, but the agency agreement must be carefully negotiated and drafted to reflect the particular deal struck by agent and author. Paragraphs should be numbered sequentially in the final version of the agreement. ➤ *Chapter 2: Agents and Packagers*

AGENCY AGREEMENT

Dated as of _____, 19___.

This Agency Agreement ("Agreement") is entered into by and between [Insert name and address of Agent or Agency] ("Agent") and [Insert name(s) and address(es) of Author(s)] (collectively "Author") and is based on the following terms and conditions.

Terms and Conditions
[An example of clauses that will appoint the Agent to representall rights in all works of the Author:]

1. Author irrevocably appoints Agent as Author's sole and exclusive agent throughout the world to represent Author in any and all matters relating to the Author's Work, including but not limited to the negotiation of Contract(s) for the disposition of Author's Work. Author represents and warrants that Author is free to enter into this Agreement, and that Author has not entered into any other agreement or obligation which interferes with this Agreement.

2. "Author's Work," as the phrase is used in this Agreement, includes but is not limited to all ideas, story materials, characters, situations, formats, and works of authorship which Author has created or creates during the term of this Agreement, or in which Author has any title or interest, including but not limited to books, articles, playscripts, screenplays, teleplays, treatments and outlines, and any and all rights in and to such work.

3. "Contract(s)," as the word is used in this Agreement, includes but is not limited to any contract or agreement, whether oral or written, for the sale, license, option, or any other disposition or exploitation of Author's Work, and/or any rights in and to Author's Work, in any and all media throughout the world.

[An example of alternative clauses to appoint the Agent formore limited representation of Author's work:]

1. Author irrevocably appoints Agent as Author's sole and exclusive agent to represent Author in any and all matters relating to print publication, electronic and audio rights in the Author's Work, including but not limited to the negotiation of Contract(s) for the disposition of such rights in Author's Work. Author represents and warrants that Author is free to enter into this Agreement, and that Author has not entered into any other agreement or obligation which interferes with this Agreement.

2. As used here, "Author's Work" shall refer to the following project only: [Insert description of the specific project[s] that will be represented by the Agent.]

3. "Contract(s)," as the word is used in this Agreement, includes but is not limited to any contract or agreement, whether oral or written, for the sale, license, option, or any other disposition or exploitation of the specified rights in the Author's Work anywhere in the world.

[Other standard clauses:]

4. Agent agrees to use her reasonable best efforts in representing Author under this Agreement. Author acknowledges and agrees that Agent has the right to represent other authors during the term of this Agreement.

5. This Agreement shall have an initial term of [Insert the number of months or years of the initial term] from the date first written above, and shall be extended from year to year thereafter unless notice of termination in writing is given by one party to the other no less than sixty (60) days prior to the expiration of the initial term or any subsequent term. Such notice shall be given in writing by registered mail to the last known address of the other party. "Term," as the word is used in this Agreement, refers to the full term of this Agreement as it may be extended as described here.

6. Author hereby irrevocably authorizes Agent to collect and receive on Author's behalf all gross monies and other consideration due and payable to Author in connection with any and all Contracts. Agent shall pay such monies and other consideration, less commissions and expenses as provided in this Agreement, within ten (10) working days after receipt by Agent.

7. Author hereby irrevocably assigns and agrees to pay to Agent, and authorizes Agent to deduct and retain as a commission for services rendered under this Agreement, a sum equal to [Insert Agent's commission rate] Percent of all gross monies and other consideration, whenever received, due and payable to Author in connection with any and all Contracts.

8. Author acknowledges and agrees that Agent may appoint sub-agents or others to assist her at her own expense. However, if Agent engages a co-agent for the disposition of any particular rights in Author's Work, then a total commission of [Insert joint commission rate] Percent shall be payable on any and all Contract(s) on which Agent and the co-agent have jointly represented Author. Such commissions shall be shared between Agent and the co-agent according to their mutual agreement.

9. On any and all Contract(s) for the disposition of rights in Author's Work outside the United States and Canada, a commission of [Insert commission rate for foreign transactions] Percent shall be payable to Agent.

10. Author agrees that Agent is entitled to the foregoing commissions on any and all gross monies or other consideration paid or payable to Author under (a) any and all Contract(s) which are entered into during the Term of this Agreement; and (b) any and all Contract(s) which are entered into within six

(6) months after the termination of this Agreement, so long as the Author's Work which is the subject of such Contract(s) was submitted by Agent to the contracting party during the Term of this Agreement. Author further agrees that Agent is entitled to retain any and all commissions payable under this Agreement notwithstanding the fact that the publisher or other contracting party demands repayment of advances or royalties from Author.

11. If Author enters into one or more Contract(s) during the Term of this Agreement, then Author agrees that Agent will remain the sole and exclusive agent for all foreign and other subsidiary rights in the Author's Work which is the subject of such Contract(s) even if this Agreement is otherwise terminated.

12. In addition to commissions otherwise payable to Agent, Author hereby agrees to pay Agent, and authorizes Agent to deduct and retain from all gross monies and other consideration payable to Author, the full amount of her out-of-pocket expenses incurred on behalf of Author, including but not limited to long distance telephone, postage, photocopying, telecopying, except that no expenses in excess of $250 shall be incurred without the Author's prior written approval. Upon termination or expiration of this Agreement, Author agrees to pay Agent any portions of such charges or expenses which have not yet been reimbursed.

13. Author hereby authorizes and instructs Agent to include a customary "agency clause" incorporating the terms of this Agreement in any Contract(s) which Agent may negotiate, and the parties agree to execute such additional documents as may be necessary to give full force and effect to this Agreement.

14. Agent and Author look forward to a long and mutually beneficial working relationship. However, in the event of any dispute under this Agreement, Agent and Author agree to submit their disputes to confidential binding arbitration under the rules of the American Arbitration Association in [Insert location of arbitration].

15. Agent and Author agree that this Agreement contains the entire agreement between them, and may not be modified or amended except by a writing signed by both parties.

Agreed and confirmed:
[Insert names and signatures of Author(s) and Agent.]

Form 4: Interview Release

It's always a good practice to secure written permission to use the information and materials gathered during research for a book, a magazine article or other work—and sometimes the publisher goes to the trouble of requiring the author to obtain such permission in the book contract. Here is one form that has been simplified in order to make it less daunting to interview subjects. A much more comprehensive agreement is required to acquire "life story rights" for commercial exploitation.

INTERVIEW RELEASE

[Insert name of Author] ("Author") has informed me that he/she is researching, writing and publishing one or more books and related works on the subject of [Insert short description of book or magazine project] (collectively "the Work"), and has asked me to grant interviews and to otherwise cooperate with Author in connection with the Work.

In order to assist Author in the preparation of the Work, I have agreed to be interviewed and to provide information and other materials to be used in connection with the Work, including my personal experiences, remarks, and recollections, as well as any photographs and documents that I may choose to give to Author ("the Interview Materials").

I hereby grant and assign to Author, and his/her licensees, successors and assigns, the following rights in connection with the Interview Materials for use as part of the Work, or any advertising, packaging or promotional materials for the Work, in any and all editions, versions and media, in perpetuity and throughout the world.

1. The right to quote or paraphrase all or any portion of the Interview Materials, and to generally use and publish the Interview Materials, including my experiences, recollections, incidents, remarks, characters, dialogue, actions, scenes, situations and information, as well as any photographs and documents that I may give to Author.

2. The right to use my name, image, voice, likeness and biographical data.

3. The right to depict and portray me, whether under my own name or under a fictitious name, in any manner that the Author may deem appropriate.

4. The right to develop, produce, distribute, advertise, promote or otherwise exploit the Work as a book or any other work in any manner that Author deems appropriate. I understand and acknowledge that Author will be the sole owner of all copyright and other rights in and to the Work.

In order to enable Author to develop the Work in any manner that Author may deem best, I hereby release and discharge the Author and his/her licensees, successors and assigns, from any and all claims, demands, or causes of action that I may have against them by reason of anything contained in the Work, or any of the above uses, including any claims based on the right of privacy, the right of publicity, copyright, libel, slander, or any other right.

In consideration of the foregoing, Author has agreed to provide me with one free copy of the Work in its first trade edition upon publication. I acknowledge and agree that I am not entitled to receive any other form of payment from Author and/or his/her licensees, successors and assigns.

Agreed and confirmed:

[Insert date, name and signature of interview subject.]

Form 5: Permissions Agreement

The cautious author or publisher will always obtain written permission to use someone else's copyrighted work, whether it's a quotation, an illustration, a photograph, or some other element. Care should be taken, too, to make sure that the permission is signed by the actual owner of rights and covers all intended uses of the copyrighted material, including audio, electronic and other media. The form provided here is intended to be filled in by the party requesting permission and countersigned by the party granting permission, but it's not unusual for the copyright owner to respond with a form of its own—and such forms are usually far more limited in scope than the one provided below!

PERMISSIONS AGREEMENT

Dated as of _____, 19____.

[Insert name and address of party granting permission] ("Licensor") and [Insert name and address of party requesting permission] ("Licensee") hereby enter into this Permissions Agreement regarding the use of selected materials from Licensor's work titled [Insert title of work from which materials are to be copied] ("Licensor's Work") in Licensee's work titled [Insert title or description of requesting party's work] ("Licensee's Work") on the terms described below.

1. Licensed Materials. This Permissions Agreement applies to the materials which appear in Licensor's Work as described here: [Insert description of materials for which permission is sought or attach materials to Permissions Agreement as an exhibit] ("the Licensed Materials").

2. License. Licensor hereby grants Licensee, and Licensee's successors, assigns and sublicensees, a non-exclusive license to copy, reproduce, print, publish, distribute and otherwise use the Licensed Materials in Licensee's Work, and any works derived from Licensee's Work, in all media, in perpetuity and throughout the world. [Or, if Licensor declines to grant such expansive rights, insert a more limited description of the media, territory and time period covered by the Permissions Agreement.]

3. Use of Licensed Materials. The Licensed Materials shall not be altered, adapted or modified in any manner without the prior written permission of Licensor, and Licensee shall include the following notice in all works where the Licensed Materials are used: [Insert precise form of copyright and/or trademark notice, acknowledgements, and any other notices that the Licensor requires the Licensee to include in the Licensee's Work.]

4. Materials: Licensor agrees to provide Licensee the following materials: [Insert description of materials, if any, that Licensor agrees to provide, e.g., negatives, text on disk, etc.]

5. <u>Fee</u>. In consideration of the rights licensed in this Permissions Agreement, Licensee agrees to pay Licensor as follows: [Insert terms of payment, if any.]

6. <u>Warranties and Reciprocal Indemnity</u>. Licensor warrants to Licensee that Licensor owns and controls the rights licensed in this Permissions Agreement, and agrees to indemnify and defend Licensee from any claim, loss or liability arising from a breach of the foregoing warranty. Except as provided above, Licensee agrees to indemnify and defend Licensor from any claim, loss or liability arising from Licensee's use of the Licensed Materials.

Agreed and confirmed:

[Insert names, titles, and signatures of Licensor and Licensee.]

Form 6: "Short-Form" Instrument of Recordation

A publisher or other purchaser of rights in a copyrighted work is entitled to record the document by which rights are acquired in the United States Copyright Office, and recordation bestows some important advantages on a copyright owner. Most authors and publishers do not wish to record the entire book publishing contract, which contains confidential financial information such as advances and royalty rates; rather, a "short form" of the contract is recorded. The form provided here is designed to summarize the rights that the publisher has acquired from the author, and then the form is sent to the Copyright Office for recordation. ➤ *Chapter 4: The Book Publishing Contract & Chapter 6: Copyright Formalities*

INSTRUMENT FOR RECORDATION
OF TRANSFER OF EXCLUSIVE RIGHTS UNDER COPYRIGHT

THIS INSTRUMENT is subject to and governed by all of the terms and conditions of that certain PUBLISHING AGREEMENT ("Agreement") dated as of [Insert date of underlying book publishing agreement] by and between [Insert name of Publisher] ("Publisher") and [Insert name of Author] ("Author") regarding the Work presently titled [Insert title of Author's work] ("the Work").

1. Pursuant to the Agreement, and by means of this instrument, AUTHOR grants, transfers, and conveys to PUBLISHER the following exclusive rights in the Work during the full term of the copyright in and to the Work: [Insert a detailed description of the "grant of rights" as it appears in the underlying book publishing agreement.]

2. AUTHOR was born on [Insert date of birth of Author], and was/is a citizen and domiciliary of the United States of America (and died on [Insert date of death of Author, if applicable]).

3. AUTHOR acknowledges that this instrument may be recorded by PUBLISHER pursuant to the United States copyright law, Title 17 of the United States Code.

Date: [Insert date of signing.]
 [Insert names and signatures of Author and Publisher.]

_____   _____
 (Signature)   (Signature)

Form 7: Warning and Disclaimer

A warning and disclaimer may be appropriate to alert the reader to
any physical, financial or legal peril that may result from making use
of the advice and information contained in the book, and to warn the
reader that the author and publisher are not guaranteeing the contents
of book. Disclaimers are also commonly used to announce that the
characters in a work of fiction are imaginary and that "any
resemblance to actual persons, living or dead, is purely coincidental."
The disclaimer shown here is widely used in publishing circles for
non-fiction books, but it is not an all-purpose disclaimer. Indeed,
whether or not a disclaimer is effective at all depends on whether
it is adequate to warn of the specific risks in a particular book.
For example, the disclaimer set forth below was used in a how-to book
on physical exercise. A different disclaimer is necessary in a novel,
a guide to mushroom-hunting or a book of legal advice; another
example of a disclaimer is the one for Kirsch's Handbook, which
appears in the introduction of the book. ➤ *Chapter 5: Preparing the Manuscript*

IMPORTANT CAUTION — PLEASE READ THIS!

Readers are strongly cautioned to consult with a physician or other health-
care professional <u>before</u> engaging in the exercises described in this book,
and to adapt the exercises in the book to meet the reader's special needs and
limitations.

This book is based on information from sources believed to be reliable, and
every effort has been made to make the book as complete and accurate as
possible based on information available as of the printing date, but its accuracy
and completeness cannot be guaranteed. Despite the best efforts of author and
publisher, the book may contain mistakes, and the reader should use the book
only as a general guide and not as the ultimate source of information about the
subject of the book.

The book is not intended to reprint all of the information available to the author
or publisher on the subject, but rather to simplify, complement and supplement
other available sources. The reader is encouraged to read all available material
and to learn as much as possible about the subject. Some of these materials
are listed under SUGGESTED READING elsewhere in this book.

The author and publisher are not engaged in rendering medical services, and the book is not intended to diagnose or treat medical or physical problems. If medical, professional or other expert assistance is required by the reader, please seek the services of a competent expert.

This book is sold without warranties of any kind, express or implied, and the publisher and author disclaim any liability, loss or damage caused by the contents of this book.

IF YOU DO NOT WISH TO BE BOUND BY THE FOREGOING CAUTIONS AND CONDITIONS, YOU MAY RETURN THIS BOOK TO THE PUBLISHER FOR A FULL REFUND.

Form 8: Notice of Reversion

When rights in a copyrighted work revert to the author upon the expiration or other termination of a copyright agreement, it is good practice to record a notice of reversion in the Copyright Office. Ideally, the notice of reversion will be signed by both the party whose rights have now terminated and the party to whom rights are reverting. If necessary, however, the following form can be adapted for signature by either one. ➤ *Chapter 8: Remaindering, Reversion and Copyright Termination*

INSTRUMENT FOR RECORDATION
OF REVERSION OF EXCLUSIVE RIGHTS
UNDER COPYRIGHT

Re: (Insert title and author of the copyrighted work in which rights have reverted, including the serial number of the Certificate of Copyright Registration.)

NOTICE IS HEREBY GIVEN THAT all rights in and to the foregoing work of authorship, including any and all rights granted by [Name and address of person who originally granted rights in the work] ("Grantor") to [Insert name and address of person to whom rights were originally granted] ("Grantee") pursuant to that certain agreement between Grantor and Grantee dated [Insert date and other identifying description of the agreement by which rights were originally granted], including but not limited to all rights under copyright, fully reverted to Grantor as of [Insert effective date of reversion].

IN WITNESS WHEREOF, I have set my hand on the date(s) and at the places set forth below.

[Insert names, signatures, and date and place where the document is signed.]

Index

Index